M.A. G. H. Bianchi

The Mythology of Greece and Rome

M.A. G. H. Bianchi

The Mythology of Greece and Rome

ISBN/EAN: 9783742849120

Manufactured in Europe, USA, Canada, Australia, Japa

Cover: Foto ©Thomas Meinert / pixelio.de

Manufactured and distributed by brebook publishing software
(www.brebook.com)

M.A. G. H. Bianchi

The Mythology of Greece and Rome

Fig. 53.—Head of Niobe. Florence.

THE MYTHOLOGY

OF

GREECE AND ROME

*WITH SPECIAL REFERENCE TO ITS
USE IN ART*

EDITED BY

G. H. BIANCHI, M.A.

LATE SCHOLAR OF ST. PETER'S COLLEGE, CAMBRIDGE
BROTHERTON SANSKRIT PRIZEMAN, 1875

WITH SIXTY-FOUR ILLUSTRATIONS

New and Revised Edition

LONDON: CHAPMAN AND HALL, Ld.

Made and Printed in Great Britain.
Richard Clay & Sons, Limited,
Printers, Bungay, Suffolk.

PREFACE.

NO apology can be needed for introducing to the public a work like the present. There has long been a want of a book which should, in a moderate compass, give a clear and readable account of these legends; for Dictionaries of Mythology do not give a view of the subject as a whole; and the price of most other works on the Greek and Roman myths would prevent their being used as class-books. These considerations have led the publishers to bring out this book in an English dress.

If any should be inclined to ask what Mythology has to do with men of the present day, the reply is plain. The works of art in our galleries and museums require a certain amount of knowledge of the mythology of the Greeks and Romans for the full appreciation of their subjects. There is hardly any litera-ture in Europe which has not been more or less coloured by these legends; and in our own day their power to inspire the poet has by no means ceased. Nay, they have incorporated themselves into our very language: "Herculean strength" is

almost as common an expression now as it was two thousand years
ago ; and we still talk of " chimerical " expectations, describe a
man as "tantalised," and use the Sphinx as the symbol of the
mysterious.

The present work, translated from the German of O. Seemann,
seems well adapted to convey a knowledge of these myths.   It
is illustrated with cuts after some of the masterpieces of ancient
and modern art.   Particular attention has been paid to this
branch of the subject, and the principal works of art in each
case are mentioned.

The distinction between Greek and Roman deities and heroes
has been preserved, but the conventional spelling has been
retained.   A full index is appended, in which the quantities of
the vowels are carefully marked.

TABLE OF CONTENTS.

6 Contents.

PART III.—THE HEROES.

8   *Contents.*

LIST OF ILLUSTRATIONS.

GREEK AND ROMAN MYTHOLOGY.

INTRODUCTION.

I.—SUBJECTS OF GREEK AND ROMAN MYTHOLOGY.

YTHS may be described as poetic narratives of the birth, life, and actions of the old heathen gods and heroes or demigods. Both myth and legend* are distinguished from the "Mährchen," or popular tale, by not being, like the latter, a mere product of the imagination, but always being founded on some preceding reality, whether that be an oft-recurring phase of nature, or a distinct and real occurrence. It is often most difficult to recognise with any precision the true germ of a myth, on account of the numerous additions and alterations made by the poets. And therefore the question, whether a particular tradition be a myth or not, is very hard to answer: on one side we are tempted to view, in the god or demigod, the hero of a tribe magnified to superhuman proportions by the admiration of

---

* The German word "sage" (legend) is really only a translation of the Greek word "mythos," and is often used in that sense. But lately the custom has tacitly sprung up of employing the term "mythos" when speaking of the life or actions of the gods, and "sage" when speaking of those of heroes.

posterity; and, on the other side, comparison of the legends of different families of nations points us to the operations of nature, not only in the demigod or the hero, but in the animals of fable and the traditions of the nursery.

A large proportion of these myths are due to men's observations of Nature, and her various active and creative forces, which appeared to their lively Southern fancy as manifestations of single supernatural beings. These were regarded, now as friendly, now as hostile, to man ; and men therefore strove as eagerly to gain their favour as to appease their wrath. Of the appearance of the deities who thus manifested themselves in the workings of nature, men necessarily formed at first very crude and fantastic ideas. But later, when men emerged from the simple conditions of the early patriarchal epoch, and began to dwell in regular political communities, they gradually ceased to regard the gods as mere personifications of natural forces. They began to regard them as beings acting in accordance with unchangeable moral laws, and endowed with forms similar to those of men (Anthropomorphism). They brought the gods into connection with each other by means of genealogies in a great measure artificial, and built up a vast political system, which has its centre in Zeus, the " father of gods and men."

Strange to say, however, it was only among the Greeks that this system of developement prevailed. The nations of Italy still continued to regard their gods as mere natural forces—that looked down on them in a cold, strange fashion—of whose form and mode of life they had no clear idea. It was only later, when the Romans came into intellectual contact with their Greek neighbours, and began to study their language and literature, that they adopted the popular Greek conceptions concerning the gods. They now transferred existing myths, and fathered them on those of their own gods and goddesses who bore the closest resemblance to the Greek divinities, and harmonised best with their natural interpretation. Thus it was that the Roman Jupiter was identified with the Greek Zeus, Juno with Hera, Minerva with Athene; though for peculiar deities, such as Janus, they could find no Greek prototype.

II.—POPULAR IDEAS CONCERNING THE GODS.

We learn most concerning the conceptions the ancients formed of their gods from the numerous Greek and Roman poets whose works have come down to us, and who contributed so largely to the construction of the myths. First, both in antiquity and importance, are the poems attributed to Homer, in which we find the whole political system of Olympus, with Zeus at its head, already constructed.

Henceforth the gods, in outward appearance at least, are endowed with forms entirely human; more grand and beautiful and majestic, but still not verging on the monstrous or fantastic.

Not only in beauty and grandeur, but also in strength and vigour, do the gods surpass men. Let but Zeus shake his ambrosial locks, and the whole of Olympus trembles. The other deities are also endowed in proportion with great strength. As corporeal, indeed, they are limited in regard to space, and cannot therefore be omnipresent; but this restriction affects them far less than mortals, for they can compass the greatest distances at lightning speed. In a moment Athene drops from the heights of Olympus down to Ithaca; and Poseidon, the ocean-god, passes in three or four steps from Samothrace to Ægæ in Eubœa. Moreover, the gods can see and hear at a much greater distance than men. In regard to hearing, indeed, they seem to have unlimited powers. Prayers ascend to them from every place, irrespective of their personal presence. In the same manner Zeus, from his high throne in Olympus, sees all that passes among men, and, sitting on the highest summit of Mount

Ida, he can follow all the events of the battle that rages before Troy.

On the other hand, the gods are subject to the same bodily wants as men. They refresh themselves in the same way with sleep, and have to support themselves with food and drink. Here again, however, they are far less fettered than mortals, for they can hold out much longer without satisfying these wants. Nor is their food so coarse as that of men; they live on ambrosia and nectar. Another natural necessity is clothing, on the tasteful ordering of which the goddesses even bestow extraordinary care, and in this, as in many other respects, greatly resemble the daughters of Eve. Although later art delights in representing some of the deities either slightly clothed or quite naked, yet we cannot justly conclude from this that the popular belief of the ancients conceived thus of those gods.

Gods endowed with frames like those of mortals must necessarily be born in the same way, and develope gradually both in mind and body. But here, again, everything proceeds with the utmost rapidity. For instance, the new-born Hermes rises from his cradle to steal the cattle of Apollo, and, coming into the world in the morning, he is found in the afternoon playing on the lyre, which he has himself invented. The most important point, however, in which they surpass mortals is that, when once in full possession of bodily and intellectual powers, they never grow old, but remain ever young and beautiful, ever free from disease and death. Compared with the race of men, who are subject to need and pain, they are the "happy," "blessed" gods, the gods "who live at ease," who can readily gratify every desire. But this does not by any means prevent their suffering occasionally from the pangs of sorrow and grief; they are vulnerable alike in body and soul, and exposed to every kind of painful sensation. So completely did the Greeks subject their gods to human passions.

As regards mental qualifications they are naturally far superior to men. In the first place, they stand higher morally; they shun all that is evil, impure, and unjust, and visit with punishment the impiety and injustice of man. This, again, does not prevent their giving way to every description of vice and folly, such as deceit, lying, hatred, cruelty, jealousy, &c. They are far from holy, therefore, in the sense in which we speak of the Supreme Being. Still less are they conceived as omniscient or omnipotent. Their powers indeed are great, and so is their knowledge. They are able to interrupt the course of nature—to send sudden storms, pestilences, and other evils—to endow themselves or others with any forms they like, and to do many other things, of which we read in fairy tales. But even Zeus, to whom a far greater measure of power is accorded than to other gods, and on whose will the government of the universe depends, is himself subjected to the immutable decrees of fate; whilst the possibility of deceiving and duping him is by no means excluded.

Where then are we to seek for the explanation of these apparent inconsistencies? We have already said that the active and creative forces of Nature were personified by the imagination of men. Let us take one of the first conceptions likely to spring up—that of the love of the heaven for the earth, from which all nature is born. Different names will be used in different localities; men will at last forget that they all once meant the same, and out of the simple personification will spring a series of divine marriages; or if one be recognised by the whole nation as the wife, the other brides will sink into mistresses.

So with the everlasting war of the sun with the clouds; we shall not only find several gods of the light in Greece, but almost every tribe had a particular hero, whose great deeds we shall generally find to be those of the sun. Yet in the midst of

all this confusion, men had a feeling that there was something
above them better and holier than they, to which that which
is good and holy alone was pleasing.   This idea was more and
more attached to Zeus himself, as the notion grew that Zeus
was the supreme god, the king of heaven.

PART I.—COSMOGONY AND THEOGONY.

BY Cosmogony, we understand the legends relating to the creation of the world; by Theogony, those relating to the origin of the gods. On both points we have to deal with the Greeks alone, since the Romans never indulged in any researches of this kind. All that their poets have to say on the subject is, without exception, borrowed from the Greeks.

According to the common account the world was formed out of Chaos. By this, however, we must not understand a huge and shapeless mass, but merely dark, unbounded space. The accounts of the poets vary very materially as to how the world proceeded from Chaos. The most popular view is that according to which Gæa or Ge (the earth) first issued from Chaos; whereupon Tartarus (the abyss beneath the earth) immediately severed itself, and Eros (the love that forms and binds all things) sprang into existence. Gæa then begot of herself Uranus (heaven), the mountains, and Pontus (the sea).

The first gods who peopled this new world were begotten of the earth partly by Uranus and partly by Pontus. From her union with Uranus sprang the Titans, the Cyclopes, and the Centimanes; from her union with Pontus various sea-deities.

1. The race of Uranus. According to Hesiod there were twelve Titans: six males—Oceanus, Cœus, Crius, Hyperion, Iapetus, and Cr.. s; and six females—Thia, Rhea, Themis, Mnemosyne, Phœbe, and Tethys. The interpretation of these divinities is

somewhat difficult, but they doubtless represented the elementary forces of nature. The Cyclopes were three in number—Brontes (thunder), Steropes (lightning), and Arges (sheet-lightning): these, we can clearly see, refer to the phenomena of the storm. The Centimanes (hundred-handed), again, are three in number—Cottus, Briareus, and Gyes. These, too, represent destructive forces of nature—perhaps the earthquake, the tempestuous sea, and the storm-wind.

2. The race of Pontus. By Pontus Gæa became the mother of the fabulous sea-deities—Nereus, Thaumas, Phorcys, Ceto, and Eurybia. These, again, had numerous descendants. Nereus represents the sea in its quiet state : we shall have to speak of him and his daughters later on. Thaumas represents to us the majesty of the sea. He is the father of Iris (the rainbow), and of the Harpies (storm-winds). Lastly, Phorcys and Ceto, from whose union the frightful Gorgons and Grææ proceeded, typify all the dangers and terrors of the sea.

Many marriages also took place among the Titans themselves. The numerous sea-nymphs are descended from Oceanus and Tethys; from Hyperion and Thia come the deities of the light—Helios (sun), Selene (moon), and Eos (dawn) ; from Cœus and Phœbe the deities of the night—Leto (dark night) and Asteria (starry night).

The most important of all the Titans, however, are Cronus and Rhea, who pave the way for the universal dominion of their son Zeus.

Uranus, fearing lest his last-born sons, the powerful Cyclopes and Centimanes, might one day seize his power, buried them directly after birth in the deep abyss beneath the earth. This displeased Gæa, their mother, who thereupon prompted the Titans to conspire against their father, and induced Cronus, the youngest and bravest of them, to lay violent hands on Uranus. Uranus was mutilated, cast into chains, and compelled by his sons to abdicate his sovereignty, which now passed to Cronus. But Cronus was not long destined to enjoy the fruits of his crime.

The curse of Uranus, who prophesied that he would suffer a like fate at the hands of his own son, was fulfilled. So anxious was he to avert such a catastrophe, that he swallowed his children immediately after their birth. Five had already suffered this fate—Hestia, Demeter, Hera, Hades, and Poseidon. But their mother Rhea, grieved at their lot, determined to rescue her next son, Zeus, by a stratagem. In the place of her child, she gave to her suspicious and cruel husband a stone wrapped in swaddling clothes, which he swallowed without further examination. Zeus, who was thus rescued, was reared by the nymphs in a grotto on Mount Dicte, in Crete. The she-goat Amalthea served as his nurse, whilst the bees brought him honey to eat. In order that the cries of the child might not betray his presence to his suspicious father, the Curetes, or attendant priests of Rhea, drowned his voice in the clashing of their weapons. Zeus remained thus hidden until he had become a mighty though youthful god. He then attacked and overthrew his father Cronus, whom he also compelled, by means of a device of Gæa, to bring forth the children that he had devoured. One part of the Titans—Oceanus, Themis, Mnemosyne, and Hyperion—submitted without hesitation to the dominion of the new ruler of the world. The others, however, refused allegiance; but Zeus, after a contest of ten years, overthrew them, with the help of the Cyclopes and Centimanes. As a punishment, they were cast into Tartarus, which was then closed by Poseidon with brazen gates. Thessaly, the land which bears the clearest traces of natural convulsions, was supposed to have been the scene of this mighty war. Zeus and his adherents fought from Olympus; the Titans from the opposite mountain of Othrys.

Comparison of the legends of other nations does not show us any such elaborate genealogy. Zeus has his counterparts almost everywhere, and Uranus himself appears in India; but Cronus, in the sense of the father of Zeus, is probably traceable to the common epithet of Zeus, Cronion, which was assumed in later

times to be a patronymic. It was natural to deduce from the
idea that one power of nature sprang from another, the expression that the god of the first power was the child of the god
of the second; it would perhaps be more correct to say that it
was the same thing to the early races of men. As to the wars,
which were so great a stumbling-block to the Greek philosophers,
we may notice that the supreme god must, of course, have been
the son of a supreme god; and yet, if his predecessor were
supreme, must have dispossessed him.

The Titans, not being actually objects of worship, were not frequently represented in ancient art. Cronus is the only exception, which may be explained by the fact that the Romans identified him with their own Saturn, or harvest-god. He is generally depicted with a severe and gloomy expression of countenance, the back of his head being veiled, as a symbol of his reserved character. In the Vatican Museum at Rome there is a bust of this kind in good preservation, an engraving of which we give (Fig. 1).

Fig. 1.—Bust of Cronus. Vatican Museum.

After his victory over the Titans, Zeus shared the empire of
the world with his two brothers, Poseidon and Hades. The
former he made ruler of the ocean and waters; the latter he set
over the infernal regions; everything else he retained for himself. This new order of things, however, was by no means

securely established. The resentment of Gæa led her to produce with Tartarus, her youngest and most powerful son, the giant Typhoeus, a monster with a hundred fire-breathing dragons' heads, whom she sent to overthrow the dominion of Zeus. A great battle took place, which shook heaven and earth. Zeus, by means of his never-ceasing thunderbolts, at length overcame Typhoeus, and cast him into Tartarus, or, according to later writers (Pindar and Virgil), buried him beneath Mount Ætna in Sicily, whence at times he still breathes out fire and flames toward heaven.

Some poets tell of another rebellion, that of the Giants, against the dominion of Zeus. These are said to have sprung from the drops of blood which fell on the earth from the mutilated body of Uranus. From the plains of Phlegra, in Thessaly, they sought to storm Olympus by piling Pelion on Ossa. But after a bloody battle, in which all the gods took part, the two were conquered, and sent to share the fate of the vanquished Titans. The dominion of Zeus was now securely established, and no hostile attack ever after disturbed the peaceful ease of the inhabitants of Olympus.

The early history of Zeus, as well as his contests for the empire of the universe, commonly called the Giganto-machia, was a favourite subject with Greek art. In the more ancient of these works the Giants do not differ, either in form or appearance, from the Gods and Heroes. In later works they are represented with the bodies of dragons, only the upper portion of the body being human. They appear thus on the celebrated cameo of the Naples Museum,

Fig. 2.—Cameo of Athenion.

where Zeus, in his chariot drawn by four fiery horses, is in the act of charging them (Fig. 2).

PART II.—THE GODS.

I.—THE GODS OF OLYMPUS.

A.—SUPERIOR DEITIES.

1. Zeus (Jupiter).—Chief of the celestial deities is Zeus, called by the Romans Jupiter, the controller and ruler of the universe. As being the god of heaven *par excellence*, the " Sky-father," he is to both nations the source of all life in nature, and from his gracious hand are shed blessing and abundance. All the phenomena of the air were supposed to proceed from him. He gathers and disperses the clouds, casts forth his lightning, stirs up his thunder, sends down rain, hail, snow, and fertilising dew on the earth. With his ægis—an impenetrable shield hung with a hundred golden tassels, in the midst of which the fearful head of the Gorgon is fastened—he produces storm and tempest. The ægis, though often meaning shield, is properly a goat-skin fastened to and supporting the true shield ; later it appears as a short cloak, and even as a breastplate, covered with scales, and fringed with serpents. It is not often found in representations of Zeus ; though a statue of him at Leyden shows it, and in a cameo he is seen with it wrapped around his left arm : similarly it was common to wrap the chlamys or scarf round the left arm, for purposes of defence. The ægis usually belongs to Athene, who borrows it from her father in the *Iliad*. She is seen wearing it in Fig. 9. In this word we probably see a confusion of two ideas, different, though of similar origin; from the same root that gives us the "springing" goat we have the storm-cloud "tossed" over the sky.

The ancients, however, were not content to regard Zeus merely as a personification of Nature; they regarded him also from an ethical standpoint, from which side he appears far more important and awful. They saw in him a personification, so to speak, of that principle of undeviating order and harmony which pervades both the physical and moral world. The strict unalterable laws by which he rules the community of the gods form a strong contrast to the capricious commands of his father Cronus. Hence Zeus is regarded as the protector and defender of all political order. From him the kings of the earth receive their sovereignty and rights; to him they are responsible for a conscientious fulfilment of their duties. Those among them who unjustly exceed their powers and pervert justice he never fails to punish. Zeus, moreover, also presides over councils and assemblies, keeps watch over their orderly course, and suggests to them wise counsels. One of the most important props of political society is the oath; and accordingly, as Zeus Horkios (ὅρκιος, *deus fidius* of the Romans), he watches over oaths, and punishes perjury. He also watches over boundaries, and accompanies the youths of the land as they march to the defence of their country's borders, giving them the victory over the invaders. All civil and political communities enjoy his protection; but he particularly watches over that association which is the basis of the political fabric—the family. The head of every household was therefore, in a certain sense, the priest of Zeus. It was he who presented the offerings to the god in the name of the family. At his altar, which generally stood in the middle of the court (in small households this was represented by the hearth), all strangers, fugitives, and suppliants found shelter. As Zeus Xenius (*hospitalis*) he protects the wanderer, and punishes those who violate the ancient laws of hospitality by mercilessly turning the helpless stranger from their door.

The superstition of early times saw in all the phenomena of the heavens manifestations of the divine will. Thus the chief deity of heaven was naturally regarded as the highest source of inspiration, and was believed to reveal his will to men in the thunder, the lightning, the flight of birds, or dreams. As the supreme oracular deity, Zeus not only had an oracle of his own at Dodona in Epirus, which was the most ancient in Greece, but also revealed the future by the mouth of his favourite son Apollo. Though he possessed no proper oracle among the Romans, yet the latter looked with all the more care and anxiety on the phenomena of the air and sky, the right interpretation of which formed a special and difficult branch of knowledge.

Zeus was the earliest national god of the Greeks. His worship extended throughout the whole of Greece, though some of his shrines had a special importance. The most ancient of them was that at Dodona, where the Pelasgian Zeus was worshipped at a time prior to the existence of any temples in Greece. He was here represented in the celebrated form of the sacred oak, in the rustling of whose branches the deity revealed himself to the faithful. He was also worshipped on the summit of Mount Tomarus, at the foot of which lay Dodona—mountain-tops being naturally the earliest seats of his worship. But all the earlier shrines were overshadowed by the great national seat of the worship of Hellenic Zeus at Olympia, on the northern banks of the river Alpheus, in Elis, where the renowned Olympian games were celebrated. The magnificent statue of Zeus, by Phidias, was an additional inducement to devotees, who flocked thither from every quarter.

Neither was the worship of Jupiter any less extensive in Italy. The most renowned of all his shrines was undoubtedly the temple erected by Tarquin on the Capitol at Rome. This, after being nearly destroyed by fire in the time of Sulla, was restored to more than its pristine splendour. The original earthen image was replaced by a statue of gold and ivory, the work of the Greek artist Apollonius, after the model of the Olympian Zeus.

Before proceeding to discuss the god as he appears in art, we must take a glance at his numerous family. The mythology of the Greeks stands in notorious contrast to that of the Romans, in attributing to Zeus a great number of mortal as well as immortal spouses, and an unusually numerous posterity. Here we must remark that, in spite of the occasional jokes of the comic poets on the numerous amours of the god, and the consequent jealousy of Hera, there was nothing farther from the intention of the Greeks than to represent the supreme deity of heaven as a sensual and lascivious being. The explanation lies partly in the great number of contemporaneous local forms of worship that existed independently of each other, and partly in the fact that the lively fancy of the Greek pictured every new production under the guise of procreation. In that part of mythology which teaches the genealogy of the gods, the earliest wife of Zeus was Metis (prudence), the daughter of Oceanus. Zeus devoured her, fearing lest she should bear a son, who would deprive him of the empire it had cost him so much to attain. It was soon after this that he produced Pallas Athene from his own head. His second goddess-wife was Themis, one of the Titans, by whom he became the father of the Horæ and the Mœræ (Fates). Dione appears as the wife of Zeus of Dodona, and the mother of Aphrodite; whilst Arcadian Zeus was wedded to Maia, by whom he had Hermes. By Demeter (Ceres) he became the father of Persephone (Proserpine, goddess of vegetation); by Eurynome, a daughter of Oceanus, of the Charites (Graces); by Mnemosyne, of the Muses; by Leto (Latona), of

Apollo and Artemis. The youngest of all his divine wives, who was recognised by later mythology as his only legitimate queen, was his sister Hera. By her he became the father of Ares (Mars), Hephæstus (Vulcan), and Hebe.

Among his mortal mistresses the most celebrated is Semele, the daughter of Cadmus, king of Thebes, and mother of Dionysus. The others—Leda, Danaë, Alcmene, Europe, and Io—will be mentioned hereafter.

The mythology of the Romans, as we have already remarked, first depicted Jupiter as devoid of all family ties. It was only after their religion had been Hellenised that men termed him the son of Saturn and Ops, made Juno his wife and Minerva his daughter.

Statues of Zeus were necessarily very numerous, both from the great extent of his worship and the great number of his temples that existed in Greece. Of all these the most renowned was the magnificent statue of Zeus at Olympia, the work of the Athenian sculptor Phidias (500–432 B.C.). The figure was seated on a lofty throne, and was more than 40 feet high. It was made of gold and ivory, or more probably a statue of wood was overlaid with plates of ivory and gold. The uncovered parts—the face, throat, breast, and hands—were of ivory. In his right hand was a figure of Victory, also of gold and ivory ; in his left was a royal sceptre, on the top of which perched an eagle. The numerous lengthy descriptions that exist can give us but a faint idea of the lofty majesty that the sculptor diffused over the countenance of the god. The object of Phidias was to represent him to mankind, not only as the omnipotent ruler of Olympus, far superior to all gods and men, both in power and wisdom ; but also as the gracious father of all, and the kindly dispenser of all good gifts. The hair, which rose straight from the brow, and then fell in equal divisions on either side, imparted to the face a lion-like expression of conscious power. This was rendered still more effective by the high forehead and strongly-formed nose. At the same time, the expression of the slightly-opened lips lent an idea of kindly benevolence. The story goes that Phidias, after completing the statue, prayed of the god a sign that he was well pleased with his work. Zeus thereupon caused a flash of lightning to descend through the open roof of the temple, and thus acknowledged his own image.

This sublime masterpiece of Phidias, which was reckoned among the seven wonders of the world, continued in existence, though not

Fig. 3.—Zeus of Otricoli. Vatican Museum.

without injury, for upwards of 800 years. It appears to have been destroyed by fire in the time of Theodosius III.

Fig. 4.—Jupiter Verospi. Vatican Museum.

C

The following are the most important of the existing statues of Zeus by Greek and Roman sculptors. The first in point of artistic worth is a bust of Zeus, in Carrara marble—now in the Vatican Museum at Rome—which was discovered in the last century at Otricoli (Fig. 3). The union of serene majesty and benevolence is the chief feature in the sublime countenance. Next comes a colossal statue in marble, known as the Jupiter of Verospi, also in the Vatican Museum (Fig. 4). Lastly, there is a bust of Zeus, discovered at Pompeii, and now in the Museum at Naples, besides an equally beautiful bronze statue in the British Museum, found at Paramythia in Epirus. On comparing all the extant art monuments of Zeus, we may gather that the object of ancient art was to present him especially as the benign ruler of the universe, sitting enthroned in

Fig. 5.—Coins of Elis with Phidias' Zeus. (After Overbeck.)

conscious majesty and blissful ease on the heights of Olympus. His characteristic features are the clustering hair, falling like a mane on either side of his fine arched brow, and the rich wavy beard. His attributes consist of the sceptre, as a symbol of his sovereignty; the thunderbolt; the eagle; the votive bowl, as a symbol of his worship; the ball beneath or near his seat, as a symbol of the universe he rules; and, lastly, a figure of Victory. His head is sometimes adorned with a garland of oak-leaves, the oak being sacred to him; and sometimes with an olive-branch or plain band, the latter being a mark of sovereignty. In Fig. 5 we give an engraving of two coins of Elis, one of which is in the Florentine and the other in the Paris Museum.

2. Hera (Juno).—Hera, according to Homer, was the eldest of the daughters of Cronus and Rhea. She is the feminine counterpart of Zeus, her brother and husband. She represents the air or atmosphere; for which reason she, like Zeus, was supposed to control the phenomena of the air and sky, and, as queen of heaven, shared with him all the honours of his position. Her conjugal relations to Zeus, which form the substance of all the myths that refer to her, afforded the poets a rich and productive material for serious and sportive poetry. They sang of the solemn marriage of Zeus and Hera, the remembrance of which was celebrated at springtide with festive offerings and marriage rites before the shrine of the goddess. Neither did they fail to tell of the conjugal strife of the royal pair, and of the cruel fate which overtook the mortal women who enjoyed the favours of Zeus. It was thus that jealousy and contention became the leading features in the character of the goddess; whereas, both in her worship and in the representations of artists, she appears as a gracious and kindly deity, the especial protectress of her own sex.

The natural signification of Hera appears to have quickly disappeared among the Greeks, and she seems to have been chiefly honoured as the guardian of the marriage tie. The nobleness of the woman who preserves inviolate the sanctity of this bond finds in her its most sublime expression. As the special patroness of marriage, she was supposed to watch over its sanctity, to vouchsafe the blessing of children, and to protect women in childbirth.

The worship of Hera was originally not very extensive. The cradle of her worship was Argos, on which account she is often termed Argive. Argos, Mycenæ, and Sparta are pointed out in the time of Homer as her favourite towns. Her worship naturally extended as her new character of goddess of marriage became more prominent. In Bœotia and Eubœa her worship

Fig. 6.—Barberini Juno.   Vatican Museum.

was very ancient, but her chief shrine was the Heræum, between Argos and Mycenæ. Here was a most magnificent statue of the goddess, made of ivory and gold, the work of the Sicyonian artist, Polycletus.*

Juno (properly Jovino) takes the same place as goddess of childbirth and patroness of marriage among the Romans as Hera did among the Greeks. In addition to this she was venerated, under the name of Juno Regina, as the tutelary deity of the city and empire of

---

* Polycletus, a native of Sicyon, was a sculptor, architect, and caster in bronze. He was a contemporary of Phidias, and, next to him, the most celebrated artist of antiquity.

Rome. Her chief shrine was on the Capitol, where she had a separate chapel in the temple of Jupiter. The Matronalia, the chief festival of the goddess, was celebrated on the first

Fig. 7.—Head of Hera, perhaps after Polycletus. Naples.

day of March, when all the matrons of the city marched in procession to her temple on the Esquiline, and there offered her flowers and libations. The victims usually sacrificed to Juno were young heifers : her sacred birds were the goose and the crow, to which the peacock of the Greek Hera was afterwards added.

The most celebrated of the art monuments that relate to Juno is the Juno Ludovisi, a colossal marble bust of remarkable beauty, which, thanks to casts and photographs, is tolerably well known. Her lofty and commanding countenance is the ideal of perfect womanly beauty, combining in a rare degree woman's chief ornaments—dignity and grace.

After this comes the Juno Barberini of the Vatican Museum, an entire and upright figure of great size (Fig. 6), distinguished by the admirable draping of the garments. The Farnese Juno, now in the Naples Museum, also deserves mention. In the same museum there is a singularly beautiful head of Hera (Fig. 7), which perhaps lays claim to reflect the conception of Polycletus.

The characteristic features of Juno are a somewhat prominent chin, expressing unbending determination of will ; somewhat curling lips, well-defined nostrils, large full eyes, and a high and noble forehead. The attributes of the goddess consist of the sceptre and diadem, significant of her power ; the veil (often omitted in the statues of later artists), as a symbol of the married woman ; the votive bowl in the hand, the pomegranate as a symbol of love, and the peacock or goose at her feet, also at times the cuckoo, as herald of spring.

3. Pallas Athene (Minerva).—The accounts which the Greeks gave of the birth of Pallas vary considerably. The most common is that which has been already mentioned. According to this, Zeus produced her from his head, which he had ordered Hephæstus to cleave open. The great goddess of war, in full armour, with poised spear, then sprang forth from her father's head, chanting a war-song, whilst a mighty commotion both on sea and land announced the great event to the world. In her physical character Pallas appears as the goddess of the dawn. The birth of the dawn from the forehead of the sky is not only a natural idea, but one which can be traced in the legends of other nations. Several of the other stories of her birth are connected with the name Tritogenia, the daughter of Tritos, a god, whose name, though not actually found in Greek mythology, may be traced in Amphitrite,

Triton, and the Lake Tritonis. This name, which originally expressed the birth of the dawn from the water, was afterwards explained in various ways, and the first part was even derived from a provincial Greek word meaning head. Looked at from her ethical side, she appears as the goddess of wisdom, a reflection and personification of that profound wisdom and sagacity with which Father Zeus controls the destinies of the world. Hence we may easily gather the other features of her character. She is, in the first place, the protectress of states; and all that their welfare requires in peace or war proceeds from her. Thus she appears as goddess of peace as well as war. In the latter capacity she accompanies the army on its march, inspires the soldiers with ardour for the fray, and rewards them with victory and rich spoils; she also affords her mighty protection to towns and cities at home. In Homer she figures, besides, as the kindly guide and protectress of individual heroes, such as Odysseus, Achilles, Diomedes. It was she who first taught mankind to manage the horse, and to build ships and chariots; she also invented the war-trumpet and flute. As goddess of war she usually wears, besides helmet, shield, and spear, the dreadful ægis. The latter, in art monuments, is represented as a breastplate covered with dragon's scales, and surrounded with serpents, in the midst of which is the dreadful head of Medusa, which has the effect of turning every one that looks on it into stone.

As goddess of peace, Athene is equally lavish in blessing. Everything necessary either to the physical or intellectual welfare of mankind was believed to proceed from her, and to be subject to her influence. Accordingly, useful inventions of all kinds are ascribed to her. It was she who first gave men the rake and the plough; it was she who invented the distaff and loom, as well as the art of dyeing woven stuffs, and many other feminine accomplishments.

By later writers this skill in art is extended to other things, and she is represented as the patroness of every branch of science, art, and manufacture.

She is also called Athene Hygiea, because she was believed to send pure atmosphere, to ward off pestilence, and to promote the growth and health of the youth of the land. We cannot wonder, therefore, that the worship of a goddess so benevolent, and exercising such an important influence on human life, was very extensive in Greece. Nowhere did she receive a higher degree of veneration than at Athens, of which city she was really the tutelary deity. Her most important shrine was the Parthenon (temple of the virgin goddess), which was erected by Pericles on the Acropolis, and the remains of which, even in the present day, excite the wonder and admiration of the world. The whole land of Attica was, indeed, in a certain measure, the peculiar property of the goddess, which she won after her well-known contest with Poseidon. Zeus had decreed the sovereignty over Attica to that deity who should bestow on the land the most useful present. Poseidon thereupon created the horse; but Athene caused the olive-tree to grow, and was thus held to have won the victory. The sacred olive-tree, which was thus called into existence, was shown in the Temple of Erechtheus on the Acropolis, and possessed such a wonderful vitality that, when the Persians burnt it after capturing the town, it immediately put forth a fresh shoot. Argos and Corinth were also renowned seats of the worship of Pallas Athene; and she also enjoyed the highest veneration in Sparta, Bœotia, Thessaly, Arcadia, and Rhodes.

The Roman Minerva, whose name was derived from a root meaning "to think," was Hellenised at a very early period, and identified with the Greek Pallas. In Rome, however, the warlike character of the goddess was completely merged in that of the peaceful inventress and patroness of the art and sciences, and of all handiwork of women. She was here worshipped, in company with Jupiter and Juno, as the tutelary deity of the city and empire, and had, in consequence, her own shrine in the temple of Jupiter Capitolinus. She also had temples on the

Aventine and Cœlian hills, to which a third was added by Pompey, in 61 B.C., in the Campus Martius.

Festivals of the goddess.—The Panathenæa, the chief festival of the Greek Pallas, were celebrated with great pomp every four years. A solemn procession passed through the streets of Athens up to the Acropolis; and an offering was made to the goddess in the shape of a costly garment (peplus), artistically embroidered by the Athenian maidens. Horse races, athletic and musical contests, took place at the same time. Another festival of less importance, called the Lesser Panathenæa, was celebrated every year at Athens in honour of the goddess.

At Rome the chief festival of Minerva, the Quinquatrus Majores, was held on the 19th of March, and was, in later times, extended to five days. It was especially observed by all engaged in intellectual pursuits, and by artists and artisans. As Minerva was also patroness of schools, the schoolboys also took part in the celebration, and enjoyed a welcome holiday.

The virgin goddess was at all times a favourite subject with ancient art. Even in the earliest times, before casting in bronze or marble sculpture was known, while the images of the gods were as yet rudely carved in wood, Pallas was a frequent subject of delineation. These wooden images usually represented the goddess as standing upright with poised spear in front of the battle, and were then called Palladia. Men delighted to believe them to have fallen from heaven, and to be a sure means of protection against hostile attack. When Greek art was in its prime, the first masters vied with each other in the representation of the goddess. Phidias outdid them all in his renowned statue of Athene Parthenos, which stood in the temple on the Acropolis. The figure was 39 feet high, and was constructed of ivory and gold. Its majestic beauty naturally formed one of the chief attractions of the magnificent temple. It disappeared, without leaving any clue behind it, during the stormy period of the invasion of the nomadic tribes. In proceeding to give an account of the most important existing statues of the goddess, we must first mention a magnificent marble bust which King Ludwig I. of Bavaria procured for the Munich collection, and which was formerly in the Villa Albani, at Rome. The goddess here wears a tight-fitting helmet, the top of which is decorated with a serpent, the emblem of wisdom. Her breastplate, which is bordered with serpents, falls like a cape over her shoulders, and is fastened in the middle by the Gorgon's head, a terrible but striking contrast to the pure and noble countenance of the goddess. A fine bust, with a delicate and youthful expression of countenance, is preserved in the Vatican Museum at Rome.

Another, not less beautiful, but with grave and almost masculine features, was discovered in the excavations of Pompeii, and is now in the Naples Museum.

Among existing (full-length) statues, the Pallas Giustiniani, of the Vatican Museum at Rome, is held to be the finest (Fig. 8). This probably once stood in a Roman temple, having been found in a place where there was formerly a temple of Minerva. This statue, in accordance with the Roman conception, bears a more peaceable character, although neither the spear nor helmet are wanting. Next come two statues found near Velletri, one of which is in the Capitoline Museum at Rome, whilst the other forms a chief ornament of the Louvre collection in Paris. Both represent the goddess in the character of a benign deity fostering all peaceful works, with a gentle but earnest expression of countenance.

Fig. 8.—Pallas Giustiniani. Vatican.

Fig. 9.—Athene Polias. Villa Albani.

The Farnese Minerva of the Naples Museum and the "Hope" copy in London betray similar characteristics. On the other hand, in a statue discovered at Herculaneum (now at Naples), Minerva appears as a warlike goddess, in an evidently hostile attitude (Fig. 10). This is also the case with the celebrated statue at the Louvre, which, on account of the necklace worn by the goddess, is generally called *Minerve au Collier ;* and again in a statue of the Villa Albani, in which a lion's skin thrown over the head takes the place of the helmet (Fig. 9).

On combining the characteristic features of Minerva, we may gather that her most prominent trait is a lofty seriousness, well befitting the chaste, grave character of the virgin goddess. The closed lips and the prominent chin betray a determined and resolute disposition, whilst her mien and bearing give token of strength and dignity.

Among the favourite animals of Minerva we may mention the serpent, the owl, and the cock. The first is a symbol of wisdom, the second of profound meditation, and the last of eager desire for the fray. The attributes of Minerva consist of the

Fig. 10.—Pallas Athene. Naples.

ægis, which serves as a shield, the spear, and the helmet. The helmet is sometimes adorned with the figures of griffins, significant of the overpowering might of the wearer. The statues are all fully clothed, in accordance with the chaste character of the goddess.

4. Apollo.—As Athene is the favourite daughter of Zeus, so Apollo ranks as the most glorious and beautiful of his sons. Like other sons of Zeus, he is a god of light, and, indeed, the purest and highest representative of this mighty power in nature. His mother, Leto (Latona), is a representative of the darkness of the night. According to the sacred legend, she was compelled when pregnant to wander about, because mankind, dreading the appearance of the mighty god, refused to receive her. This myth was afterwards altered by later writers, who assign the jealousy of Hera as the cause of her wanderings. Leto at length found a refuge on Delos, which was once a floating island, and had to be fastened to the bottom of the sea by means of lofty columns. As the bright god of heaven, to whom everything impure and unholy is hateful, we find Apollo, soon after his birth, preparing to do battle with the evil powers of darkness. With his arrows he slew both the giant Tityus and the serpent Python, the latter a monster that inhabited the valley of the Plistus, near Delphi, and destroyed both men and cattle. These and similar myths are merely a panegyric on the conquering power exercised by the genial warmth of Spring over the dark gloom of Winter.

But though Apollo thus appears as the foe of all that is evil and impure, ancient myths, nevertheless, represent him also as a terrible god of death, sending virulent pestilences and dealing out destruction to men and animals by means of his unerring arrows. This may be easily explained, however, by glancing at the natural signification of the god. The rays of the sun do indeed put to flight the cold of winter, but as their heat increases they themselves ultimately become the cause of disease and death. This is beautifully portrayed in the fable of the death of Hyacinthus.

To proceed further in the analysis of his character as god of light, Apollo next appears as the protector of streets and houses. A conical pillar was usually erected at the side of the doors of houses as a symbol of him, and a defence against all sorceries. Connected with this is his repute as a god of health ; one who is indeed able to send disease and death, but who, on the other hand, is all-powerful to protect against physical maladies. This feature in his character, however, is more extensively developed in the person of his son, Asclepius (Æsculapius). But it is not only outward ills that this wonder-working deity can cure : as the true redeemer from sin and crime, he alone can afford consolation to guilty souls. Even those pursued by the Furies he sometimes receives in tenderness and pity, a fine instance of which is found in the story of Orestes. It is here that we must seek the explanation of his character as god of music ; in the fact that it exercises so soothing and tranquillising an influence on the soul of man. His favourite instrument was the lyre, which he was wont to play with masterly skill at the banquets of the gods, whilst the Muses accompanied him with their wondrous strains. Apollo was therefore regarded as the leader of the Muses (Musagetes) ; and all the great singers of antiquity, such as Orpheus and Linus, are mythically represented as his sons.

But Apollo attained his greatest importance among the Greeks as god of prophecy. His oracles continued to exercise an important influence on social and political life, even down to the latest times. The inspiration of Apollo was distinguished by the fact that the god revealed the future less by means of outward signs than by inducing an ecstatic condition of mind bordering on madness in those persons through whom he wished to proclaim his oracles. These were generally women and maidens, who, either at oracular shrines proper, or dwelling alone as Sibyls, gave forth the responses of the god. In early times they were somewhat numerous. There was an oracle at Clarus, near Colophon ; an oracle at Didyma, near Miletus ; and an oracle on the Ismenus, near Thebes. These were eventually all thrown into the shade by that of Delphi. The responses of this oracle exercised, during a long period of Grecian history, an all-powerful influence, especially on the Dorian tribes. The convulsions of the Pythia, or priestess of Apollo, were brought about partly by the chewing of laurel leaves, and partly by the gaseous vapours that issued from a cleft in the earth beneath the sacred tripod. The ecstatic condition in which she gave the responses, which were comprehensible only to the initiated priests, manifested itself in a foaming at the mouth and in convulsions of the body.

Delphi naturally became the chief seat of the worship of Apollo. The gorgeous temple was rebuilt in the time of the Pisistratidæ, after the destruction of the old one by fire. Its wealth from offerings became so great that their value was computed at 10,000 talents (more than £2,000,000). In the neighbourhood of Delphi the Pythian games were celebrated in the third year of every Olympiad.

The shrine of the god at Delos, his birthplace, was little less renowned. The sanctuary itself was situated at the foot of Mount Cynthus; but the whole island was sacred to the god, for which reason no one was buried there. Here, too, games, said to have been instituted by Theseus, were celebrated every four years in honour of the god. Apollo had, besides, a great number of less celebrated shrines and temples, not only in Greece, but also in Asia Minor, and wherever the Greek colonies extended.

The Apollo of the Romans, as his name indicates, was transferred to Rome from Greece. At a comparatively early period men began to feel the want of a prophetic deity, as the Roman gods, although they vouchsafed hints as to the future, confined their responses to a mere Yea or Nay. Moreover, in the character of god of healing, he was early admitted into the Roman system, as we gather from the fact that the first temple really dedicated to Apollo was erected in 429 B.C., under the pressure of a grievous pestilence. The worship of Apollo was especially exalted by the Emperor Augustus, who ascribed his victory at Actium chiefly to the assistance of the god. He accordingly erected a magnificent temple to Apollo on the Palatine, which was embellished with the celebrated statue of Apollo Citharœdus, by Scopas.

Fig. 11.—Apollo Belvedere. Vatican.

This remark leads us to contemplate the different statues of the god. Apollo constantly bears a very youthful appearance, and is always beardless. His figure is strong and handsome, his head covered with fair clustering locks, and his face expressive of majesty, but marked withal by a cheerful serenity. Such is the original and

Fig. 12.—Head of Apollo Belvedere.

fundamental type, which was usually followed in the representation of the god. It was principally developed by Scopas and Praxiteles, who belonged to the later Attic school, which flourished from the end of the Peloponnesian war to the reign of Alexander the Great.

D

The principal creation of Scopas was a marble statue, representing the god as a Pythian Citharœdus with the lyre in his hand, clothed in a long robe reaching to the feet. This invaluable work was procured by Augustus for the temple he erected to Apollo on the Palatine. Praxiteles, a younger contemporary of Scopas, acquired considerable renown by his bronze figure of a youthful Apollo pursuing a lizard (Apollo Sauroctonus). In existing art monuments sometimes the conception of a warlike, vengeful deity obtains, in which case the god is represented as nude, or nearly so, and armed with quiver and bow. At other times he wears a mild and benevolent aspect ; he is then distinguished by his lute, and completely enveloped in a chlamys. Of the former kind is the most beautiful and celebrated of all his existing statues, the Apollo Belvedere, which was discovered in 1503, near Nettuno, the ancient Antium, and is now in the Vatican. The proud self-consciousness of a conquering deity is inimitably expressed in his whole attitude. He stands with his right hand and leg against the trunk of a tree, his left arm outstretched, with the ægis, probably as a symbol of fear and terror, in his hand. The serpent creeping up the tree is a symbol of the powers of darkness vanquished by the god (Fig. 11). It may also be taken as the symbol of life and healing, like the serpent of Asclepius (see p. 96). We have also given a larger engraving of the head of the Belvedere Apollo, in order to afford a clearer idea of its wondrous beauty (Fig. 12).

The so-called Apollino, of the Florence gallery, a youthful figure resting after battle, is a work of scarcely less beauty. The shape of the body, which is entirely nude, is wonderfully soft and delicate. With his left arm the god leans upon a tree ; in his left hand he negligently holds the bow, whilst his right hand is raised to his head in a meditative fashion. The Farnese Apollo of the Naples Museum possesses an equally graceful form. The god is here represented as a musician ; in his left hand he holds the lyre, whilst his right glides over the strings. The animated expression of his face, indicating his entire devotion to his art, is exquisitely beautiful. The goose at his feet, which was regarded even by the ancients as a music-loving bird, appears to drink in with rapture the heavenly tones.

In those works which represent the god as a Pythian lute-player in a long Ionian garment, we perceive an almost feminine figure and a visionary expression of face. The most important works of this kind are the Apollo Citharœdus of the Munich collection (Fig. 13), formerly called the Muse of Barberini, which is marked by a somewhat quieter attitude ; and the so-called Apollo Musagetes of the Vatican collection, which is characterised by a lively dancing movement of the figure, and is generally regarded as an imitation of the masterpiece of Scopas already mentioned. A pure and heavenly inspiration seems to pervade the features of the laurel-crowned god; his mighty lyre, to the tones of which he appears to be singing, is suspended from a band across the chest, and is aptly adorned with the portrait of Marsyas, his vanquished rival.

Fig 13.—Apollo Citharœdus. Munich.

Lastly, the graceful statue of Apollo Sauroctonus (Lizard-slayer) deserves mention. Many copies of it still exist, the chief of which is a marble statue in the Vatican collection. The delicate figure of the god, midway between youth and boyhood, leans carelessly against the trunk of a tree, up which a lizard is creeping. The god is eagerly watching its movements, in order to seize a favourable moment to nail it to the tree with his arrow.

The principle attributes of Apollo are the bow, arrows, quiver, laurel crown, and lyre. To these may be added, as symbols of his prophetic power, the tripod and the omphalos (navel), the latter being a representation of the earth's centre in the temple at Delphi, on which he is often depicted as sitting. The god also appears standing on the omphalos ; as in the case of a marble statue lately found in the theatre of Dionysus. His sacred animals were the wolf, the hind, the bat, the swan, the goose, and the dolphin ; the three last being music-loving creatures.

5. Artemis (Diana).—Artemis is the feminine counterpart of her twin brother Apollo, with whom she entirely harmonises when regarded from her physical aspect. Like him, she is a beautiful and propitious deity ; but like him, too, she can deal out, at times, death and destruction among mankind. Like Apollo, she promotes the growth of the young plant, and is equally the foe of all that is evil and impure. Like him, she is skilled in the use of the bow, of which she avails herself, however, not only for the destruction of monsters, but also at times to chastise the insolence of man—witness the death of the children of Niobe. Her favourite amusement is the chase ; armed with quiver and bow she ranges mountain and valley, accompanied by a band of nymphs. The chase ended, she delights to bathe in some fresh spring, or to lead off some favourite dance on the flowery meadows, surrounded by her nymphs, all of whom she overtops by a head. Then the heart of her mother, Leto, rejoices as she gazes on the innocent sports of her lovely daughter.

As a virgin goddess she was especially venerated by young maidens, whose patroness she remained till their marriage, and to whom she afforded an example of chastity. The story of

Actæon, who was changed into a stag and then torn to pieces by his own dogs, shows that she did not suffer any injury to her virgin modesty to go unpunished. (For this story see the Theban legends.)

Originally, Artemis appears to have been the goddess of the moon, just as her brother Apollo is unmistakably identical with the sun. This conception, however, continued to grow fainter and fainter, until, in the later days of confusion of religions, it was again revived. Artemis was frequently confounded with Selene or Phœbe (Luna).

The national Artemis of the Greeks was originally quite distinct from the Artemis Orthia, a dark and cruel deity, to whom human sacrifices were offered in Laconia. Lycurgus abolished this barbarous custom, but caused instead a number of boys to be cruelly whipped before the image of the goddess on the occasion of her annual festival. This is the same Artemis to whom Agamemnon was about to offer, in Aulis, his daughter Iphigenia, previous to the departure of the Greeks for Troy. The Scythians in Tauris likewise had a goddess whom they propitiated with human sacrifices. This caused her to be confounded with Artemis Orthia, and the story arose that Iphigenia was conveyed by the goddess to Tauris, from which place she subsequently, assisted by her brother Orestes, brought the image of the goddess to Greece.

The Ephesian Artemis, known to us as "Diana of the Ephesians," was distinct from all that have been mentioned. She was, in fact, an Asiatic, not a Hellenic deity.

The Roman Diana, who was early identified with the Greek Artemis, was likewise originally a goddess of the moon. As such, she possessed a very ancient shrine on Mount Algidus, near Tusculum. Like the Greek Artemis, she was also regarded as the tutelary goddess of women, and was invoked by women in childbirth. This was also the case with Artemis, although the

Fig. 14.—Diana of Versailles.

matrons of Greece looked for more protection in this respect at the hands of Hera. She gained, however, a certain political importance in Rome after having been made by Servius Tullius the tutelary deity of the Latin League. As such, she possessed a sacred grove and temple on the Aventine.

Artemis is a favourite subject with the masters of the later Attic school. She is always represented as youthful, slender and light of foot, and without womanly fulness. Her devotion to the chase is clearly betokened by the quiver and bow which she generally bears, and by the high girt robe and Cretan shoes, which allow her to pass unencumbered through the thickets of the forest.

Among existing statues, the most celebrated is the so-called Diana of Versailles, which came from the Villa of Hadrian, at Tibur (Fig. 14). It is now a chief ornament of the Louvre collection, and is a worthy companion to the Belvedere Apollo, although it does not quite equal this in beauty. In this statue the goddess does not appear as a huntress, but rather as the protectress of wild animals. She is conceived as having just come to the rescue of a hunted deer, and is in the act of turning with angry mien on the pursuers. With her right hand she grasps an arrow from the quiver that hangs at her back, and in her left she holds the bow.

A really beautiful statue of the Vatican collection depicts the goddess in a most striking attitude. She has just sent forth her deadly arrow, and is eagerly watching its effect. The hound at her side is just about to start in eager pursuit of the mark, which was evidently therefore a wild animal. In her left hand is the bow, still strung, from which her right hand has just directed the arrow. Her foot is likewise upraised in triumph, and her whole deportment expresses the proud joy of victory. The chief attributes of Diana are bow, quiver, and spear, and also a torch, as an emblem of her power to dispense light and life. The hind, the dog, the bear, and the wild boar were esteemed sacred to her.

6. Ares (Mars).—Ares, the son of Zeus and Hera, represents war from its fatal and destructive side, by which he is clearly distinguished from Athene, the wise disposer of battles. He was, it is probable, originally a personification of the angry clouded sky. His home, according to Homer, was in Thrace, the land of boisterous, wintry storms, among whose warlike inhabitants he was held in high esteem, although his worship was not so extensive in Greece.   Homer, in the *Iliad*, paints in particularly lively colours the picture of the rude "manslaying" god of war. He here appears as a deity who delights only in the wild din of battle, and is never weary of strife and slaughter.   Clad in brazen armour from head to foot, with waving plume, helmet, and high-poised spear, his bull's hide shield on his left arm, he ranges the battlefield, casting down all before him in his impetuous fury.   With strength he combines great agility, and is, according to Homer, the fleetest of the gods.   Strong though he be, however, he is overmatched in battle by Athene ; a palpable indication that prudent courage often accomplishes more than impetuous violence.

The usual attendants and servants of Ares are Fear and Terror.   By some writers they are described as his sons, yet in Homer they fight against him.   There is little to be said of the principal seats of his worship in Greece.   In Thebes he was regarded as the god of pestilence ; and Aphrodite, who elsewhere appears as the wife of Hephæstus, was given him to wife. By her he became the father of Harmonia, who married Cadmus, and thus became the ancestress of the Cadmean race in Thebes. According to an Athenian local legend, his having slain a son of Poseidon gave rise to the institution of the Areopagus.   He was here regarded as the god of vengeance.   A celebrated statue by Alcamenes adorned his temple at Athens.   Among the warlike people of Sparta the worship of Ares was also extensive.

This deity was regarded with a far greater degree of veneration in Rome, under the appellation of Mars, or Mavors.   He seems to have occupied an important position even among the earliest Italian tribes.   It was not as god of war, however—for which, amid the peaceful pursuits of cattle-rearing and husbandry, they cared little—but as the god of the spring triumphing over the powers of winter that he was worshipped.   It was from his bounty that the primitive people looked for the prosperous growth of their flocks and the fruits of their fields; it was Mars on whom they called for protection against bad weather and destructive pestilence.

In warlike Rome, however, this deity soon laid aside his peaceful character, and donned the bright armour of the god of war. He was even regarded as being, after Jupiter, the most important god of the state and people of Rome. Numa himself gave him a flamen of his own, and created or restored in his honour the priesthood of the Salii. The occasion, according to the sacred legend, was on this wise. As King Numa one morning, from the ancient palace at the foot of the Palatine, raised his hands in prayer to Jove, beseeching his protection and favour for the infant state of Rome, the god let fall from heaven, as a mark of his favour, an oblong brazen shield (ancile). At the same time a voice was heard declaring that Rome should endure as long as this shield was preserved. Numa then caused the sacred shield, which was recognised as that of Mars, to be carefully preserved. The better to prevent its abstraction, he ordered an artist to make eleven others exactly similar, and instituted for their protection the college of the Salii, twelve in number, like the shields, who were selected from the noblest families in Rome. Every year in the month of March, which was sacred to Mars, they bore the sacred shields in solemn procession through the streets of Rome, executing warlike dances and chanting ancient war-songs. From the days of Numa the worship of "Father Mars" continued to acquire an ever-increasing popularity. Before the departure of a Roman army on any expedition, the imperator retired to the sanctuary of the god in the old palace, and there touched the sacred shields and the spear of the statue of Mars, crying aloud at the same time, "Mars, watch over us!" According to popular belief, the god himself went unseen before the host as it marched to battle, whence he was called "Gradivus." In the war with the Lucanians and

Bruttians (282 B.c.), when the consuls were hesitating whether to begin the attack, an unknown youth of extraordinary stature and beauty encouraged the troops to begin the assault on the enemy's camp, and was himself the first to scale the wall. When he was afterwards sought for, in order that he might receive his richly merited reward, he had disappeared, leaving no trace behind him. As it could have been none other than Father Mars, the consul, Fabricius, decreed him a thanksgiving of three days' duration.

Mars naturally received a due share of all booty taken in war. Defeat was ascribed to his wrath, which men strove to avert by extraordinary sin-offerings.

Popular belief made Mars the father, by a vestal virgin, of Romulus and Remus, the legendary founders of the city. His wife appears to have been Nerio; but she enjoyed no honours at Rome.

In attendance on Mars we find Metus and Pallor, who answer to the Greek deities already mentioned; and also his sister Bellona, corresponding to the Enyo, who was worshipped in Pontus and Cappadocia, though not in Greece proper. Bellona had a temple in the Campus Martius.

The Campus Martius (Field of Mars), the celebrated place of exercise of the Roman youth, stretched from the Quirinal westwards to the Tiber, and was dedicated to the god of war. Augustus, after the overthrow of the murderers of Cæsar, his adoptive father, erected a temple to Mars, which was built in Greek style, and far surpassed in grandeur and splendour all the other temples of the god. Three columns of it are still standing, mute witnesses of vanished splendour. A large number of religious festivities were celebrated in the month of March in honour of Mars. The procession of the Salii formed the chief feature of the festival; but there were also races and games. On the Ides of October also a chariot race took place in honour of Mars, at which the singular custom prevailed of offering the near horse of the victorious team to the god. The inhabitants of the two oldest quarters of the city contended for the head of the slaughtered animal, and whoever got it was supposed to reap great blessings from its possession.

Ancient artists represented Marsasatall and powerful young man, whose activity, however, is as apparent as his strength. His characteristic features are short curly hair, small eyes, and broad nostrils, significant of the violence and passionateness of his nature. The most celebrated of existing statues is the Mars Ludovisi of the Villa Ludovisi, at Rome. It has often been conjectured that this is an imitation of the renowned work of Scopas. The deity is depicted as resting after battle ; and, in spite of the usual turbulence of his dis-

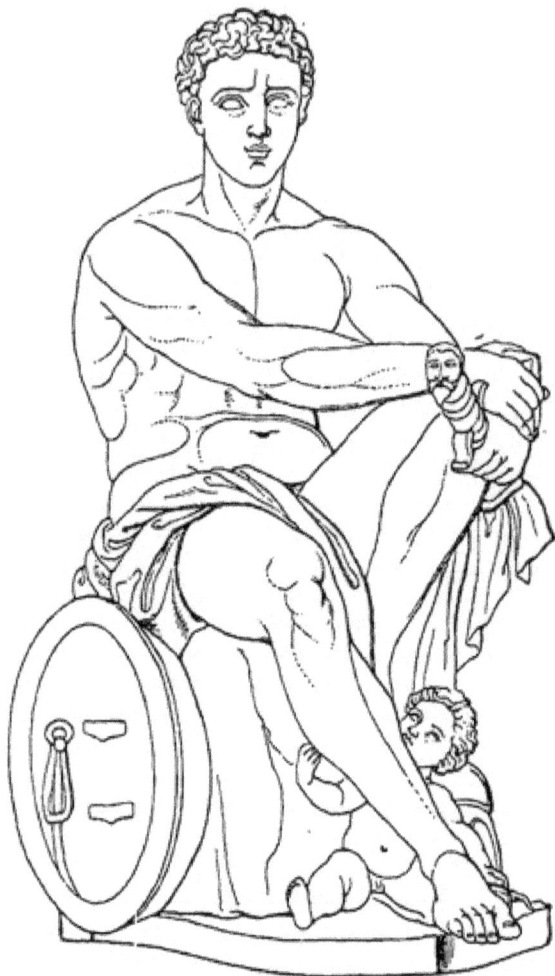

Fig 15 —Mars Ludovisi.

position, he here appears to have surrendered himself to a more gentle frame of mind. The little god of love crouching at his feet gazes into his face with a roguish, triumphant smile, as though rejoiced to see that even the wildest and most untameable must submit to his sway, and thus shows us what has called forth this gentle mood. (Fig. 15.) The Mars Ludovisi is an original work,

Greek in its origin, though belonging to a somewhat late period. The Borghese Mars of the Louvre, on the other hand, is undoubtedly of Roman origin. It is supposed to represent Ares bound by the craft of Hephæstus.

Besides these two principal statues, the bust of Mars of the Munich collection deserves mention. It is distinguished by a peculiarly expressive head, of which we give an engraving (Fig. 16).

The attributes of Mars are the helmet (decorated with the figures of wolf-hounds and griffins), shield, and spear. The animals sacred to him were the wolf, the horse, and the woodpecker.

Fig 16.—Bust of Ares. Sculpture Gallery at Munich.

7. Aphrodite (Venus).—

In the *Iliad*, Aphrodite is represented as the daughter of Zeus and Dione, the goddess of moisture, who, as the wife of the god of heaven, was held in high esteem among the old Pelasgians. The same notion of the goddess being produced from moisture is seen in the legend, which relates that Aphrodite was born of the foam of the sea, and first touched land on the island of Cyprus, which was henceforth held sacred to her. She was probably a personification of the creative and generative forces of nature, and figured among the Greeks as goddess of beauty and sexual love. We must not forget that this conception does not cover the whole character of the goddess. She not only appears as Aphrodite Pandemus (the earthly Aphrodite), a goddess of the spring, by whose wondrous power all germs in the natural and vegetable world are quickened, but we also hear of Aphrodite Urania, a celestial deity, who was venerated as the dispenser of prosperity and fertility; and also an Aphrodite Pontia (of the sea), the tutelary deity of ships and mariners, who controlled the winds and the waves, and granted to ships a fair and prosperous passage. As the worship of Aphrodite was extremely popular among the numerous islands and ports of the Grecian seas, we can well imagine that it was in this latter character that she received her greatest share of honour.

The poets paint Aphrodite as the most beautiful of all the goddesses, whose magic power not even the wisest could withstand. Even wild animals were conscious of her influence, and pressed round her like lambs. She was endowed with the celebrated love-begetting magic girdle, which she could lay aside at will and lend to others. And as she thus gave rise to passion in others, she herself was not free from its influence. This is evidenced by the numerous stories of her amours with the gods or favoured mortals, which it is so difficult to bring into harmony with each other. Sometimes Ares, sometimes Hephæstus, is said to be her husband. The latter account, which originated in Lemnos, was the more popular; doubtless because its very strangeness in mating the sweetest and most lovely of the goddesses with the lame and ugly god of fire had a certain charm. No children are mentioned as springing from the union of Aphrodite with Hephæstus; but Eros and Anteros, as well as Demus and Phobus, are said to be her children by Ares. Other legends, generally of a local character, unite her to Dionysus, or to Hermes.

The story of her love for the beautiful Adonis clearly represents the decay of nature in autumn, and its resuscitation in spring. Adonis, whom Aphrodite tenderly loved, was killed, when hunting, by a wild boar. Inconsolable at her loss, Aphrodite piteously entreated Father Zeus to restore his life.

Zeus at length consented that Adonis should spend one part of the year in the world of shadows, and the other in the upper world. Clearly the monster that deprived Adonis of life is only a symbol of the frosty winter, before whose freezing blast all life in nature decays. In the story of Troy, Aphrodite plays an important part. She was the original cause of the war, having assisted Paris in his elopement with Helen. This was his reward for his celebrated judgment, in which he awarded the prize of beauty to Aphrodite in preference to Hera or Athene. Besides the Trojan prince Anchises enjoyed her favours, and she became by him the mother of the pious hero Æneas.

The goddess appears ever ready to assist unfortunate lovers; thus she aided the hero Peleus to obtain the beautiful sea-nymph Thetis. On the other hand, she punishes with the utmost severity those who from pride or disdain resist her power. This appears in the legend of Hippolytus, son of Theseus, King of Athens, whom she ruined through the love of his stepmother Phædra; also in the story of the beautiful youth Narcissus, whom she punished by an ungratified self-love, because he had despised the love of the nymph Echo.

The Seasons and the Graces appear in attendance on Aphrodite. Their office is to dress and adorn her. She is also accompanied by Eros, Pothus, and Himerus (Love, Longing, and Desire), besides Hymen, or Hymenæus, the god of marriage.

The Roman Venus (the Lovely One) was regarded by the earlier Italian tribes as the goddess of spring, for which reason April, the month of buds, was held sacred to her. She early acquired a certain social importance, by having ascribed to her a beneficent influence in promoting civil harmony and sociability among men. After her identification with the Aphrodite of the Greeks, she became more and more a goddess merely of sensual love and desire. She had three principal shrines—those of Venus Murcia, Venus Cloacina, and Libitina. The first of these surnames points to Venus as the myrtle goddess (the myrtle being an emblem of chaste love); her temple was situated on the brow of the Aventine, and was supposed to have been erected by the Latins, who were planted there by Ancus Marcius.

The temple of Venus Cloacina (the Purifier) was said to have been erected in memory of the reconciliation of the Romans and Sabines, after the rape of the Sabine women. The surname of Libitina points to her as goddess of corpses. All the apparatus of funerals were kept in this temple, and her attendants were at the same time the public undertakers of the city.

To these ancient shrines was added another in the time of Julius Cæsar, who erected a temple to Venus Genetrix, the goddess of wedlock, in fulfilment of a vow made at the battle of Pharsalus.

Aphrodite, or Venus, is notoriously an especially common subject of representation among the artists of antiquity. The task of giving expression to the most perfect female beauty, arrayed in all the charms of love, by means of chisel or brush, continually spurs the artist to fresh endeavours. It was especially among the masters of the later Attic school, who devoted themselves to the representation of the youthful and beautiful among the gods in whom the nude appeared least offensive, that statues of Venus were attempted. The Venus of Cnidus, by Praxiteles, was the most important work of that master; and the people of Cnidus were so proud of it that they engraved her image on their coins. The fact that they ventured to portray the goddess as entirely nude may be regarded as a sign both of the falling away of the popular faith and of the decay of art.

Henceforth, except in the case of statues for the temples, it became an established custom to represent Venus and other kindred deities as nude. Venus is further distinguished by a fulness of form, which is, nevertheless, combined with slenderness and grace. The countenance is oval; the eyes are not large, and have a languishing expression; the mouth is small, and the cheeks and chin full and round.

Of the numerous existing statues we can here mention only the most important. First among them in artistic worth is a marble statue larger than life, which was found in 1820 on the island of Melos (Milo), and is now in the Louvre at Paris (Fig. 17). In this statue only the upper part of the body is nude, the lower portions, from the hips downward, being covered with a light garment. One scarcely knows which to admire most in this splendid statue—the singularly dignified expression of the head, or the charming fulness and magnificent proportions of the limbs. The arms are quite broken off, so that we cannot determine the conception of the artist with any certainty. It is supposed that the goddess held in her hand either an apple, which was a symbol of the Isle of Melos, or the bronze shield of Ares. Her looks express proud and joyous self-consciousness.

In the Venus of Capua (so called because found among the ruins of the Amphitheatre) she again appears as a victorious goddess (Venus Victrix). This statue is now in the Museum at Naples.

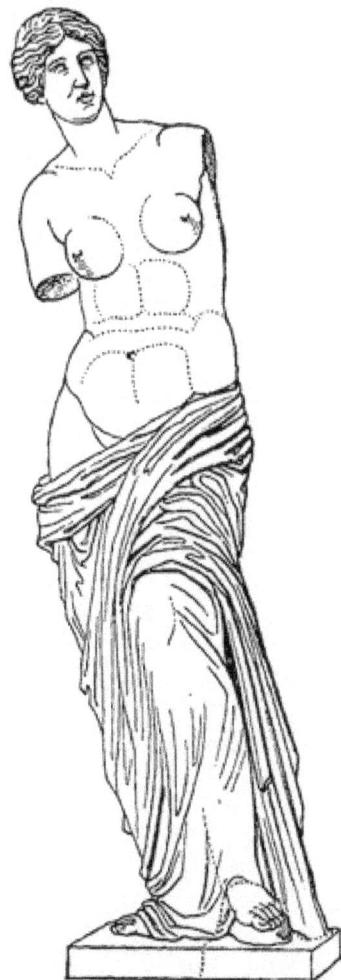

Fig. 17.—Venus of Milo. Louvre.

The shape of the nude body is not so vigorous or fresh as that of the Venus of Milo, but somewhat soft and ill-defined.

The Medicean Venus, formerly in the Villa Medici at Rome, is better known. It is a work of the later Attic school, in which, at the end of the second century B.C., Greek art once more blooms for a while. It is the work of the Athenian artist Cleomenes, though probably chiselled in Rome. As Venus Anadyomene (rising from the sea) the goddess appears entirely nude. This is the most youthful in appearance of all her statues, and is distinguished by the perfect regularity and beauty of its form, though there is no trace of the lofty dignity of the goddess. " What a descent," says Kraus in his *Christian Art*, " is there from the Venus of Milo to this coquette, whose apparently bashful posture is only meant to challenge the notice of the beholder."

The "Venus crouching in the bath " of the Vatican collection, and the "Venus loosing her sandal" of the Munich Gallery, are creations similar in style. In some imitations of the Cnidian Venus, the most important of which are in Rome and Munich, the goddess wears a more dignified

Fig. 18.—Venus Genetrix. Villa Borghese.

demeanour; and also in the wonderfully graceful Venus Genetrix of the Villa Borghese, at Rome (Fig. 18).

The attributes of Venus vary much according to the prevailing conception of the goddess. The dove, the sparrow, and the dolphin, and among plants the myrtle, the rose, the apple, the poppy, and the lime-tree, were sacred to her.

E

8. Hermes (Mercurius).—Hermes was the son of Zeus and Maia, a daughter of Atlas. He was born in a grotto of Mount Cyllene in Arcadia, whence he is called Cyllenius. We know the stories of his youth chiefly from the so-called Homeric Hymn. From this we learn how Hermes, soon after his birth, sprang from his mother's lap to seek the oxen of Apollo. Finding outside the cave a tortoise, he stretched strings across its shell, and thus made a lyre, to which he sung the loves of Zeus and Maia. Then hiding the lyre in his cradle, he went out to seek for food. Coming to Pieria in the evening, he stole thence fifty cows from the herds of Apollo, and drove them to the river Alpheüs. Here he slew two of them, and roasted the flesh, but could not swallow it. Then returning home in the early morning, he passed through the key-hole like the morning breeze, and lay down in his cradle. Apollo, however, soon remarked the theft, and hurried after the impudent robber. Hermes now played the innocent, and obstinately denied the charge; but Apollo was not to be deceived, and forced the young thief to accompany him to the throne of Zeus to have their quarrel decided. Zeus ordered Hermes to restore the cattle, but Apollo gladly made them over to Hermes on receiving the newly-invented lyre. Thus Hermes became the god of shepherds and pastures, whilst Apollo henceforth zealously devoted himself to the art of music.

As a token of their thorough reconciliation, Apollo gave his brother god the golden Caduceus, or magic wand, by means of which he could bestow happiness on whomsoever he would ; and henceforth both dwelt together in the utmost harmony and love, the favourite sons of their father Zeus.

Various interpretations have been given of the nature of Hermes. Some have seen in him the thunderstorm, some the dawn, and some the morning breeze. The name Hermes, compared with the corresponding Indian words, seems to make his connection with the morning certain. Several points in the legend just related guide us to the breeze rather than the dawn; the invention of music, the kine carried off—which, nevertheless, he cannot eat (the wind cannot consume as fire does what it breaks down and carries off)—and the passing through the key-hole "like the morning breeze." So also his function of guide and conductor of the soul, which we shall speak of presently.

The following are the most important features in the character of Hermes :—Not only does he promote the fruitfulness of flocks and herds, but he also bestows prosperity and success on all undertakings, especially those of trade and commerce. As the guardian of the streets and roads, and the friendly guide of those travelling on business, Hermes must have appeared especially worthy of honour among the Greeks, who were at all times sharp and greedy men of business. Accordingly, men erected in his honour, on the roads, what were called Hermæ—mere blocks of stone, or posts, with one or more heads : these latter were at cross-roads, and also served as finger-posts. Hermæ* were also often to be seen in the streets of towns and in public squares. Not only did Hermes protect and guide merchants whilst travelling, but he also endowed them with shrewdness and cunning to out-wit others. And as a god who had himself commenced his career by a dexterous theft, he was fain to allow thieves and rogues to invoke his protection before entering on their opera-tions ; just as in the present day robbers and bandits in Italy or Greece see nothing strange in asking their patron saint to bestow on them a rich prey. Every chance gain—in gambling, for instance—and every fortunate discovery were attributed to Hermes.

Though playing such an important part in human life, Hermes also appears as the fleet messenger and dexterous agent of Zeus.

---

* In this meaning, however, some have derived the word from a different root, and supposed it to mean originally only "pillars."

It is in this guise that the epic poets love to depict him. With his golden-winged shoes he passes more swiftly than the wind over land and sea, executing the commissions of his father Zeus or the other inhabitants of Olympus. Thus he is sent by Zeus to command the nymph Calypso to release Odysseus, and to warn Ægisthus against the murder of Agamemnon. At times, difficult tasks are allotted to him; for instance, the destruction of the hundred-eyed guardian of Io, on which account Homer calls him the Argus-slayer. Doubtless in this myth the hundred-eyed Argus represents the starry heavens; Argus is slain by Hermes, that is, in the morning the stars cease to be visible. As messenger and herald of the gods, he is a model for all earthly heralds, who, in ancient times, were the indispensable agents of kings in every difficult business. Hence he bears the herald's staff, or *caduceus.* This is the same wand once given him by Apollo, consisting of three branches, one of which forms the handle, whilst the other two branch off like a fork, and are joined in a knot. The origin of this herald's staff appears to have been the olive branch wreathed with fillets of wool. It was only at a later period that the two last were converted into serpents. By means of this wand Hermes can either induce deep sleep or rouse a slumberer, but he uses it chiefly in guiding souls to the infernal regions. This leads us to speak of the important office of Hermes as Psychopompus, or conductor of the soul. Every soul, after death, commenced its journey to the region of shadows under the guidance of the god. On extraordinary occasions, where, for instance, the spirits were summoned in the oracles of the dead, Hermes had to reconduct the souls of the departed to the upper world, thus becoming a mediator between these two regions, in other respects so far divided.

As dreams come from the lower world, Hermes was naturally regarded as the deity from whom they proceeded; on which account people were wont to ask him for good dreams before going to sleep.

The highest conception of Hermes, however, is that of the god who presides over the bringing up of children; and, indeed, what god was more fitted to be presented as an example to Grecian youth than the messenger of the gods, equally dexterous in mind and body? He is the fleetest of runners and the most skilful of disc-throwers and boxers; and though he does not, like Apollo, represent any of the higher forms of intellectual life, still he possesses in the highest degree that practical common sense which was so greatly valued among the Greeks. The wrestling school and the gymnasium were consequently regarded as his institutions, and adorned with his statues. In further development of his relation to the education of the young, later poets even made him the inventor of speech, of the alphabet, and of the art of interpreting languages. The custom which prevailed among the Greeks of offering him the tongues of the slaughtered animals, shows clearly that they also considered him as the patron of eloquence.

There is little to be said of the Roman Mercury. As his name (from *mercari*, to trade) signifies, he was considered by the Romans solely as god of trade. His worship was introduced at the same time as that of Ceres—some years after the expulsion of the Tarquins, at a season of great scarcity—but appears to have become confined to the plebeians. The guild of merchants regarded him as their tutelary deity, and offered sacrifices to him and his mother Maia on the Ides of May.

The plastic representation of Hermes made equal progress with his ideal development. The first statues of the god, founded on the ancient Hermæ already mentioned, represented him as a shepherd, sometimes as the herald and messenger of the gods, always as a powerful, bearded man. Later, he assumed a more youthful appearance, and was represented as a beardless youth in the very prime of strength, with broad chest, lithe but powerful limbs, curly hair, and small ears, mouth, and eyes; altogether a wonderful combination of grace and vigour. If we add to this the expression of kindly benevolence which plays around his finely-cut lips, and the inquiring look of his face as he bends forward thoughtfully, we have the principal characteristic features of the god.

Among existing statues, a full-sized "Hermes at rest," in bronze,

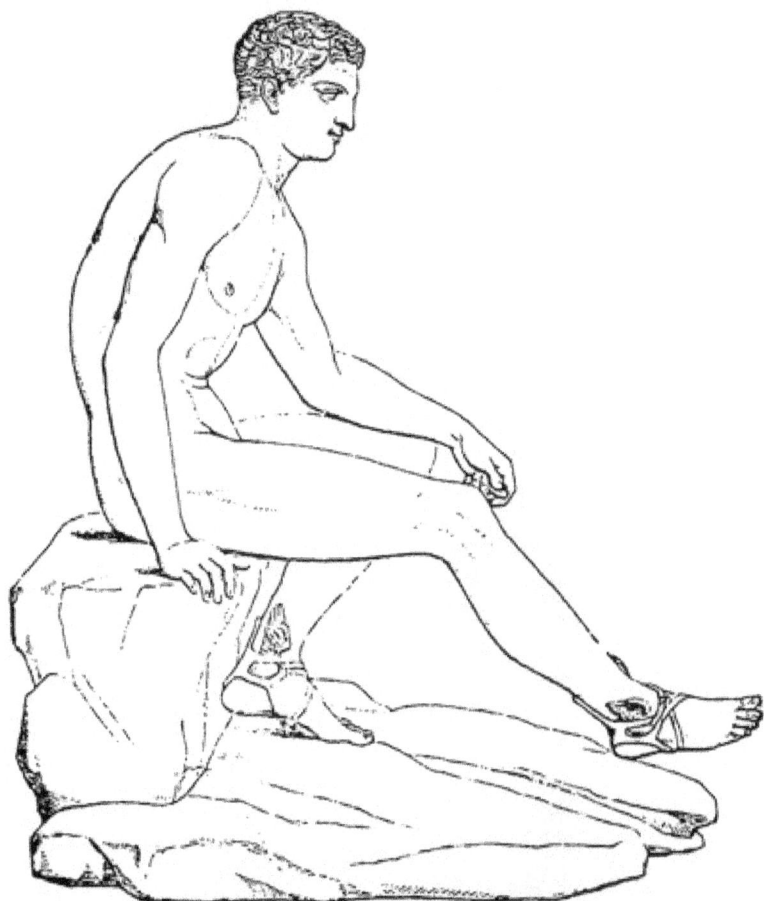

Fig. 19.—Resting Hermes.   Bronze Statue at Naples.

which was found at Herculaneum, and is now in the Naples Museum, is perhaps most worthy of mention.   He here appears as the messenger of the gods, and has just sat down on a rock to rest.   The winged sandals form his only clothing, and these are, strictly speaking, not really sandals, but simply straps covering the foot, to which wings are fastened close to the ankles (Fig. 19).

Fig. 20. —Statue of Hermes.   Capitoline Collection.

A splendid marble statue of the Vatican collection, which was once taken for Antinous, portrays the god as the patron of wrestling ; the Caduceus which he holds in his left hand is, however, a modern addition. In the Hermes Ludovisi of Rome we have a graceful representation of Hermes Logius, the patron of the art of rhetoric. The wings are here not placed on the feet, or even directly on the head, as is often the case, but are fastened to a low round travelling-hat.

A pretty bronze statuette in the British Museum depicts Hermes as the god of trade and commerce, with a well-filled purse in his hand. Such is also the conception of a fine statue of the Capitoline collection at Rome (Fig. 20). The principal attributes of the god have already been incidentally mentioned : they are wings on the feet, head, or cap ; the herald's staff, the votive bowl, and the purse.

9. Hephæstus (Vulcan).

—Hephæstus, the god of fire and the forge, was commonly regarded as a son of Zeus and Hera. He was so lame and ugly that his mother in shame cast him from heaven into the sea. But Eurynome and Thetis, the Oceanids, took pity on him, and tended him for nine years in a deep grotto of the sea, in return for which he made them many ornaments. After being reconciled to his mother, he returned to Olympus under the guidance of Dionysus. According to another not less popular account, it was not his mother who treated him so cruelly, but Zeus. Hephæstus, on the occasion of a quarrel between Zeus and Hera, came to the help of his mother, whereupon the angry god of heaven seized him by the foot and hurled him from Olympus. The unfortunate Hephæstus fell for a whole day, but alighted at sundown on the isle of Lemnos with but little breath in his body. Here the Sintians, who inhabited the island, tended him till his recovery. Later writers say that it was from this fall that he became lame. The same fundamental idea lies at the root of these various legends, viz., that fire first came down from heaven in the form of lightning. Hephæstus originally represented the element of fire, and all the effects of fire are accordingly referred to him. The fires of the earth break forth from the open craters of volcanoes · it must therefore be Hephæstus who is working in the midst of the fiery mountain, where he has his forges and his smithies. So says the legend of Mount Mosychlus, in Lemnos, the chief seat of his worship. Scarcely less celebrated, from its connection with him, was Mount Ætna, in Sicily. After it was observed that the wine was particularly good in the neighbourhood of volcanic mountains, the story of the intimate friendship between Hephæstus and Dionysus was concocted.

The most beneficial action of fire is manifested in its power to melt metals and render them useful to man in the shape of implements and tools of all kinds. Hence the conception of the character of Hephæstus tended ever more and more to represent him as the master of all ingenious working in metals, and as the patron of artificers and craftsmen using fire. In this character he was brought into close connection with the art-loving goddess Athene, and hence we see why both these divinities enjoyed so many kindred honours and had so many festivals in common at Athens, the chief seat of Greek science and art. It was also chiefly in the character of artificer that Hephæstus was treated of by the poets, who delight to describe the gorgeous brazen palace which he built himself on Olympus, in which was a huge workshop with twenty cunningly-devised pairs of bellows. He also constructed there the imperishable dwellings of the gods. Many also were the ingenious implements which he constructed, such as the walking tables, or tripods, which moved of their own accord into the banqueting-chamber of the gods, and then returned to their places after the meal was over. He also made himself two golden statues of maidens, to assist him in walking, and bestowed on them speech and motion. Among the other works of his mentioned by the poets are the ægis and sceptre of Zeus, the trident of Poseidon, the shield of Heracles, and the armour of Achilles, among which, also, was a shield of extraordinary beauty.

The worship of Hephæstus was not very extensive in Greece.

The most important seat of his worship was the isle of Lemnos, where he was supposed to dwell on Mount Mosychlus with his workmen, the Cabiri, who answer to the Cyclopes of Ætna. He was held in great esteem at Athens, where, at different festivals, torch races were held in his honour. Young men ran with burning torches, and whoever first reached the goal with his torch alight received the prize. He was, moreover, highly venerated by the Greeks in Campania and Sicily, a fact which may be easily explained by the fiery mountains of these places.

The Romans called this god Vulcanus, or, according to its more ancient spelling, Volcanus. They honoured in him the blessings and beneficial action of fire. They also sought his protection against con-

Fig. 21.—Hephæstus. Bronze Figure in the British Museum.

flagrations. Under the influence of the Greek writers, the original and more common conception of the god gave place to the popular image of the smith-god, or Mulciber, who had his forges in Ætna, or on the Lipari Isles, and who vied with his comrades in wielding the hammer. In correspondence with the Greek myths, Venus was given him to wife ; by this men doubtless sought to convey the idea that truly artistic works can only be created in harmony with beauty.

The chief shrine of the god in Rome was the Volcanal, in the Comitium, which was not really a temple, but merely a covered fire-place. In the Campus Martius, however, was a real temple close to the Flaminian Circus, where the festival of the Volcanalia was celebrated with every kind of game on the 23rd day of August.

Greek and Roman artists generally represented this god as a powerful, bearded man of full age. He is distinguished by the shortness of his left leg, by the sharp, shrewd glance of his cunning eye, and his firm mouth. His attributes are the smith's tools, the pointed oval workman's cap, and the short upper garment of the craftsman or humble citizen.

With the exception of some small bronzes in London and Berlin, and a newly discovered marble bust of the Vatican collection, we possess no antique statues of the god worth mentioning. The engraving (Fig. 21) is from a bronze in the British Museum.

10. Hestia (Vesta).—It must have been at a comparatively late period that Hestia, the daughter of Cronus and Rhea, attained a general veneration, as her name is not mentioned either in the *Iliad* or *Odyssey.* Hestia is the guardian angel of mankind, who guards the security of the dwelling, and is, in consequence, regarded as the goddess of the family hearth, the centre of domestic life. The hearth possessed among the ancients a far higher significance than it does in modern life. It not only served for the preparation of meals, but was also esteemed the sacred altar of the house ; there the images of the household gods were placed, and thither, after the old patriarchal fashion, the father and priest of the family offered sacrifice on all the

important occasions of domestic life. No offering was made in
which Hestia, the very centre of all domestic life, had not her
share.

And as the state is composed of families, the goddess of the
domestic circle naturally becomes the protectress of every political community. On this account, in Greek states the Prytaneum,
or seat of the governing body, was dedicated to Hestia; there
she had an altar, on which a fire was ever kept burning. From
this altar colonists, who were about to leave their native land in
search of new homes, always took some fire—a pleasing figurative
indication of the moral ties between the colony and the mother
country.

As the hearth-fire of the Prytaneum was an outward and
visible sign to the members of a state that they were one great
family, so the Hestia of the temple at Delphi signified to the
Greeks their national connection and the unity of their worship.
Her altar in this temple was placed in the hall before the cave
of the oracle ; on it was placed the celebrated omphalus (navel
of the earth, likewise an emblem of the goddess), Delphi being
regarded by the Greeks as the centre of the whole earth. Here,
too, a fire was kept ever burning in honour of Hestia. The
character of the goddess was as pure and untarnished as flame
itself. Not only did she herself remain a virgin, though wooed
by both Poseidon and Apollo, but her service could be performed
only by chaste virgins. She does not appear to have had a
separate temple of her own in Greece, since she had a place in
every temple.

The service of Vesta occupied a far more important place in
the public life of the Romans. Her most ancient temple, which
was supposed to have been built by Numa Pompilius, was
situated on the slope of the Palatine opposite the Forum. It
was built in a circle, and was of moderate dimensions, being,
indeed, little more than a covered fire-place. In it the eternal

fire, a symbol of the life of the state, was kept burning. Here, too, the service was performed by virgins, whose number was at first four, but was afterwards increased to six. Their chief occupation was to maintain the sacred fire, and to offer up daily prayers at the altar of the goddess for the welfare of the Roman people. The extinction of the sacred flame was esteemed an omen of coming misfortune, and brought severe punishment on the negligent priestess. The choice of vestals lay with the Pontifex Maximus. They were chosen between the ages of six and ten years, always out of the best Roman families. For thirty years they remained bound to their sacred office, during which time they had to preserve the strictest chastity. After the lapse of thirty years they returned to civil life, and were permitted to marry if they liked.

Another sanctuary of Vesta existed in Lavinium, the metropolis of the Latins, where the Roman consuls, after entering on their office, had to perform a solemn sacrifice. The festival of Vesta was celebrated on the 9th of June, on which occasion the Roman women were wont to make a pilgrimage barefooted to the temple of the goddess, and place before her offerings of food.

In the domestic life of the Romans the hearth and the hearth-goddess Vesta occupied as important a position as among the Greeks. The worship of Vesta is closely connected with that of the Penates, the kindly, protecting, household gods, who provided for the daily wants of life, and about whom we shall have more to say before concluding the subject of the gods.

Agreeably to the chaste, pure character of the goddess, she could only be represented in art with an expression of the strictest moral purity; she generally appears either sitting or standing, her countenance characterised by a thoughtful gravity of expression. Her principal attributes consist of the votive bowl, the torch, the simpulum, or small cup, which was used in making libations, and the sceptre. In consequence of the dignity and sanctity of her character,

Fig. 22.—Vesta Giustiniani. Torlonia Collection.

she was always represented as fully clothed, which may account for the fact that the ancients had so few statues of the goddess. We may, therefore, consider it fortunate that such a splendid example as the Vesta Giustiniani, which belongs to the private collection of Prince Torlonia, at Rome, has come down to us. It is supposed to be an original work of the best period of Greek art. The goddess is represented as standing in a calm posture, her right hand pressed against her side, whilst with the left she points significantly towards heaven, as though wishing to impress on mankind where to direct their prayers and thoughts (Fig. 22).

11. Janus.—Among the most important gods of the Romans was the celebrated Janus, a deity quite unknown to the Greeks. In his original character he was probably a god of the light and sun— the male counterpart, in fact, of Jana, or Diana, and thus very similar to the Greek Apollo. As long as he maintained this original character, derived from nature, he was regarded as the god of all germs and first beginnings, and possessed, in consequence, an important influence both on the public and private life of the Romans. .We must confine ourselves to mentioning some of the most important traits resulting from this view of his character. First, Janus is the god of all beginnings of time. He begins the new year, whose first month was called January after him, and was dedicated to him. Thus, New Year's Day *(Kalendæ Januariæ)* was the most important festival of the god; on this occasion the houses and doors were adorned with garlands and laurel boughs, the laurel being supposed to exercise a potent influence against all magic and diseases. Relatives and friends exchanged small presents (principally sweets; for example, dates and figs wrapped in laurel leaves) and good wishes for the coming year. The god himself received offerings of cake, wine, and incense, and his statue was adorned with fresh laurel boughs. This offering was repeated on the first day of every month, for Janus opened up every month; and as the Kalends were sacred to Juno, he was therefore called Junonius. In the same way Janus was supposed to begin every new day, and called *Matutinus Pater*. He also appears as the doorkeeper of heaven, whose gates he opened in the morning and closed in the evening.

From being the god of all temporal beginnings, he soon became the patron and protector of all the beginnings of human activity. The Romans had a most superstitious belief in the importance of a good commencement for everything, concluding that this had a magical influence on the good or evil result of every undertaking. Thus, neither in public nor private life did they ever undertake anything of importance without first confiding the beginning to the protection of Janus. Among the most important events of political life was the departure of the youth of the country to war. An offering was therefore made to the god by the departing general, and the temple, or covered passage sacred to the god, was left open during the continuance of the war, as a sign that the god had departed with the troops and had them under his protection. The consul never neglected, when he entered on his office, to ask the blessing of Janus, and the assemblies never began their consultations without invoking Janus. In the same way the private citizen, in all important occurrences and undertakings, sought by prayers and vows to acquire the favour of Janus. The husbandman, before he commenced either to sow or to reap, brought to Janus Consivius an offering of cake and wine. The merchant, when he entered on a journey of business, and the sailor, when he weighed anchor and started on a long and dangerous voyage, never omitted to invoke the blessing of the god. This view of the god also explains the custom of calling on Janus first in every prayer and at every sacrifice, since, as keeper of the gates of heaven, he also appeared to give admittance to the prayers of men.

As the god of all first beginnings, Janus is also the source of all springs, rivers, and streams of the earth. On this account the fountain nymphs were generally looked on as his wives, and Fontus and Tiberinus as his sons.

The power of Janus in causing springs to rise suddenly from the earth was experienced, to their cost, by the Sabines. The latter, in consequence of the rape of their women, had overrun the infant state of Rome, and were about to introduce themselves into the town on the Palatine through an open gate, when they suddenly found themselves drenched by a hot sulphur spring that gushed violently from the earth, and were obliged to retire.

In the legend alluded to, Janus appears as the protector of the gates of the city. As the god who presided over the fortunate entrance to and exit from all houses, streets, and towns, Janus was held in high honour among the people. His character as guardian of gates and doors brought him into close connection with the Penates and other household gods; hence the custom of erecting over the doors an image of the deity with the well-known two faces, one of which looked out and the other in.

Janus had no temple, in the proper sense of the word, at Rome. His shrines consisted of gateways in common places of resort and at cross-roads, or of arched passages, in which the image of the god was erected. The Temple of Janus in the Forum at Rome, which has been already alluded to, was a sanctuary of this kind closed with doors, and was probably the most ancient in the city. Its doors stood open only in time of war.

Roman art never succeeded in executing a plastic representation peculiar to Janus, the double head being only an imitation of the Greek double Hermæ. In course of time entire figures of Janus appeared, but these always had a double face. They were generally bearded, but in later times one face was bearded, the other youthful. Not one specimen of these works of art has been preserved, so that we only know these forms from coins. The usual attributes of Janus were keys and staff.

12. Quirinus.—Quirinus was also a purely Roman divinity, but having been reckoned among the great deities of heaven, he must therefore be mentioned here. In his symbolic meaning he bore a great resemblance to Mars; and as Mars was the national god of the Latin population of Rome, so Quirinus was the national god of the Sabines who came to Rome with Titus Tatius. Together with Jupiter and Mars, he formed the tutelary Trinity of the Roman empire. His shrine was on the Quirinal, which was originally inhabited by the Sabines, and which was named after him. Numa gave Quirinus a priest of his own. He had a special feast on the 17th of February, but his worship appears to have assimilated itself more and more to that of Mars. He was subsequently identified with Romulus.

F

B.—SECONDARY DEITIES.

1. *Attendant and Ministering Deities.*

1. Eros (Amor).—Of the deities who appear in the train of Aphrodite, Eros alone seems to have enjoyed divine honours; Longing and Desire being no more than allegorical figures typifying some of the influences that emanate from the goddess of love. Eros was commonly reputed the son of Aphrodite and Ares, and was generally depicted as a boy of wondrous beauty, on the verge of youth. His characteristic weapon is a golden bow, with which he shoots forth his arrows from secret lurking-places, with an unfailing effect that represents the sweet but consuming pangs of love. Zeus himself is represented as unable to withstand his influence —an intimation that love is one of the most terrible and mighty forces of nature. As unrequited love is aimless, Anteros was conceived by the imagination of the poets as the brother and com-

Fig. 28.—Head of Eros.   Vatican.

panion of Eros, and consequently a son of Aphrodite.   As the little Eros, says the myth, would neither grow nor thrive, his mother, by the advice of Themis, gave him this brother as a playfellow ; after which the boy was glad so long as his brother was with him, but sad in his absence.

Eros was not only venerated as the god who kindles love between the sexes, but was also regarded as the author of love and friendship between youths and men. On this account his statue was generally placed in the gymnasia between those of Hermes and Heracles ; and the Spartans sacrificed to him before battle, binding themselves to hold together faithfully in battle, and to stand by one another in the hour of need.

This deity was termed by the Romans Amor, or Cupido, but this was solely in imitation of the Greek Eros, since he never enjoyed among them any public veneration.

The significant fable of the love of Cupid for Psyche, a personification of the human soul, is of comparatively late origin, though it was a very favourite subject in art.

Artists followed the poets in the delineation of Eros, in so far as they generally depicted him as a boy on the confines of youth. An Eros by the re-nowned artist Praxiteles was esteemed one of the best works of antiquity. It was brought to Rome by Nero, but was de-stroyed by fire in the reign of Titus. In later times the god of love was represented as much younger, because the mischievous pranks attributed to him by the poets were more adapted to the age of child-hood.

Fig. 24.—Eros trying his Bow. Capitoline Museum.

A considerable number of statues or statuettes of Eros have come down to us from antiquity. Among the most celebrated is the Torso (mutilated statue) of the Vatican, of the glorious head of which we give an engraving (Fig. 23). There is also an "Eros trying his bow" (Fig. 24) in the Capitoline Museum at Rome, and an "Eros playing with dice" in the Berlin Museum. Lastly, there is the celebrated group of the Capitoline Museum, which represents the embraces of Cupid and Psyche.

Eros generally appears with wings in the art monuments of antiquity. His insignia are bow and arrows, in addition to a burning torch. The rose was held especially sacred to him, for which reason he often appears crowned with roses.

In connection with Venus and in company with Amor we find Hymenæus, a personification of the joys of marriage, who was, however, only recognised by later writers and by later art. He is portrayed as a beautiful youth, winged like Eros, but taller, and of a more serious aspect. His indispensable attribute is the marriage torch.

2. The Muses.—Pindar gives the following account of the origin of the Muses. After the defeat of the Titans, the celestials besought Zeus to create some beings who might perpetuate in song the mighty deeds of the gods. In answer to this prayer,

Fig. 25.—Polyhymnia. Berlin Museum.

Zeus begot with Mnemosyne (Memory) the nine Muses. They sing of the present, the past, and the future, while Apollo's lute accompanies their sweet strains, which gladden the hearts of the gods as they sit assembled in the lofty palace of Father Zeus, in Olympus. Looked at in connection with nature, there is little doubt but that the Muses were originally nymphs of the fountains. The veneration of the Muses first arose in Pieria, a district on the eastern declivity of Mount Olympus in Thessaly, from whose steep and rocky heights a number of sweet rippling brooks descend to the plains. The perception of this natural music led at once to a belief in the existence of such song-loving goddesses. Their seat was subsequently transferred from the declivities of Olympus to Mount Helicon in Bœotia, or to Mount Parnassus, at the foot of which the Castalian fountain, which

Fig. 26.—Melpomene. Vatican.

was sacred to them, had its source. Originally the Muses were only goddesses of song, though they are sometimes represented with instruments on vases. In early times, too, they only appear as a chorus or company, but at a later period separate functions were assigned to each, as presiding over this or that branch of art. Their names were Clio, Melpomene, Terpsichore, Polyhymnia, Thalia, Urania, Euterpe, Erato, and Calliope.

Fig. 27.—Euterpe. Vatican.

According to the art-distribution made, probably, at the time of the Alexandrine school, Calliope represents epic poetry and science generally, her attributes being a roll of parchment and a pen. Clio is the muse of history, and is likewise characterised by a roll and pen, so that it is sometimes difficult to distinguish her from Calliope. Euterpe represents lyric poetry, and is distinguished by her double flute. Melpomene, the muse of tragedy, generally appears with a tragic mask, a club or sword, and a garland of vine leaves. Terpsichore is the muse of dancing, and has a lyre and plectrum. To Erato is assigned erotic poetry, together with geometry and the mimic art; she generally bears a large stringed instrument. Thalia, the muse of comedy, is distinguished by a comic mask, an ivy garland, and a crook. Polyhymnia presides over the graver chant of religious service ; she may be recognised by her dress, wrapped closely round her, and her grave, thoughtful countenance, but is without attribute of any kind. Lastly, Urania, the muse of astronomy, holds in one hand a celestial globe, and in the other a small wand.

Several European museums possess ancient groups of the Muses, among which, perhaps, the finest is that preserved in the Vatican. From this group are copied our engravings of Melpomene and Euterpe (Figs. 26 and 27). The original of Polyhymnia (Fig. 25) is in the Berlin Museum.

The Romans venerated a number of fountain-nymphs of song and prophecy under the name of Camenæ, among whom the Egeria of the history of Numa is well known. The Roman writers seem to have identified these goddesses with the Muses at pleasure.

3. The Charites (Gratiæ).—The Charites generally appear in the train of the goddess of love, whom it was their duty to clothe and adorn. They are often found, however, in attendance on other gods, since all that is charming and graceful, either to the senses or the intellect, was supposed to proceed from them.

Their names are Aglaïa, Euphrosyne, and Thalia. They were commonly represented as the daughters of Zeus and Eurynome, the Oceanid. Later writers, however, make them the daughters of Dionysus and Aphrodite. They were venerated as the source of all that makes human life more beautiful and pleasant, without whom there could be no real enjoyment of life. Thus, even the gods would not sit down to banquets without the Charites ; and whenever men came together to feast, they first called on them and offered them the first bowl. Music, eloquence, art, and poetry received the higher consecration only at their hands ; whence Pindar terms his songs a gift from them. Wisdom, bravery, kindly benevolence, and gratitude—in fine, all those qualities which become men most, and make them agreeable in the eyes of their fellow-men, were supposed to proceed from the Charites.

The Graces of the Romans were simply transferred from the mythology of the Greeks, and have, therefore, the same meaning as the Charites.

Art represented the Charites or Graces as blooming maidens, of slender, comely form, characterised by an expression of joyous innocence. In their hands they often hold flowers, either roses or myrtles. They are less often distinguished by definite attributes than by a mutual intertwining of arms. In earlier Greek art they always appear fully clothed; but gradually their clothing became less and less, until at length, in the age of Scopas and Praxiteles, when nude figures had become common, it entirely disappeared. There are, however, few ancient statues of the Charites in existence.

4. Themis and the Horæ (Seasons).—In intimate connection with the Charites we find the Horæ, the daughters of Zeus and Themis. They were generally represented as three in number—Eunomia, Dice, and Irene. They represent the regular march of nature in the changes of the seasons, and Themis, who personifies the eternal laws of nature, and as the daughter of Uranus and Gæa ranks among the most ancient deities, is consequently their mother. Themis is the representative of the reign of law among gods and men; at Zeus' command she calls together the assemblies of the gods. She also occupies a similar position on earth, as presiding over national assemblies and the laws of hospitality. Her daughters, the Horæ, appear in a similar though in a subordinate and attendant character. In Homer they figure as the servants of Zeus, who watch the gates of heaven, now closing them with thick clouds, now clearing the clouds away. They also appear as the servants and attendants of other divinities, such as Hera, Aphrodite, Apollo, and the Muses. Like their mother, they preside over all law and order in human affairs; and under their protection thrives all that is noble and beautiful and good.

We know but little concerning the worship of the Horæ among the Greeks. The Athenians celebrated a special festival in their honour, but they recognised only two—Thallo, the season of blossom, and Carpo, the season of the ripened fruit. The adoption of four Horæ, corresponding to the four seasons of the year, appears to have arisen at a later period.

In plastic art Themis is generally represented with a balance in one hand and a palm branch in the other. The Horæ generally appear as lovely girls dancing with their garments tucked up, and adorned with flowers, fruit, and garlands. Subsequently they were

Fig. 28.—The Horæ. Relief from the Villa Albani.

distinguished by various attributes, typical of the different seasons. Such is the case in the engraving (Fig. 28), after a relief in the Villa Albani.

5. Nice (Victoria).—Nice is nothing but a personification of the irresistible and invincible power exercised by the god of heaven by means of his lightning. She also appears in the company of Pallas Athene, who was herself honoured by the Athenians as the goddess of victory. Victory does not seem to have had many separate temples or festivals, since she generally appears only in attendance on her superior deities.

Far more extensive was the veneration of Victoria at Rome, a fact for which the warlike character of the people easily accounts. Her chief shrine was on the Capitol, where successful generals were wont to erect statues of the goddess in remembrance of their exploits. The most magnificent statue of this kind was one erected by Augustus in fulfilment of a vow after

Fig. 29.—Victoria.   United Collections in Munich.

his victory at Actium. The proper festival of the goddess took place on the 12th of April.

In both Greek and Roman art Victory was represented as a winged goddess. She is distinguished by a palm branch and laurel garland, which were the customary rewards of bravery among the ancients. Large statues of the goddess are seldom met with, though she is often depicted on vases, coins, and small bronzes. The museum of Cassel has a small bronze statue of the goddess, whilst a fine *alto-relievo* in terra-cotta exists in the Royal Collection at Munich (Fig. 29).

6. Iris.—Iris was originally a personification of the rainbow, but she was afterwards converted into the swift messenger of the gods, the rainbow being, as it were, a bridge between earth and heaven.   In this character she makes her appearance in Homer, but, later still, she was again transformed into a special attendant of Hera.   Her swiftness was astounding; "Like hail or snow," says Homer, "that falls from the clouds," she darts from one end of the world to the other—nay, dives to the hidden depths of the ocean and into the recesses of the lower world, executing the commands of the gods.

In art Iris was represented with wings, like Nice, to whom she, in many respects, bears a strong resemblance. She may be distinguished from the latter, however, by her herald's staff (Caduceus). A very much injured specimen, from the east pediment of the Parthenon at Athens, is now preserved in the British Museum.

7. Hebe (Juventas).—Hebe was the daughter of Zeus and Hera, and, according to her natural interpretation, represented the youthful bloom of Nature. In the fully developed mythology of the Greeks she appears as the cupbearer of the gods, to whom, at meals, she presents the sweet nectar. It may at first seem strange that the daughter of the greatest of the divinities of Greece should be relegated to so inferior a position. This, however, is easily explained by the old patriarchal custom of the Greeks, by which the young unmarried daughters, even in royal palaces, waited at table on the men of the family and the guests.

In post-Homeric poetry and legend Hebe no longer appears as cupbearer of the gods, the office having been assigned to Ganymedes. This was either in consequence of the promotion of the son of the King of Troy, or on account of Hebe's marriage with the deified Heracles.

Hebe occupies no important place in the religious system of the Greeks; she seems to have been chiefly honoured in connection with her mother Hera, or now and then with Heracles.

Juventas, or Juventus, is the corresponding deity of the Romans; but, as was the case with so many others, they contrived to bring her into a more intimate connection with their political life by honouring in her the undying and unfading vigour of the state. She had a separate chapel in the temple of Jupiter Capitolinus.

With regard to the artistic representation of Hebe, statues of this goddess appear to have been very rare in ancient times ; at least, among all the numerous statues that have been discovered, none can be safely identified with Hebe. She is the more often met with on ornamental vases and reliefs, on which the marriage of Heracles and Hebe is a favourite subject. She is usually depicted as a highly-graceful, modest maiden, pouring out nectar from an upraised vessel. She appears thus in the world-renowned masterpiece of the Italian sculptor Canova, so well known from casts. In default of an ancient statue, we give an engraving of this work (Fig. 30).

8. Ganymedes.—A similar office in Olympus was filled by the son of Tros, the King of Troy, Ganymedes, who was made immortal by Zeus,

Fig. 30.—Hebe. From Antonio Canova.

and installed as cupbearer of the gods. Neither Homer nor Pindar, however, relate the episode of Zeus sending his eagle to carry off Ganymedes. This feature of the story, which is a favourite subject of artistic representation, is first found in Apollodorus. The Roman poet, Ovid, then went a step farther, and made the ruler of Olympus transform himself into an eagle, in order to carry off his favourite.

The rape of the beautiful boy is often portrayed in ancient art. The most famous monument is a bronze group of Leochares, an artist who flourished in the fourth century B.C. A copy of it still exists in the celebrated statue of Ganymedes in the Vatican collection. In

Fig. 31.—Ganymedes and the Eagle. From Thorwaldsen.

modern art the story has been treated with still greater frequency. There is an extremely beautiful group of this kind by Thorwaldsen, in which Ganymedes is represented as giving the eagle drink out of a bowl (Fig. 31).

2. *The Phenomena of the Heavens.*

1. Helios (Sol).—Helios (Latin *Sol*), the sun-god, belongs to that small class of deities who have preserved their physical meaning intact. His worship was confined to a few places, the most important of which was the island of Rhodes. An annual festival, attended with musical and athletic contests, was here celebrated with great pomp in honour of the sun-god. He is portrayed by the poets as a handsome youth with flashing eyes and shining hair covered with a golden helmet. His daily office was to bring the light of day to gods and men, which he performed by rising from Oceanus in the east, where the Ethiopians live, and completing his course along the firmament. For this purpose the post-Homeric poets endow him with a sun-chariot drawn by four fiery horses ; and though Homer and Hesiod do not attempt to explain how he passed from the west where he sets, to the east where he rises, later poets obviate the difficulty by making him sail round half the world in a golden boat (according to others a golden bed); and thus he was supposed again to arrive at the east. In the far west Helios had a splendid palace, and also a celebrated garden, which was under the charge of the Hesperides. He is described as the son of the Titans Hyperion and Thea, whence he himself is called a Titan. By his wife Perse, a daughter of Oceanus, he became the father of Æëtes, King of Colchis, celebrated in the legend of the Argonauts, and of the still more celebrated sorceress Circe. Another son of Helios was Phaëthon, who, in attempting to drive his father's horses, came to an untimely end.

Helios sees and hears everything ; whence he was believed to bring hidden crimes to light, and was invoked as a witness at all solemn declarations and oaths.

All the stories relating to Helios were gradually transferred to the Roman Sol, who was originally a Sabine deity, chiefly by means of the Metamorphoses of Ovid. The untiring charioteer of the heavens was also honoured as the patron of the race-course ; but he never attained a prominent position in religious worship.

Helios, or Sol, is depicted as a handsome youth, his head encircled by a crown, which gives forth twelve bright rays corresponding to the number of the months, his mantle flying about his shoulders as he stands in his chariot. It was chiefly in Rhodes, however, that Helios was made the subject of the sculptor's art. Here, in 280 B.C., was erected in his honour the celebrated colossal statue which has acquired a world-wide celebrity under the name of the Colossus of Rhodes, and which was reckoned as one of the seven "wonders of the world." It was the work of Chares of Lindus, and was 105 feet in height.

2. Selene (Luna).—As Artemis is the twin sister of Apollo, so is Selene the twin sister of Helios; he representing the sun, she the moon. Selene, however, never really enjoyed divine honours in Greece. The poets depict her as a white-armed goddess, whose beautiful tresses are crowned with a brilliant diadem. In the evening she rises from the sacred river of Oceanus, and pursues her course along the firmament of heaven in her chariot drawn by two white horses. She is gentle and timid, and it is only in secret that she loves beautiful youths and kisses them in sleep. Poets delight to sing of the secret love she cherished for the beautiful Endymion, the son of the King of Elis. She caused him to fall into an eternal sleep, and he now reposes in a rocky grotto on Mount Latmus, where Selene nightly visits him, and gazes with rapture on his countenance.

In later times she was often confounded with Artemis, Hecate, and Persephone. The same remarks apply to the Roman Luna. The latter, however, had a temple of her own on the Aventine, which was supposed to have been dedicated to her by Servius Tullius. Like her brother Sol, she was honoured in Rome in connection with the circus, and was held to preside over the public games.

In sculpture, Selene, or Luna, may be recognised by the half moon on her forehead, and by the veil over the back of her head; she also bears in her hand a torch. The sleeping Endymion was a frequent subject of representation on sarcophagi and monuments.

3. Eos (Aurora).—Eos, the goddess of the dawn, was also a daughter of Hyperion and Thea, and a sister of Selene and Helios. She was first married to the Titan Astræus, by whom she became the mother of the winds—Boreas, Zephyrus, Eurus, and Notus (north, west, east, and south winds). This is a mythological mode of intimating the fact that the wind generally rises at dawn. After Astræus, who, like most of the Titans, had rebelled against the sovereignty of Zeus, and had been cast into Tartarus, Eos chose the handsome hunter Orion for her husband. The gods, however, would not consent to their union, and Orion was slain by the arrows of Artemis, after which Eos married Tithonus, the son of the King of Troy. She begged Zeus to bestow on him immortality, but, having forgotten to ask for eternal youth, the gift was of doubtful value, since Tithonus at last became a shrivelled-up, decrepid old man, in whom the goddess took no pleasure.

Memnon, King of Æthiopia, celebrated in the story of the Trojan war, was a son of Eos and Tithonus. He came to the assistance of Troy, and was slain by Achilles. Since then, Eos has wept without ceasing for her darling son, and her tears fall to the earth in the shape of dew.

Eos is represented by the poets as a glorious goddess, with beautiful hair, rosy arms and fingers—a true picture of the invigorating freshness of the early morning. Cheerful and active, she rises early from her couch, and, enveloped in a saffron-coloured mantle, she harnesses her horses Lampus and Phaëthon (Brightness and Lustre), in order that she may hasten on in front of the sun-god and announce the day.

The views and fables connected with Eos were transferred by the Roman writers to the person of their goddess Aurora* without undergoing any alteration.

---

* The Mater Matuta of the Romans was a deity very similar to the Eos of the Greeks. She was the goddess of the early dawn, and was held in

Representations of this goddess are found now and then on vases and gems. She either appears driving a chariot and four horses, as harnessing the steeds of Helios, or as gliding through the air on wings and sprinkling the earth with her dew.

4. The Stars.—Only a few of the stars are of any importance in mythology. Phosphorus and Hesperus, the morning star and the evening star, which were formerly regarded as two distinct beings, were represented in art in the guise of beautiful boys with torches in their hands. There were also several legends relating to Orion, whom we have already alluded to as the husband of Eos. He himself was made a constellation after having been slain by the arrows of Artemis, while his dog was Sirius, whose rising announces the hottest season of the year. All kinds of myths were invented about other constellations; among others, the Hyades, whose rising betokened the advent of the stormy, rainy season, during which the sailor avoids going to sea. The story went that they were placed among the constellations by the gods out of pity, because they were inconsolable at the death of their brother Hyas, who was killed by a lion whilst hunting. Connected with them are the Pleiades, *i.e.*, the stars of mariners, so called because on their rising in May the favourable season for voyages begins. They were seven in number, and were likewise set in the heavens by the gods. Finally, we must not forget to mention Arctus, the Bear. Tradition asserted that this was none other than the Arcadian nymph Callisto, who had been placed among the constellations by Zeus when slain in the form of a she-bear by Artemis. She had broken her vows of chastity, and borne a son, Arcas, to Zeus.

5. The Winds.—The four chief winds have been already alluded to as the sons of Eos. They were especially venerated

---

high estimation among the Roman women as a deity who assisted them in childbirth. Like the Greek Leucothea, she was also regarded as a goddess of the sea and harbours, who assisted those in peril.

G

by those about to make voyages, who then solicited their favour with prayers and offerings. Otherwise, they maintained their character of pure natural forces, and were, consequently, of little importance in mythology. The rude north wind, Boreas, or Aquilo, was especially dreaded on acccount of his stormy violence, and was hence regarded as a bold ravisher of maidens. Thus an Attic legend asserts that he carried off Orithyia, the daughter of Erechtheus, as she was playing on the banks of the Ilissus. She bore him Calaïs and Zetes, well known in the story of the Argonauts. Boreas, however, stood in high favour among the Athenians, who erected an altar and chapel to him, because, during the Persian war, he had partially destroyed the fleet of Xerxes off Cape Sepias.

As Boreas is the god of the winter storm, so Zephyrus appears as the welcome messenger of Spring; on which account one of the Horæ was given him to wife. Zephyrus was called Favonius by the Romans, to intimate the favourable influence he exercised on the prosperous growth of the vegetable world.

These, together with the other chief winds, Notus (south wind) and Eurus (east wind) were sometimes said to reside in separate places ; at other times they were said to dwell together in the Wind-mountain, on the fabulous island of Æolia, where they were ruled over by King Æolus.

3. Gods of Birth and Healing.

1. Asclepius (Æsculapius).—It was only in later times that the necessity of having special gods of birth and healing made itself felt ; at all events, Asclepius, or Æsculapius, as he is called by the Romans, does not appear as a god in Homer. The worship of this deity, who was said to be the son of Apollo, appears to have originated in Epidaurus, the seat of his principal shrine, and thence to have become generally diffused. In Epidaurus his priests erected a large hospital, which enjoyed a great reputation. The common method of cure consisted in allowing those who were sick to sleep in the temple, on which occasion, if they had been zealous in their prayers and offerings, the god appeared to them in a dream and discovered the necessary remedy.

The worship of this deity was introduced into Rome in the year 291 B.C., in consequence of a severe pestilence which for years had depopulated town and country. The Sibylline books were consulted, and they recommended that Asclepius of Epidaurus should be brought to Rome. The story goes that the sacred serpent of the god followed the Roman ambassadors of its own accord, and chose for its abode the Insula Tiberina at Rome, where a temple was at

Fig. 32.—Asclepius. Berlin.

once erected to Æsculapius. A gilded statue was added to the temple in the year 13 B.C. The method already mentioned of sleeping in the temple was also adopted here.

In art, Asclepius is represented as a bearded man of ripe years, with singularly noble features, from which the kindly benevolence of a benefactor of mankind looks forth. He is generally accompanied by a serpent, as a symbol of self-renovating vital power, which he is feeding and caressing, or which is more commonly represented as creeping up his staff. Such is the conception in the engraving (Fig. 32), which is after a statue preserved at Berlin. As the god of healing, he has also other attributes—a bowl containing the healing draught, a bunch of herbs, a pine-apple, or a dog; the latter being a symbol of the vigilance with which the physician watches disease.

Fig. 33.—Head of Asclepius. British Museum.

There are numerous extant statues of the god, although the great statue in gold and ivory of the temple at Epidaurus has been entirely lost. A fine head of colossal proportions was discovered on the Isle of Melos, and is now an ornament of the British Museum (Fig. 33). There is, on the other hand, a very fine statue without a head in existence at Athens, near the temple of Zeus. There are, moreover, celebrated statues in Florence, Paris, and Rome (Vatican); in the last case, of a beardless Æsculapius.

2. Inferior Deities of Birth and Healing.—The Greeks also honoured Ilithyia as a goddess of birth. This appears to have been originally a surname of Hera, as a deity who succoured women in childbirth. Hygiea was looked on as a goddess of health, and was described as a daughter of Asclepius.

The Romans had no need of a special goddess presiding over birth, although they honoured a deity often identified with

Fig. 34.—Night and the Fates. From Carstens.

Hygiea, whom they called Strenia, or Salus. As guardian of
the chamber of birth, they honoured Carna, or Cardea, who was
supposed to drive away the evil Striges (screech owls) that came
at night to suck the blood of the new-born child. Carna was
further regarded as the protectress of physical health. Another
of these inferior deities, of whom men sought long life and con-

tinued health, bore the name of Anna Perenna (the circling year).

4. *Deities of Fate.*

1. Mœræ (Parcæ).—The Mœræ, better known by the Latin name of Parcæ, really denote that portion of a man's life and fortune which is determined from his birth; so that, in this sense, there are as many Mœræ as individuals. The Greeks, however, who were wont to revere all such indefinite numbers under the sacred number three, generally recognised three. These they regarded as the dark and inexplicable powers of fate, daughters of the night. Their names were Clotho (spinner), Lachesis (allotter), and Atropos (inevitable).

Only two Parcæ were originally known to the Romans, but a third was afterwards added to make their own mythology harmonise with that of the Greeks.

The popular conception of the Parcæ as grave hoary women was not followed in art, where they always appear as young. In the first instance, their attributes were all alike, separate functions not yet having been allotted to them. But at a subsequent period it was Clotho who spun, Lachesis who held, and Atropos who cut the thread of life. This arrangement was first adopted by later artists, who generally give Clotho a spindle, Lachesis a roll of parchment, and Atropos a balance, or let the last point to the hour of death on a dial. Such is the case in a talented creation of Carstens, in which the conception of modern times is brought into harmony with the ideal of antiquity (Fig. 34).

2. Nemesis, Tyche (Fortuna), and Agathodæmon (Bonus Eventus).

—Nemesis really denotes the apportionment of that fate which is justly deserved, and a consequent repugnance to that which is not. Homer does not acknowledge Nemesis as a goddess, and so it is probable that her claim to public veneration dates from a later period. She was regarded as a goddess of equality, who watches over the equilibrium of the moral universe, and sees that happiness and misfortune are allotted to man according to merit. Hence arose, subsequently, the idea of an avenging deity, who visits with condign punishment the crimes and wickedness of mankind. In this character she resembles the Furies. The Romans likewise introduced Nemesis into their system; at least her statue stood on the Capitol, though popular superstition never regarded her with a friendly eye.

The various conceptions of Nemesis are again displayed in works of art. The kindly, gentle goddess, who dispenses what is just, is depicted as a young woman of grave and thoughtful aspect, holding in her hand the instruments of measurement and control (cubit, bridle, and rudder). As the stern avenger of human crimes, she appears with wings in a chariot drawn by griffins, with a sword or whip in her hand.

Tyche, the goddess of good fortune, was, according to common accounts, the daughter of Oceanus and Tethys. She was usually honoured as the tutelary deity of towns, and as such had temples and statues in many populous cities of Greece and Asia. In course of time, however, the idea gained ground that Tyche was the author of evil as well as of good fortune. She resembled, in this respect, the Fortuna of the Romans, who was regarded as the source of all that is unexpected in human life. Servius Tullius was said to have introduced into Rome the worship of Fortuna, whose favourite he had certainly every reason to regard himself. He erected a temple to her under the name of Fors Fortuna, and made the 24th of June the common festival of the goddess. Later, her worship became still more extensive. Under the most different surnames, some of which referred to the state (*Fortuna populi Romani*), and others to every description of private affairs, she had a great number of temples and chapels erected in her honour. She had also celebrated temples in Antium and Præneste.

Ancient artists endowed this goddess with various attributes, the most important of which was the rudder, which she held in her hand in token of her power to control the fortunes of mankind. She is also endowed with a sceptre for the same purpose, and with a horn of plenty as the giver of good fortune; sometimes she is also represented with the youthful Plutus in her arms. The later conception of an impartial goddess of fate is apparent in those art-monuments which depict her standing on a ball or wheel. Among the larger existing works, we may mention a copy preserved in the Vatican of a Tyche by Eutychides of Sicyon, which was formerly exhibited in Antioch. The goddess here wears a mural crown on her head as the tutelary deity of towns, and has a sheaf of corn in her right hand.

Besides Fortuna, the Romans honoured a deity called Felicitas as the goddess of positive good fortune. Lucullus is said to have erected a temple to her in Rome, which was adorned with the works of art brought by Mummius from the spoils of Corinth. Even this did not suffice for the religious needs of the people, and we find that the belief in personal protecting deities grew rapidly among both Greeks and Romans. These deities were termed by the Greeks "dæmones," and by the Romans "genii." They were believed to be the invisible counsellors of every individual, accompanying him from birth to death, through all the stages of life, with advice and comfort. Offerings of wine, cake, incense, and garlands were made to them, particularly on birthdays.

II.—THE GODS OF THE SEA AND WATERS.

---

1. Poseidon (Neptunus).—Poseidon, or Neptunus, as he was called by the Romans, was the son of Cronus and Rhea. Homer calls him the younger brother of Zeus, in which case his subjection to the latter is only natural. According to the common account, however, Zeus was the youngest of the sons of Cronus, but acquired the sovereignty over his brothers by having overthrown their cruel father. Poseidon was accordingly indebted to his brother for his dominion over the sea and its deities, and was therefore subject to him. He usually dwelt, not in Olympus, but at the bottom of the sea. Here he was supposed to inhabit, with Amphitrite his wife, a magnificent golden palace in the neighbourhood of Ægæ. Originally, like Oceanus and Pontus, he was a mere symbol of the watery element, but he afterwards attained an entirely independent personality. Even in Homer he no longer appears as the sea itself, but as its mighty ruler, who with his powerful arms upholds and circumscribes the earth. He is violent and impetuous, like the element he represents. When he strikes the sea with his trident, the symbol of his sovereignty, the waves rise with violence, dash in pieces the ships, and inundate the land far and wide. Poseidon likewise possesses the power of producing earthquakes, cleaving rocks, and raising islands in the midst of the sea. On the other hand, a word or look from him suffices to allay the wildest tempest. Virgil, in the first book of the *Æneid*, has given a beautiful description of the taming of the fierce elements by the god.

Poseidon was naturally regarded as the chief god of all the seafaring classes, such as fishermen, boatmen, and sailors, who esteemed him as their patron and tutelary deity. To him they addressed their prayers before entering on a voyage, to him they brought their offerings in gratitude for their safe return from the perils of the deep.

Poseidon, therefore, enjoyed the highest reputation among the seafaring Ionians. His temples, altars, and statues were most numerous in the harbours and seaport towns, and on islands and promontories. Among the numerous shrines of this deity we may mention that of Corinth, in the neighbourhood of which were celebrated in his honour the Isthmian games, which subsequently became a national festival in Greece, Pylus, Athens, and the islands of Rhodes, Cos, and Tenos.

It was only natural that many legends, local and provincial, should exist about a god who played such an important part in the lives of seafaring folk. In the Trojan epos he figures as a violent enemy of Troy, his indignation having been provoked by the injustice of the Trojan king, Laomedon. Poseidon had built the walls of Troy at the king's request with the aid of Apollo, but Laomedon having cheated him in the matter of the stipulated reward, Poseidon thereupon sent a terrible sea-monster, which laid waste the crops and slew the inhabitants. They had recourse to the oracle, which counselled the sacrifice of the king's daughter Hesione. The unhappy maiden was exposed to the monster, but was rescued by Heracles. The fable of this monster, which is manifestly a symbol of the inundation of the sea, is repeated in many succeeding stories (*e.g.*, in the story of Perseus, who rescued in a similar way Andromeda, the daughter of the king of Æthiopia). There are numberless stories, in which Poseidon appears as the father of the different national heroes. The most important is, perhaps, the legend of Theseus, of which we shall speak later on. There was scarcely a Grecian town or district which did not lay claim to divine origin for the person of its founder or ancestral hero. Again, the conception of the wild stormy nature of the sea caused Poseidon to be represented as the father of various giants and monsters. By the nymph Thoösa he became the father of the savage Polyphemus, slain by Odysseus, who thus provoked the implacable enmity of Poseidon. The giant Antæus, who fought with Heracles, was also said to be a son of Poseidon; besides many other monsters, such as Procrustes, Cercyon, and the Aloïdæ.

The favourite animal of Poseidon was the horse, which he was supposed to have created. This may, perhaps, be due to the fact that the imagination of the Greeks pictured to itself the horses of Poseidon in the rolling and bounding waves. In Athens the origin of the horse was referred to the contest between Athene and Poseidon, as to who should make the land the most useful present. In Corinthian legend Poseidon appears as the father of the winged horse Pegasus by Medusa. This story is connected with the taming of the horse, which was ascribed to Poseidon. On account of his intimate connection with the horse, Poseidon was especially regarded as the patron

Fig. 35.—Poseidon.   Dolce Gem.

of the games, and had, in consequence, an altar of his own on all race-courses. The competitors, before the races, solicited his favour with prayers and sacrifices.

The dolphin and the pine-tree were held sacred to Poseidon, the latter probably because it was so extensively used in shipbuilding. Black steers, horses, rams, and wild boars were sacrificed to him.

The Romans not being a seafaring people, Neptune never stood in such high estimation among them as among the Greeks. In Rome his prominent characteristic was his connection with the horse and the race-course. These were placed under his special protection, for which reason the only temple he had in Rome stood in the Circus Flaminius.

The representation of Poseidon, or Neptune, in art harmonises tolerably well with the descriptions of the poets. He is accordingly represented as similar to his brother Zeus in size and figure, with broad deep chest, dark wavy hair, and piercing eyes. Artists intimated the greater violence of his nature by giving him more angularity of face, and a more bristling and disordered head of hair than Zeus. The expression of his countenance is more grave and severe, and the kindly smile that plays around the mouth of Zeus is altogether wanting. Ancient statues of Poseidon are comparatively rare. The Vatican Museum possesses a fine bust, and also a marble statue of the god. He is generally distinguished by the trident in his right hand; sometimes in its place we find a tiller. A band similar to a diadem denotes his dominion over the sea. Our engraving of the god is after a beautiful gem of the Dolce collection (Fig. 35).

2. Amphitrite.—After Poseidon had attained an almost exclusive veneration as god of the sea, Amphitrite, one of the Nereids, was given him to wife. According to the usual account, he carried her away from Naxos. Others say that she fled to Atlas to avoid the rude wooing of the god, but Poseidon's dolphin found her and fetched her back. She had three children by Poseidon—Triton, Rhode, and Benthesicyme.

In plastic art, Amphitrite is generally depicted as a slim and beautiful young woman, either nude or half clothed, riding in the chariot of Poseidon at his side, or by herself. On gems she also appears enthroned on the back of a mighty Triton, or riding a sea-horse or dolphin. Her hair generally falls loosely about her shoulders. She is distinguished by the royal insignia of the diadem and sceptre, at times she also wields the trident of her husband.

The worship of Amphitrite was entirely unknown to the Romans, who recognised the sea-goddess Salacia as the wife of Neptune.

3. Triton and the Tritons.—Triton was the only son of Poseidon and Amphitrite ; he never appears, however, to have enjoyed divine honours. This perhaps explains how it came to pass that he was subsequently degraded to the level of a fabulous sea-monster. The poet Apollonius Rhodius describes him as having a body, the upper parts of which were those of a man, while the lower parts were those of a dolphin. Such too is his appearance in works of art. Poets and artists soon revelled in the conception of a whole race of similar Tritons, who were regarded as a wanton, mischievous tribe, like the Satyrs on land.

The Tritons, as sea-deities of fantastic form, are of little importance in higher art, though they were all the more frequently employed in fountains and water-works. The fore-legs of a horse were sometimes added to the human body and dolphin's tail, thus giving rise to the figure termed the Ichthyocentaur.

4. Pontus and his Descendants.—We have already spoken of Pontus and his race in our account of the Theogony. Here we can only mention those of his children who either enjoyed divine honours, or are of importance in art. The eldest among them was Nereus.

1. *Nereus and his Daughters.*—Nereus presents to us the calm and pleasant side of the sea. He appears as a kindly, benevolent old man, the good spirit of the Ægean sea, where he dwells with his fifty lovely daughters, the Nereids, ever ready to assist the storm-beaten sailor in the hour of need. Like all water-spirits, Nereus possessed the gift of prophecy, though he

did not always choose to make use of it. Heracles sought him
on his way to the garden of the Hesperides, in order to learn
how he might get possession of the golden apples. In spite of
his urgent entreaties, Nereus endeavoured to elude him by
assuming every kind of shape, though he was at length vanquished by the persistence of the hero, who would not let him
go until he had obtained the necessary information.

By his wife Doris, the daughter of Oceanus, he became the
father of fifty, or, according to some, of a hundred daughters,
who were all venerated as kindly, beneficent sea-nymphs. They
are a charming, lovely tribe, who win the hearts of the sailors—
now by their merry sports and dances, now by their timely
assistance in the hour of danger. This joyous band generally
forms the train of Poseidon and Amphitrite. Besides Amphitrite,
the chosen bride of Poseidon, we find among them Thetis, the
beautiful mother of Achilles, so celebrated in ancient poetry,
who usually figures as their leader. Her beauty and grace
were so great that Zeus himself became her lover. He surrendered her, however, to Peleus, son of Æacus, because an
oracle had declared that the son of Thetis should become greater
than his father.

In art Nereus generally appears as an old man with thin grey
locks. He is commonly distinguished by a sceptre, or even a trident.
The Nereids were depicted as graceful maidens, in earlier times
slightly clothed, but later entirely nude, riding on dolphins, Tritons,
or other fabulous monsters of the deep.

2. *Thaumas, Phorcys, Ceto.*—Whilst Nereus and his daughters represent the sea in its peaceful aspect, Thaumas, the
second son of Pontus, represents it as the world of wonders.
By Electra, a daughter of Oceanus, he became the father of Iris,
the messenger of the gods, and also of the Harpies. The latter
personify the storm-winds. Originally fair maidens, they wore
afterwards represented as winged creatures, half man and half

bird; they had the faces of maidens, but their bodies were covered with vultures' feathers; they were pale and emaciated in appearance, and were continually tormented with an insatiable hunger. They are best known from the story of the Argonauts, where they appear as the tormentor of the blind king Phineus, whose table they continually robbed of its viands, which they either devoured or spoiled. They were regarded by the ancients as the ministers of sudden death, and were said to be either two or three in number. Phorcys and Ceto, the brother and sister of Thaumas, present to us the sea under its terrible aspect. This pair, from whose union sprang the Gorgons, the Grææ, and the dragon of the Hesperides, typify all the terrors and dangers of the deep. We shall have more to say concerning the Gorgons and Grææ in the story of Perseus.

5. Proteus.—Proteus is a deity of inferior rank. He is represented as an old man (the servant of Poseidon) endowed with the gift of prophecy. He plays the same part in the story of Troy as Nereus does in that of Heracles. His usual abode was the island of Pharos. It was thither that Menelaus turned after he had been driven to the coast of Egypt, on his return from Troy, to seek the advice of the " unerring old man of the sea." But Proteus, being in no amiable mood, sought to elude the importunity of the hero by converting himself into a lion, a dragon, a panther, a wild boar, and many other forms. At length, however, he was vanquished by the persistence of Menelaus, and vouchsafed an answer. He was supposed to be the keeper of the fish who inhabit the depths of the sea, and of the other marine animals.

In works of art he generally appears like a Triton, *i.e.*, with body ending in a fish's tail. He is usually distinguished by a crook.

6. Glaucus.—Among the inferior sea-deities, Glaucus deserves mention as playing a part in the story of the Argonauts.

He was really only a local god of the Anthedonians in Bœotia, and his worship was not extended to other places in Greece. But though he had no splendid temples, he stood in very high estimation among the lower classes of sailors and fishermen; indeed we find universally that the common people, in all their cares, turned rather to the inferior deities, whom they supposed to stand closer to them, than to the higher and more important gods. According to the story, Glaucus was originally a fisherman of Anthedon, who attained in a wonderful manner the rank of a god. One day, after having caught some fish, he laid them half dead on the turf close by. He was astonished to see, however, that on coming in contact with a certain herb, which was unknown to him, they were restored to life and sprang back into the sea. He himself now ate of this wonderful herb, and immediately felt himself penetrated by so wondrous a sensation of bliss and animation that, in his excitement, he too sprang into the sea. Oceanus and Thetis hereupon cleansed him from all his human impurities, and gave him a place among the sea-gods. He was venerated on many of the islands and coasts of Greece as a friendly deity, ever ready to assist the shipwrecked sailor or the castaway.

In art he is represented as a Triton, rough and shaggy in appearance, his body covered with mussels or sea-weed. His hair and beard show that luxuriance which characterises sea-gods.

7. Ino Leucothea, and Melicertes.—Like Glaucus, Ino, the daughter of Cadmus, attained at once immortality and divine rank by a leap into the sea. She was a sister of Semele, the mother of Dionysus, and the wife of Athamas, king of Orchomenus. It was she who, after the unhappy death of Semele, took charge of the infant Dionysus. Hera, however, avenged herself by driving Athamas mad, whereupon he dashed Learchus, his eldest son by Ino, against a rock. He was about to inflict the same fate on Melicertes, his second son, when in frantic haste the unhappy mother sought to save her child by flight. Athamas, however, pursued her as far as the Isthmus, when Ino, seeing no hope of escape, cast herself from the rock Moluris into the sea. Here she was kindly received by the Nereids, who converted both her and her son into sea-deities. She henceforth bore the name of Leucothea, and her son that of Palæmon. They were both regarded as benevolent deities of the stormy sea, who came to the assistance of those who were shipwrecked or in other peril. They appear in this guise in the *Odyssey*, where Odysseus, who saw only certain death before him, is represented as having been saved by a scarf thrown to him by Leucothea.

8. The Sirens.—The Sirens must also be reckoned among the sea-deities. They are best known from the story how Odysseus succeeded in passing them with his companions without being seduced by their song. He had the prudence to stop the ears of his companions with wax, and to have himself bound to the mast. The Sirens were regarded as the daughters either of the river-god Achelous by one of the nymphs, or of Phorcys and Ceto. Only two Sirens are mentioned in Homer, but three or four were recognised in later times and introduced into various legends, such as that of the Argonauts, or the Sicilian story of the rape of Persephone. Demeter is said to have changed their bodies into those of birds, because they refused to go to the help of their companion, Persephone, when she was carried off by the god of the lower world.

In art they are represented, like the Harpies, as young women with the wings and feet of birds. Sometimes they appear altogether like birds, only with human faces; at other times with the arms and bodies of women, in which case they generally hold instruments of music in their hands. As their songs were death to those who were seduced by them, they are often depicted on tombs as spirits of death.

9. The Race of Oceanus.—Lastly, we must enumerate among the water-deities the numerous descendants of Oceanus,

H

viz., the Oceanids, and also the rivers that are spread over the earth. The latter were believed to have their common source in the ocean encircling the earth, and thence to flow beneath the ground until they reached the surface in springs.

Oceanus himself appears in the myths which treat of the genealogy of the gods as the eldest son of Uranus and Gæa, and therefore, like his wife Tethys, a Titan. As he did not take part in the rebellion of the other Titans against the dominion of Zeus, he did not share their dreadful fate, but was allowed to remain in undisturbed enjoyment of his ancient domain. He was supposed to dwell on the most western shores of the earth, which he never left even to attend the assemblies of the gods.

On account of their great importance to the fertility of the soil, the river-gods enjoyed a great reputation among the Greeks, although their worship was entirely of a local nature. Only Achelous, the greatest of all the Greek rivers, appears to have enjoyed general veneration. The river-gods were believed to dwell either in the depths of the rivers themselves, or in rocky grottoes near their sources. They were depicted either as delicate youths, or as men in their prime, or as old men, according to the magnitude of the river. They all possess a conformity with the nature of their element, viz., that power of transformation which we discover in the other sea-deities. They also appear, like other water-spirits, to possess the gift of prophecy.

Among the Romans all flowing waters were held sacred. Fontus, the son of Janus, was especially esteemed as the god of springs and fountains in general; but, as among the Greeks, each river had its special deity. The most important of these was Tiberinus. The springs were popularly supposed to be inhabited by nymphs gifted with the powers of prophecy and magic, who sometimes honoured mortals with their favours, as Egeria did King Numa.

In art the river-gods were commonly represented in the guise of those animals whose forms they were most in the habit of assuming. They thus appear as serpents, bulls, or even as men with bulls' heads. They were also portrayed, however, in purely human guise, with the exception of having small horns on either side of the head. Their attributes consist of urns and horns of plenty, symbols of the blessings that proceed from them.

III.—THE GODS OF THE EARTH AND LOWER WORLD.

We now come to a class of deities who stand in the most decided contrast to the gods of the heaven and the sea, whom we have previously described. It consists of those deities whose power is incessantly exerted either on the surface or in the depths of the earth, and who are accordingly brought into the closest connection with the life of man. The worship of these deities assumed among the Greeks a passionate and excited character, at first entirely strange to the Romans, though it gradually crept in here also.

Though the ancients saw in the earth, on the one hand, the fruitful source of all life in nature, they did not seek to disguise the fact that it is, on the other hand, also the open sepulchre into which all earthly existence sinks when its time is over. The worship of these deities was therefore celebrated with festivals of joy and mirth at the season of the revival of nature, and with mournful solemnities at the season of its decay. The devotees manifested both their mirth and mourning in a loud, noisy, passionate manner, usually designated orgiastic. An element of mystery never failed to introduce itself into the worship of these deities, who, in virtue of their dwellings, were able to inspire a greater feeling of awe than the bright forms of the gods of heaven. Their wrath also, which manifested itself in the sterility of the soil, was the subject of especial fear.

Mysteries proper, or secret rites, existed only among the Greeks, but never found their way into the religious systems of Italy. We shall enumerate first the deities of the upper world, who preside over the growth of flocks and the fruits of the earth, and then those who inhabit the lower world.

1. Gæa (Tellus).—First among them is Gæa, or Mother Earth herself. This deity appears in the Cosmogony (or myths relating to the formation of the universe) as one of the primeval creative forces, having herself proceeded immediately from Chaos. In later times she acquired a more personal and plastic character, although she never attained any real importance in the religious system of the Greeks, owing to the existence of more definite and substantial deities, such as Rhea, Hestia, Demeter, and Themis. The worship of Tellus in Rome was more important, although here, too, it was somewhat thrown into the shade by the worship of Ceres and kindred deities.

The chief significance of Gæa lies in the fact that she is the source of all life and increase in nature. She is hence regarded as a mother who tends with loving care all her children. Under this aspect her praises are sung by Hesiod, and also in an ancient Dodonaic hymn. Like Demeter and other deities who dispense prosperity and abundance, she appears as tending and nourishing the young, and is often represented thus on ancient monuments.

At the same time Gæa is the common grave of mankind, and draws all things, with inexorable severity, down into her dark womb. She thus becomes a goddess of death and the lower world, and was on this account invoked, together with the Manes, as a witness of all solemn compacts and oaths.

A very ancient shrine of this goddess existed at Delphi, and the oracle there had once, said the Delphians, belonged to her.

In Rome, where she was also venerated as a goddess of marriage, her temple stood on the site of the house of Spurius Cassius. Festive offerings were made to her before and after seed-time. On the occasion of the Paganalia, she and Ceres were propitiated by the sacrifice of a pregnant sow, which was supposed to promote the prosperity of the coming year.

2. Rhea Cybele (Magna Mater Idæa).—Rhea is well known as the daughter of Uranus and Gæa, and the wife of Cronus, by whom she became the mother of Zeus and the other Cronidæ. She seems to have enjoyed only a limited measure of divine honours, until she was identified with the Phrygian goddess Cybele, who, like the Egyptian Isis, was an Asiatic symbol of fertility. She was worshipped throughout Lydia and Phrygia under the appellation of the "Mighty Mother." Thence her worship, which was of a peculiarly noisy character, made its way through the Greek colonies into Greece itself, and towards the end of the second Punic war was, at the instance of the Sibylline books, introduced into Rome. Attalus, king of Pergamus, was on this occasion good enough to present the Romans with a sacred stone, which was regarded by the inhabitants of Pessinus as the great mother herself. After its arrival at Ostia, this stone was carried to Rome amid a solemn procession of Roman matrons. The day of its arrival (10th April) was ever afterwards kept as a festival, at which games were celebrated under the superintendence of the prætor. The worship of Cybele, however, never seems to have become naturalised in Rome, perhaps because Romans were not allowed to officiate as her priests.

The true home of the worship of Cybele was the district of Pessinus, a rough and rocky mountain land. It was here that she made her noisy processions, seated in a chariot drawn by lions or panthers, amid the boisterous music of her weird attendants, the Corybantes and Curetes. The myths that relate to the goddess bear a wild, fantastic character, similar to that of her rites. The best known among them is the story of her favourite, Attis, or Atys. He was a Phrygian youth of a beauty so exceptional that the great mother of the gods chose him for her husband. At first he returned her affection, but afterwards he proved faithless, and was about to marry a daughter of the king of Pessinus. But the vengeance of the angry goddess overtook him, for when the wedding guests were assembled at the festive banquet the goddess appeared in their midst, and filled those present with panic fear, and troubled their minds. Atys fled to the mountains, where he slew himself in a fit of frenzy. Afterwards, the goddess instituted a great mourning in memory of him, which took place about the time of the vernal equinox. The priests of the goddess marched, amid the loud noise of kettle-drums and fifes, to the mountains, in order to search for the lost youth ; and when at length he, or an image representing him, was found, the priests, in an ecstasy of joy, danced about in wild excitement, gashing themselves with knives.

Representations of Rhea Cybele are rare. A statue representing her seated on a throne is shown in the Vatican. Her usual attribute is a kettle-drum.

3. Dionysus, or Bacchus (Liber).—Dionysus, or Bacchus,

was regarded by Greeks and Romans alike as the god of wine and vineyards. In his more extended meaning he represents the blessings of the autumn. It is he who causes the fruits to ripen for the use of man ; it is likewise he who dispenses to mankind all the advantages of civilisation and refinement, and of well-ordered political affairs.

Thebes was described as the birth-place of the god. His mother was Semele, the daughter of Cadmus, whom Zeus, the great god of heaven, honoured with his love. This very love, however, proved fatal to Semele, for the ever-jealous Hera came to her in the guise of her nurse, Beroë, and succeeded in exciting her suspicions as to the truth of her lover's divinity. She insidiously persuaded Semele to make her lover swear to do what she desired, and then to put him to the test. Semele did so, and then besought Zeus to appear to her in the full majesty of his divine form. In vain did Zeus adjure her to take back her foolish request; she insisted on its fulfilment, and perished miserably, being burnt to ashes by the flame of Zeus, who approached her in a flash of lightning. Her unborn child was preserved by Zeus, who ordered Hermes to carry it to the nymphs of Nysa to be brought up. A later legend makes Ino, the sister of Semele, the foster-mother of Dionysus. The locality of this Nysa is somewhat uncertain, but it is generally supposed to be a district of Mount Pangæus in Thrace.

Dionysus, after growing up amid the solitude of the forest and strengthening himself by his contests with its wild beasts, at length planted the vine. Both the god and his attendants soon became intoxicated with its juice; after which, crowned with wreaths of laurel and ivy, and accompanied by a crowd of nymphs, satyrs, and fauns, he ranged the woods, which resounded with the loud and joyful cries of his inspired worshippers. The legend says that his education was then completed by Silenus, the son of Pan. In company with his preceptor and the rest of his train, he then set forth to spread his worship and the cultivation of the vine among the nations of the earth. He did not confine himself to mere vine-planting, however, but proved a real benefactor of mankind by founding cities, and by introducing more civilised manners and a more pleasant and sociable mode of life among men. On such as refused his favours his wrath fell with dreadful effect. Agave, the mother of the Theban king Pentheus, who had refused to receive him, and the rest of the Theban women, were driven mad by him; and in their frenzy they mistook the king for a wild boar and tore him to pieces.

The most celebrated among the myths which testify to the wondrous power of Dionysus is the story of the punishment of the Tyrrhenian pirates.   On the occasion of his passage from Icaria to Naxos, these pirates put Dionysus in chains, purposing to take him to Italy, and there sell him as a slave.   At a nod from the youthful god the chains fell from his limbs; he appeared as a lion, while a bear was seen at the other end of the ship.   Vines and ivy tendrils wound themselves round the mast and sails of the ship, which stood still, whilst the strains of the

Fig. 36.—Dionysus and Lion.   From the Monument of Lysicrates.

nymphs burst forth.   The sailors, terrified by the transformation of the god, leaped overboard, and were changed into dolphins. A fine representation, in relief, of this scene still exists on the monument of Lysicrates, at Athens.   The most beautiful feature in it is the figure of the god playing with his lion in the most joyous unconsciousness (Fig. 36).   With the name of Naxos, which was a chief seat of his worship, is connected the celebrated story of his marriage with Ariadne, the daughter of Minos, king of Crete.   The Attic hero, Theseus, after escaping the dangers of the Labyrinth by her means, had taken her away with him from

Crete in order to marry her. He deserted her, however, whilst asleep on the island of Naxos, either of his own accord or because warned of the god in a dream. The indescribable anguish and consternation of Ariadne, on awaking to find herself alone and deserted on a foreign strand, was only equalled by her joyous surprise when Bacchus, returning from his travels in India, found her and made her his bride. The poets, indeed, do not relate that Zeus then bestowed on her that immortality which he had already given his son on account of his glorious achievements and extraordinary merit toward mankind; but such appears to have been the popular tradition. At Athens a sort of harvest thanksgiving was celebrated in honour of both Dionysus and his bride, at which vines with the grapes on them were borne in solemn procession through the streets of the city.

The worship of Dionysus extended not only over the whole of Greece, but also to Italy, Asia Minor, Thrace, and Macedonia, and to every place where the vine was cultivated by the Greeks. The god was extolled as Lyæus, the deliverer from care, and great festivals were instituted in his honour, which were of a disorderly character, but very popular among the common people. At the time of the winter solstice there was mourning, because at this season the vine seemed to die away, and the god was believed to be suffering persecution at the hands of the evil spirits of winter, and obliged to flee in consequence to the sea or lower world. It was, therefore, thought right to suffer with him, and people manifested their grief at his disappearance by every kind of wild gesture. At the winter festivals of Dionysus, which were celebrated every other year, only women and girls took part. The festivals of the god at the beginning of spring, when the new wine was tasted for the first time, were purely festivals of gladness, like the greater Dionysia at Athens. On these occasions the reawakening of nature was celebrated with boundless joy and boisterous mirth. All kinds of jokes and mischievous pranks were indulged in, and festive processions and theatrical performances followed each other in quick succession.

The following festivals were celebrated at Athens in honour of Dionysus :—

1. The *Lesser* or *Rural Dionysia.* This was the vintage festival proper, which did not take place in Attica till the end of November or beginning of December, because they liked to let the grapes hang as long as possible. A he-goat was first solemnly sacrificed to the god; this was followed by a festive procession bearing the sacred things, and the festival concluded with all kinds of country amusements, dancing, masquerading, and revelling. The chief amusement of the young men was dancing on the leather bag. Out of the skin of the slaughtered goat was made a leather bag, which was inflated and smeared with oil: the young men then attempted to dance on it.

2. The *Lenæa*, or feast of the wine-press, was celebrated in the month of January at Athens, in the place where, according to an old tradition, the first wine-press had stood. Here stood the Lenæon, one of the two chief temples of the god. The chief feature of the festival was a magnificent procession with the sacred symbols of the god. This was followed by a great banquet, the viands for which were furnished by the city of Athens. The new wine which was drunk on these occasions did not tend to diminish the hilarity of the worshippers, so that all kinds of mischievous jokes were perpetrated.

3. The *Anthesteria* were celebrated in February, on the 11th, 12th, and 13th days of the month Anthesterion. They were supposed to commemorate the return of Dionysus from the lower world, or, in other words, the reawakening of nature from the sleep of winter. The first day was called πιθοιγία (cask-opening), because on this day the new wine was first broached. The

second and chief day of the festival was called χόες (cups). A procession and a great banquet took place, at which the guests were crowned with flowers. Many liberties were permitted to the slaves on this occasion, as at the Roman Saturnalia. The third day was called χύτροι (pots), because vessels were displayed filled with all kinds of boiled vegetables. These were regarded in the light of offerings for the souls of the dead, who were popularly supposed to revisit the upper world on this occasion.

4. The *Greater* or *City Dionysia* formed the chief festival of the god, and the proper spring-feast of the Athenians. It was celebrated with extraordinary splendour in the month of March, and lasted several days, bringing together a vast concourse of strangers from all parts. The city, renowned alike for the refined artistic taste and the keen wit of its inhabitants, then donned its holiday garb, and innumerable merry antics were played by the crowds assembled in the streets and squares. The

Fig. 37.—The so-called Sardanapalus in the Vatican.

chief feature of the festival was a solemn procession, in which an old wooden statue of the god was borne through the streets. There were likewise banquets and comic processions in masks, and grand representations of new comedies and tragedies. The proceedings concluded with the presentation of prizes to the successful competitors.

The Italian nationalities likewise celebrated a festival on the 17th of March, called the Liberalia, in honour of Liber, or Liber Pater, the Italian god of the vine. It was distinguished throughout by the simple countrified character of the proceedings, and resembled the Lesser Dionysia of the inhabitants of Attica. People amused themselves with all kinds of jokes and antics, and with masquerades, the masks for which were cut from the bark of trees. The chief object of the festival was to pray for the fertility of the vines. These innocent festivals had nothing to do with the voluptuous Bacchanalia which were afterwards introduced into Rome in imitation of the Greek mysteries, and which the most rigorous interference of the authorities was unable to suppress.

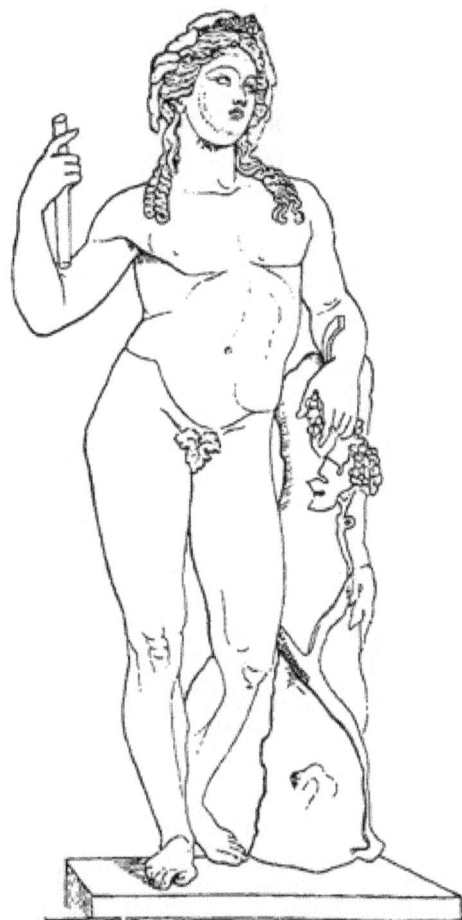

Fig. 38.—Youthful Dionysus. From the Chateau Richelieu, now in the Louvre.

If we try to conceive briefly the significance of the worship of

Dionysus in the religion of the ancients, we shall find that in his primitive character the god was a personification of the active, productive power of nature. As Demeter was supposed to give corn and the other fruits of the field, so Dionysus was supposed to give the fruits of trees, and especially of the vine. He was likewise regarded as the author of the blessings of civilisation, so that, on this point, he supplements the idea of the great culture-goddess Demeter, with whom, both among the Greeks and Romans, he had many temples and festivals in common. Looking at his character from another side, we find him coming into contact with Apollo, since he was supposed not only to endow men with a kindly, cheerful disposition, but also to inspire them with a love of music, on which account he was honoured with Apollo as the friend and leader of the Muses.

Artistic representations of Dionysus have come down to us on numerous monuments. In earlier art he was generally depicted as majestic and grave, and on that account represented with a beard. We have given an instance of this earlier conception in the so-called Sardanapalus of the Vatican (Fig. 37). In later art he became more youthful, and was characterised by a delicate roundness of form. The statues of this period are distinguished by the almost feminine expression of face with which they endow the god, as well as by the rounded limbs and the graceful ease of every attitude. The statue of a youthful Dionysus in the Louvre at Paris is an instance of this later mode of conception (Fig. 38). So likewise is the head of Dionysus at Leyden, which is distinguished by a sweet expression of reverie. His soft hair, which falls about his shoulders in delicate ringlets, is generally intertwined with a garland of vine leaves or ivy (Fig. 39). The other attributes of the god are the thyrsus, or Bacchic wand, the diadem, the skin of a wild beast falling across his chest, which often forms his sole clothing, and the drinking-cup in his hand. He is

Fig. 39.—Marble Head of Youthful Dionysus at Leyden.

Fig. 40.—Sleeping Ariadne. Vatican.

generally accompanied by lions, tigers, or panthers; and the bull
and ram, as the symbols of fertility, were held sacred to him,
while the latter was also his usual sacrifice. Among plants,
besides the vine and the ivy, the laurel was held sacred to him on
account of its powers of inspiration.

Of all the prominent personages in the stories of Dionysus, Ariadne has received most attention at the hands of the sculptor. The most celebrated of such ancient monuments is a marble figure of great beauty, larger than life, representing the sleeping Ariadne. It is now preserved in the Vatican Museum at Rome (Fig. 40). Among the

Fig. 41.—Dannecker's Ariadne.   Frankfort-on-the-Main.

productions of modern sculptors, the Ariadne of Dannecker, at Frankfort-on-the-Main, which represents her as the bride of Theseus, riding on a panther, justly enjoys a very high reputation (Fig. 41).

4. The Nymphs.—We now come to a class of inferior terrestrial divinities who are often found in the train of Bacchus. The most numerous and important of these are the Nymphs. They personify the restless activity and energy of nature, over the whole of which their power extends. They manifest their presence in the murmuring, rippling streams and brooks, as well as in the sprouting vegetation of wood and meadow. They are tender, graceful maidens, who, though kindly disposed towards men, yet avoid human habitations, and prefer the peaceful solitude of the woods and mountains, where they lead a merry, joyous life among the clefts and grottoes.

Sometimes they devote themselves to useful pursuits, and spin and weave; sometimes they engage in graceful dances, and sing merry songs, or bathe their delicate limbs in the white spray of lonely brooks. They gladly join the train of those superior deities supposed to preside in the realms of nature. Thus we see them joining in the Bacchic revelry with Dionysus, or figuring in the train of Aphrodite, or ranging field and wood as they hunt in the company of Artemis.

According to the divisions of nature, over which the Nymphs were supposed to preside, we may distinguish the following classes :—

1. The *Water-Nymphs*, to whom, in their wider signification, the Oceanids and Nereids also belong. Here, however, we have only to deal with the water-nymphs of the brooks and fountains of the land, who are distinguished by the name of *Naiads.* As the kindly nourishers of plants, and as thereby ministering indirectly to the sustenance of both man and beast, they enjoyed a large measure of veneration among the ancients, although, being inferior deities, they could claim no temples of their own. Like the sea-nymphs, they possessed the gift of prophecy, and appear as the patrons of poetry and song.

2. *Nymphs of the Mountains,* or *Oreads,* to whom belong the nymphs of the valleys and glens (Napææ). These were very numerous, and received special names from the particular mountains or districts they inhabited. The most celebrated among them was the Bœotian nymph Echo. She was consumed by love for the beautiful youth Narcissus, a son of the river-god

Cephisus, and finding that he did not reciprocate her affection, she pined away in ever-increasing grief, until at length her emaciated frame was changed into rock, and nothing but her voice remained. But Aphrodite avenged this injury to her sex on Narcissus, who had in his vain self-love thus contemned the beautiful nymph. As he was hunting one day on Mount Helicon, he bent down to quench his thirst from a spring clear as crystal, and the goddess caused him to fall in love with his own shadow, which was reflected in the water. The object of his desires being unattainable, he too pined away from grief, and the flower named after him has ever since continued an emblem of heartless beauty.

3. The *Dryads*, or *Hamadryads* (wood-nymphs). These appear to have been a conception of later times. It was supposed that their existence depended on that of the trees they inhabited, so that when the latter were destroyed the nymphs also perished. Not sharing immortality, therefore, they cannot properly be reckoned among the gods.

The veneration of nymphs was very ancient in Greece, and was thence transferred to Rome. Goats, lambs, milk, and oil were offered to them.

In art they are depicted as lovely maidens, generally only slightly clad, and adorned with flowers and garlands. The Naiads are also represented as drawing water, or with attributes relating to their element.

5. **The Satyrs.**—In contrast to the Nymphs, or female personifications of the life of Nature, we find a number of inferior wood and water-deities of the male sex, called Satyrs, Sileni, and Panes, between whom it is difficult to distinguish clearly. Generally by Satyrs (Fauni) we understand the wood and mountain-spirits proper, who are inseparably connected with Dionysus, whose attendant train they form. Coarse sensuality and a wanton spirit of mischief are the leading features of their

I

character. On account of their animal propensities they were fabled to be only half human in appearance, with blunt noses and otherwise ignoble features, bristling hair, goat-like ears, and a goat's tail. Like the Muses, they love music and dancing, their instruments being the Syrinx and the flute, together with cymbals and castanets. Like their master, they were passionately addicted to excessive indulgence in wine; but whereas in the former this produced only a rapturous enthusiasm and an exalted frame of mind, with them its effects were purely sensual, and excited them to insane and unseemly pranks of all kinds.

The Satyrs were not an uncommon subject of representation among ancient artists. The conception was based on the original hideous half-man, half-animal type; and in art, as well as in poetry, the blunt nose, the pointed ears, and the goat's tail form their characteristic features. The Bacchic insignia of a band round the brow and an ivy garland also belong to them. There are some particularly fine antique statues of satyrs in the art-collections of Munich and Rome.

Fig. 42.—Head of Satyr. Munich Sculpture Gallery.

The engraving (Fig. 42) shows the highly-expressive face of a satyr in the Munich collection.

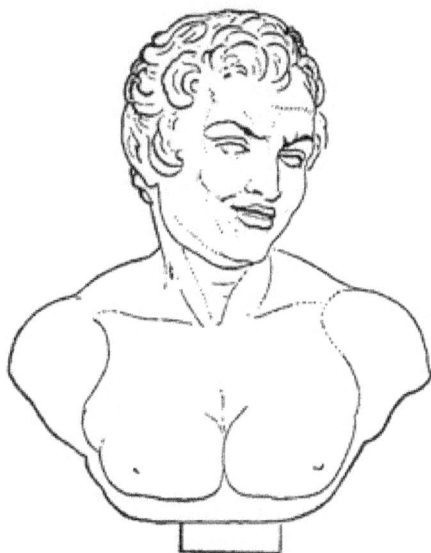

6. Silenus.—Silenus, according to the common tradition, was an old satyr who tended and brought up Dionysus, and afterwards became the faithful companion of his wanderings. He is depicted by the poets as a somewhat elderly man, with blunt nose and bald head, hairy chest and thighs, and a stomach so large that he can scarcely walk. He generally appears riding on an ass in front of the Bacchic company, with a satyr on either side supporting his half-drunken form.

The artists of antiquity seem to have devoted themselves frequently to the subject of Silenus. They either represented him as the nurse and preceptor of the youthful Bacchus, holding the child in his arms and regarding him with a look of affection, in which the comic element is entirely lacking, or they present him to us as the insatiable but good-natured wine-bibber. His standing attribute is the wine-skin, besides which, like other members of the Bacchic train, he bears a thyrsus and ivy garland.

Besides Silenus, who was celebrated as the preceptor of Dionysus, there was a whole tribe of Sileni. Whether this is due to the fact that the older satyrs were called Sileni, or whether they form a special class of deities presiding over the flowing, gushing water, cannot be determined with any certainty.

Among the Sileni were two personages who play a part in the story of Dionysus. These were Marsyas and Midas. The former, like all satyrs, was an accomplished master of the flute, and challenged Apollo to a trial of skill which proved fatal to him. The conditions of the contest were that he who was vanquished should put himself entirely in the power of his adversary. Apollo won, and made a cruel use of his victory by hanging Marsyas on a pine tree and flaying him alive.

Midas was the mythic founder of the kingdom of Phrygia, in Asia Minor, whither he had emigrated from Macedonia. Tradition makes him a son of Cybele, and, as her favourite, endowed with fabulous wealth. But, like many of the sons of men in the present day, the richer he grew the greater was his thirst for gold, until it betrayed him at length into an act of great folly. One day, the drunken Silenus strayed from the company of Bacchus into the garden of Midas. The latter received him with great hospitality, and after entertaining him sumptuously for ten days brought him to Bacchus. Pleased with his kindness, the god rewarded him with the gratification of any wish he might make. Midas now wished that everything he touched might turn to gold. Naturally the gratification of this wish well-nigh proved his ruin ; and he only escaped by washing, at the command of the god, in the river Pactolus, which has ever since washed down gold in its sands. A later fable makes Midas the judge in the rivalry of Apollo and Pan, on which occasion he decided in favour of the latter, for which the god changed his ears into those of an ass. Modern criticism has seen in the rich Midas one of the many personifications of the sun, who, as he rises over the earth, turns all things to gold.

7. Greek and Roman Wood-Spirits.—1. *Pan.*—Pan was a very ancient god of the woods and meadows. He was at first honoured only by the inhabitants of the mountain-land of Arcadia and by other pastoral tribes. Subsequently his divinity was more generally acknowledged and more highly esteemed. Common accounts make him the son of Hermes by the nymph Penelope, a daughter of Dryops. His mother was not a little terrified at his birth, since he was hairy all over, and had horns and goat's feet. His father wrapped him in a hare-skin, and bore him to Olympus, where the assembled gods showed no small pleasure at the sight of the strange little wood-demon. From time immemorial Pan was regarded by the shepherds of Greece as their most doughty protector ; for which reason the mountain caves in which they gathered their herds together at night, or in threatening weather, were held sacred to him. There were many such caves of Pan in the mountains of Arcadia, and also one at the foot of the Acropolis at Athens, besides others on Mount Parnassus in Bœotia, and elsewhere. Pan was esteemed a god of great cheerfulness and activity of character, who loved to range the woods as a huntsman, and was on this account regarded with little less veneration by huntsmen than by shepherds. He was also looked on as the patron of fishing and bee-keeping.

As the god of shepherds, Pan was also a lover of music, and on returning in the evening from the chase, says the Homeric story, he was wont to play sweet tunes on his pan-pipe (Syrinx), whilst the Oreads, or mountain-nymphs, sang the praises of the gods and led off their spirited dances. The poets have founded a story on his discovery of the Syrinx. They invented a fabulous nymph called Syrinx, with whom Pan was supposed to have fallen violently in love. The nymph, however, did not return his affection, and fled from his embraces. Pan pursued her, and in her extremity she sought the aid of Gæa, who transformed her into a reed. Out of this reed Pan, by joining seven pieces together, made an instrument which he called the Syrinx, after the nymph.

Pan was as passionately fond of dancing as of music. According to Pindar, he was the most accomplished dancer among the gods. His favourite amusement was to dance in company with the mountain-nymphs, on which occasions he regaled them with every kind of droll leap, in the performance of which his goat's feet stood him in good stead.

As a wood-deity, Pan also possessed the gift of prophecy; indeed, according to some, it was he who first imparted this gift to Apollo. He certainly had a very ancient oracle at Acacesium in Arcadia.

Wild mountainous country and the thick untrodden forest are both alike apt to impress the lonely traveller with feelings of awe. All such sensations of sudden and unaccountable fear were ascribed to Pan (Panic). He was also said to delight in terrifying travellers with all kinds of strange noises. Hence, at a later period, arose the story that in the contest with the Titans he rendered good service to Zeus by blowing on a shell trumpet which he had invented, whereupon the Titans were seized with a sudden terror. This, however, is only another version of Triton's services at the battle with the giants. It is well known that the Athenians introduced the worship of Pan, to which they had been hitherto strangers, into their city after the battle of Marathon, in consequence of the assistance which they believed they had received from the god.

Such are the more ancient and simple features of the character of Pan. He assumed a higher significance when men began to regard him as the companion of the "Mighty Mother," and assigned him a place in the Bacchic circle. Men now saw in him a productive force of nature like the Phrygian Attis; indeed, in consequence of a misinterpretation of his name, he was made the creator and god of the universe. He seems to have originally signified the "purifying" breeze, which at one time whistled through the reeds, or at another moaned dismally in the forest, frightening the belated traveller.

After he had once been introduced into the company of Dionysus, poets and artists alike set themselves to work to invent a number of Panes and little Pans (Panisci), who were easily confounded with the Satyrs and Sileni.

The chief shrine of Pan was at Acacesium in Arcadia. Cows, goats, and sheep were sacrificed to him, besides offerings of milk, honey, and new wine.

In art we must distinguish the earlier and later types of the god. In the former, which dates from the best days of Greek art, he is conceived as entirely human in appearance, with the exception of two sprouting horns on either side of the forehead. Later, he was depicted with larger horns, a long goat's beard, and goat's feet. We give an engraving of this

Fig. 43.—Pan.   From a Mural Painting at Herculaneum.

later conception (Fig. 43), which is taken from a mural painting at

Naples.   The usual attributes of Pan are a Syrinx and shepherd's crook, sometimes also a pine garland.

2. *Silvanus.*—Among the Roman wood-deities, Silvanus occupies a position most akin to that of Pan, although they are not exactly identical.   His name, derived from *silva* (wood), points him out as the god of the forest, where he was supposed to dwell, a deity kindly disposed towards mankind, and propitious to the welfare of trees, plants, and cattle.   At times, however, he appears, like Pan, as a mischievous sprite, who delights to trick and terrify the lonely traveller.   His sphere of activity was not confined to the woods, since he was also regarded as the author of fruitfulness in gardens and orchards.   In this character Silvanus bears a close resemblance to Terminus, the god of boundaries and landed property, inasmuch as he preserves fields, gardens, and houses from harm.   The first of the fruits of the field were offered to him.   He had two shrines in Rome, one on the Viminal and another on the Aventine.

Artists and poets agree in representing Silvanus as an old man with a rustic head-gear, scattering blooming lilies and other flowers. He is usually distinguished by a pruning-knife.

3. *Faunus and Fauna.*—Closely resembling Silvanus is another deity called Faunus, one of the most ancient national gods of Italy.   He appears as the good spirit of the mountains, pastures, and plains.   He was regarded by the shepherds as their best protector, since he made their cattle fruitful and drove off noxious beasts of prey.   In the former character he was also called Inuus (the fertiliser); in the latter Lupercus (the warder-off of wolves).

Like Pan, he appears to have his seat in the woods, whence he sometimes terrifies and annoys travellers.   At night, too, he creeps into men's houses, and torments them with evil dreams and horrible apparitions (Incubus).

Like Pan, too, Faunus possessed the gift of prophecy, and answered both by direct revelations and by dreams. In this character he was called Fatuus, and had a celebrated oracle in the grove at Tibur, on the spring Albunea. Having once invented a number of Fauns, the poets soon began to identify them with the Satyrs of the Greeks.

In honour of this decidedly national deity, different festivals were celebrated, at which rams were sacrificed and libations of wine and milk made. The Faunalia were celebrated on the Nones of December, on which occasion the guests at the festive board surrendered themselves to the most unrestrained mirth, and granted many liberties also to their slaves. The Lupercalia, however, formed the proper expiatory festival of Faunus. This festival was celebrated on the 15th of February, and was remarkable for the number of ancient customs which were observed. The chief of these was the course of the Luperci, or priests of Faunus, who, after making their offering, ran from the shrine of the god (Lupercal), on the Palatine, through the streets of Rome, their only clothing being an apron cut from the skin of the slaughtered animal. They struck all whom they met with thongs, also cut from the same blood-stained skin. Barren women placed themselves in the way of the Luperci, believing that by means of the strokes the reproach of barrenness would be taken away from them. As a day of atonement, this day was termed *dies februatus* (from *februare*, to purify), whence the name of the month.

The feminine counterpart of Faunus, though not his wife, was Fauna, a propitious, kindly goddess of the plains. She is also called Maia, or Bona Dea. The women made an offering to her every year at night, on which occasion males were strictly excluded.

In art Faunus bears exactly the same appearance as Pan, with whom, indeed, he was often identified.

8. Priapus.—The worship of Priapus, the god of fields and gardens, appears to have been long of a purely local character, confined principally to the districts on the Hellespont, since he is not even mentioned by earlier writers. He was the son of Dionysus and Aphrodite, and presided over the exuberant fertility of nature. He was supposed to exercise influence over the fruitfulness of flocks and herds, whilst fishing and the rearing of bees were also placed under his protection. His special sphere, however, was the protection of gardens and vineyards. Asses were sacrificed to him, a fact which gave rise to all sorts of comical stories relating to the hostility of Priapus to this animal. Besides this, he received the first fruits of the garden and field and drink-offerings of milk and honey. The worship of Priapus was introduced into Italy at the same time as that of Aphrodite, and he was identified with the native Mutunus.

This deity was scarcely noticed in higher art. In the gardens of Italy, however, rough-hewn pillars of wood, similar to those of Hermes, were erected in his honour. He is usually distinguished by a pruning-knife and club.

9. Saturnus and Ops.—Before passing to Demeter, or Ceres, the great goddess of civilisation, to whom by Greeks and Romans alike the blessings of the harvest were ascribed, and who forms the best link between the gods of the upper and lower worlds, we must pause to consider some gods of agriculture and cattle-rearing peculiar to the Romans. Among them are Saturn and Ops, who belong to the most ancient national deities of Italy. To Saturn was ascribed the introduction of agriculture, together with the cultivation of the vine and other fruits. He was, therefore, venerated as the great benefactor of mankind, who not only promoted the physical welfare of men, but who also introduced a higher standard of civilisation. After the Romans had become acquainted with the mythology of the Greeks, they identified him with Cronus. In consequence of this, the story arose that, after his dethronement by Jupiter, Saturn fled to Italy, where he was hospitably received by Janus. There he is said to have brought together the inhabitants, who had hitherto wandered about without any fixed homes, and to have united them in regular political communities, over which he himself ruled. This was the golden age. In remembrance of the happy age when men were not yet troubled by sorrow or need, the Saturnalia were celebrated during three days, beginning from the 17th of December. This festival, which with changed meaning still continues in the Carnival of the present day, was celebrated in Rome with particularly great splendour. Unbounded festivity reigned throughout the whole town, and vented itself in every description of joke and prank. The distinctions of class were suspended, the courts and schools kept holiday, and the shops were closed. The chief day was the 19th of December, which was especially a festive day for the slaves, for on this day there were practically no slaves in Rome. No services were required of them, and they were allowed to don the clothes of their masters and to eat and drink as much as they liked, whilst their masters waited on them at table. And this custom allowed a class, otherwise subject to so many afflictions, to forget their sorrows for at least one day in a year. Wealthy Romans generally kept open house on this day, and vied with each other in the splendour of their hospitalities ; and of course a solemn sacrifice was made to Saturn. The woollen bandages which, during the greater part of the year, enveloped the feet of his statue in order that he might not depart without vouchsafing a blessing, were on this day unloosed, and throughout the night the temple was illuminated with wax tapers. This festival, which was extremely popular among the Romans, was also celebrated with games in the circus.

The chief temple of Saturn, which was begun by Tarquinius Superbus and finished in the first years of the Republic, was situated on the ascent to the Capitol from the Forum. Beneath it was a vault containing the state treasury, or *ærarium*, the guardianship of the state treasures being committed to this god as the dispenser of every blessing.

Regarded as the wife of Saturn, and therefore identified with Rhea, Ops was the goddess of the seed-time and harvest. On this account her worship was closely connected with that of Saturn, and she had a place in his temple on the Capitoline. A festival was celebrated in honour of her on the 25th of August, when the newly-gathered corn was threshed.

When taken together, Saturn and Ops were regarded as deities who presided over marriage and the education of children, it being an easy step from the deity of the sprouting, ripening seed, to that of the budding, thriving season of human life.

Saturn is always represented as an old man, and is generally distinguished by a pruning-knife or sickle.

10. **Vertumnus and Pomona.**—Vertumnus and Pomona much resemble Saturn and Ops, the only difference being that the former exert their influence solely on the growth and welfare of the fruits of the garden and orchard. Vertumnus properly signifies the self-changing one; referring, probably, to the manifold changes which the fruit undergoes from the time of its first appearance in blossom to that of its maturity. For the same reason the god was said to possess the faculty of assuming any shape he liked. The first of the flowers and fruits were offered to him. Pomona, as her name signifies, was the goddess of the fruit harvest, and called by the poets the wife of Vertumnus. Each deity had a special priest (flamen), though the latter naturally held only an inferior position.

In art Vertumnus generally appears as a beautiful youth, his head crowned with a garland of ears of corn or laurel, with a horn of plenty, as a symbol of the blessings he bestows, in his right hand. He is sometimes distinguished by a dish filled with fruit, or a pruning-knife. Pomona is generally represented as the season of Autumn, a beautiful maiden with boughs of fruit-trees in her hand.

11. Flora.—Among the inferior deities of the plain was Flora, the goddess of blossoms and flowers, who was held in great honour by the Sabines, and everywhere in the interior of Italy. Her worship is said to have been introduced into Rome by Numa, who assigned the goddess a priest of her own. She attained a higher significance by becoming a goddess of maternity, whom women invoked before their confinement. Her festival was celebrated with great rejoicings from the 28th of April to the 1st of May (Floralia). The doors of the houses were adorned with flowers, and wreaths were worn in the hair. After the first Punic war, the festival, which was remarkable throughout for its merry and tumultuous character, was also celebrated with games, hares and deer being hunted in the circus.

Artists appear to have represented Flora as the season of Spring, in the guise of a beautiful girl crowned with flowers. There is a fine marble statue of this kind, larger than life, in the museum at Naples, called the Farnese Flora.

12. Pales.—Pales was the ancient pastoral goddess of the Italian tribes, from whom the name Palatine, which originally meant nothing but a pastoral colony, was derived. She was especially venerated by the shepherds, who besought her to send fruitfulness and health to their flocks. A festival in her honour was celebrated on the 21st of April, the anniversary of the foundation of the city (Palilia), at which very ancient rustic customs were observed. The most remarkable of these was the kindling of a large straw fire, through which the shepherds rushed with their flocks, thinking thus to purify themselves from their sins. Milk and baked millet-cakes were offered to the goddess. There is no statue of her now in existence.

13. Terminus.—Terminus, although he had nothing to do either with the welfare of the crops or the fruitfulness of the flocks, may yet be reckoned among the field deities, as the god who specially presided over boundaries. All landmarks were held sacred to him, and their erection was attended with religious ceremonies. In order that his people might fully appreciate the sanctity of boundaries, King Numa instituted a special festival in honour of the god, called the Terminalia, and annually celebrated on the 23rd of February. The proprietors of lands bordering on each other were wont on this occasion to crown the boundary stone with garlands, and to make an offering of a flat cake to the god.

In his wider signification Terminus was regarded as the god under whose protection the boundaries of the state reposed, and in this character he had a chapel in the temple of Minerva on the Capitol. A statue of the god also stood in the midst of the temple of Jupiter Capitolinus, which is explained by the following story:—After Tarquinius had conceived the plan of building the great temple of Jupiter on the Capitol, the limited space necessitated the removal of several existing shrines, which could only occur with the consent of the deities themselves. They all expressed by means of auguries their readiness to make way for the highest god of heaven, except Terminus, who refused, and whose shrine had therefore to be included in the temple of Jupiter.

Statues of Terminus are exactly like the Hermæ of the Greeks, and have no importance in art.

14. Demeter (Ceres).—Demeter was a daughter of Cronus and Rhea. Her name signifies Mother Earth, and she is, therefore, an expression of the ancient conception of the earth-goddess, with a special reference to nature and human civilisation. She was also named Deo, and by comparison of these two words, her name has been interpreted as Dawn-Mother, from the same root as Zeus, the sky. The thriving of the crops was ascribed to her influence; she was further regarded as the patroness of all those arts which are more or less intimately connected with agriculture, and which men first learned from her. Demeter thus rises to the rank of a goddess of civilisation. She rescued men by means of agriculture from the lower grades of hunters and shepherds, and brought their former rude and barbarous manners into subjection to law and morality. She thus becomes that "bountiful daughter of Heaven," who, as Schiller sings in his *Lay of the Bell,*

> "of old
> Called the wild man from waste and wold,
> And, in his hut thy presence stealing,
> Roused each familiar household feeling;
> And, best of all the happy ties,
> The centre of the social band,—
> The instinct of the Fatherland."

Regarded in this light, she comes into contact with Dionysus, whose beneficial influence on human civilisation and manners we have already described. This accounts for the intimate connection of these two deities in the Eleusinian mysteries, where Dionysus-Iacchus even appears as the son of Demeter and the husband of Cora-Persephone. Owing to the important part she played in the institution of law and order among mankind, she was venerated as the goddess of marriage, marriage being the necessary foundation of civil society. She was also regarded as the tutelary goddess of national assemblies.

Of the numerous legends which are linked with the name of this goddess, none perhaps is more celebrated, or more pregnant with meaning in regard to her worship, than the rape of her daughter Persephone, or Cora. The latter was once playing with the daughters of Oceanus in a flowery meadow, where they were picking flowers and making garlands. Persephone happened to quit her companions for a moment to pluck a narcissus she had perceived, when suddenly the ground opened at her feet, and Pluto, or Hades, the god of the infernal regions, appeared in a chariot drawn by snorting horses. Swift as the wind he seized and carried off the terrified maiden in spite of her struggles, and vanished again into the regions of darkness before her companions were aware of the catastrophe. All this occurred, however, with the knowledge of Zeus, who had, unknown to Demeter, promised her daughter to Pluto. When Demeter missed her darling child, and none could tell her where she had gone, she kindled torches, and during many days and nights wandered in anxiety through all the countries of the earth, not even resting for food or sleep. At length Helios, who sees and hears everything, told Demeter what had happened, not disguising, however, that it had occurred with the consent of Zeus. Full of wrath and grief, the goddess now withdrew from the society of the other gods into the deepest solitude. Meanwhile all the fruits of the earth ceased, and a general famine threatened to extinguish the human race. In vain Zeus sent one messenger after another, beseeching the angry goddess to return to Olympus. Demeter swore that she would neither return nor allow the fruits of the earth to grow until her daughter was restored to her. At length Zeus was fain to consent, and despatched Hermes to the lower world to bring Persephone back. Persephone joyfully prepared to obey this command, but as she was about to depart Hades gave her a pomegranate-seed to eat, whereupon she found herself bound to him and unable to return. By means of Zeus, however, a compact was made by which Persephone was to spend two-thirds of the year in the upper world with her mother, and the remaining portion with her husband. And thus every year at springtide she ascends from her subterraneous kingdom to enjoy herself in her mother's company, but returns again late in autumn to the regions of darkness and death.

It is not difficult to discover the meaning of this myth. It is simply an allegorical representation of the spectacle that is annually renewed before our eyes—the dying away and coming to life again of the vegetable world. Whilst Cora is dwelling during the winter months in the realms of Hades, Nature appears to wear a garb of mourning for her lost daughter. In the Eleusinian mysteries this inevitable decease and re surrection of the vegetable world was conceived as a symbol of higher meaning, setting forth the immortality of the soul. Every living being shares the fate of Cora ; every life becomes the prey of cold, inexorable death, only to arise from the darkness of the grave more beautiful and glorious than before.

Closely connected with this beautiful and expressive myth is another which refers to the institution of the Eleusinian mysteries. When Demeter, after the loss of her daughter, was wandering over the earth in the guise of a poor old woman, she came to Eleusis. The daughters of Celeüs, the king of the city, found her sitting on a stone by the Maidens' Well as they came thither to draw water, and offered the old woman service in their father's house as nurse to their youngest brother Demo. phon. The goddess consented, and was kindly received in the house of Celeüs, where she was at once installed as nurse to the young prince. She became so fond of the child that she resolved to make him immortal by anointing him with ambrosia, and then laying him at night in the glow of the fire. She was discovered at her work, however, by the mother of the child, whose cries disturbed her, and thus prevented her from fulfilling her benevolent intention. She now revealed herself to Celeüs, and commanded him to build her a temple in Eleusis. When it had been hastily completed, with the help of the goddess, she initiated Celeüs and some other princes of Eleusis—Triptolemus, Eumolpus, and Diocles—in the solemn rites of her service. On Triptolemus, who is called the son of Celeüs, she imposed the task of disseminating a knowledge of agriculture and of her own worship throughout the earth, and for this purpose lent him her own chariot and dragons. On this he travelled through the countries of the earth, making known everywhere the blessings of agriculture, and uniting men in regular political communities. He was not well received in all places, and the goddess had sometimes to step in and punish those who contemned her benefits. Such was the case with the Scythian king Lynceus and the Thessalian prince Erysichthon; but at length her cause triumphed, and the worship of the bountiful goddess spread itself over the whole world.

The chief seat of her worship was the city of Eleusis, which was beautifully situated on the bay of Salamis. It retained this honour even after it had lost its independence and come into the possession of the Athenians. The Eleusinian mysteries were celebrated both here and at Athens, in honour of Demeter and the deities associated with her. They probably contained a symbolical history of Cora.

There was a distinction between the greater and lesser mysteries. The latter were celebrated at Athens in the month of Anthesterion (February), and were a kind of preparation for the greater mysteries, which took place in September, and were celebrated during nine days, partly at Athens and partly at Eleusis. In these secret rites only those could take part who had been initiated. The chief feature of the festival was a great and solemn procession on the sixth day from Athens to Eleusis, a distance of about twelve miles. All those who took part in it—often as many as 30,000—were crowned with myrtle, and bore torches in their hands, as the procession started from Athens at the earliest dawn.

The festival of the Thesmophoria, which was celebrated at the beginning of November, in honour of Demeter in her character of lawgiver and goddess of marriage, was less im-

K

Fig. 44.—Demeter Enthroned.   Painting from Pompeii.   Naples.

portant than the Eleusinia. It lasted for five days, and only married women were allowed to take part in it.

The Ceres of the Romans, though undoubtedly an ancient Italian goddess, was the very counterpart of the Greek Demeter, with whom, after the successful introduction of her worship during the first years of the Republic, she was entirely identified.

The chief festival of Ceres and her associate deities, Liber and Libera, fell on the 19th of April, which, as the proper spring month, was especially dedicated by the inhabitants of Italy to deities presiding over agriculture. The Cerealia were opened by a grand procession, in which every one was clothed in white. It was further celebrated with solemn sacrifices and games in the circus, the management of which lay with the plebeian ædiles.

The usual sacrifice, both among Greeks and Romans, was the sow (the symbol of fruitfulness), but, besides this, cows and the first fruits of the trees and hives were offered to her.

In the representations of the goddess an expression of lofty dignity is blended with condescending benevolence and gentleness. Her principal attributes are a torch, a sheaf of corn, a garland of ears of corn interwoven in her hair, and a basket filled with flowers at her side. Among the few antique statues, a large marble figure in the Capitoline Museum at Rome deserves especial mention. The engraving (Fig. 44), which is after a Pompeian painting, depicts Demeter as the bountiful goddess of agriculture. She is seated on a throne, and holds a torch consisting of two calices in her right hand, and a bunch of corn in her left.

15. Persephone (Proserpina).—In Persephone, the goddess of the lower world, whom the Athenians preferred to call by her mystic name of Cora, two distinct conceptions are embodied. On the one hand she appears as the wife of the dark god of the lower world—like him, a gloomy, awe-inspiring deity, who pitilessly drags down all that lives into the hidden depths of the earth ; whence the grave is called the chamber of

Persephone. Such is the view of her taken by Homer and later epic poets. These represent her as sitting enthroned at the side of her grim lord, the joyless queen of the infernal regions, to dwell in which were worse than to be a slave on earth. On the other hand she appears as Cora, the lovely daughter of the all-bountiful Mother Earth; a personification, in fact, of that never-dying force of nature which, year by year, causes the most luxuriant vegetation to spring up before our eyes, only, however, to die away again in the autumn. In a somewhat narrower sense Persephone may be regarded as a type of the grain, which long remains in the ground where it has been sown as though dead, but afterwards breaks forth into new life. It was only natural to associate with this last conception ideas of the immortality of the soul, of which, in the secret doctrines of the mysteries, Persephone was a symbol. Though we know but little concerning the details of the mysteries, we are yet aware that their chief object was to disseminate better and purer ideas of a future life than the popular faith of the Greeks afforded. It was commonly believed that the souls of men after death led a dull, miserable existence in the world of shadows. Those initiated in the mysteries, however, were taught that death was only a resurrection of the soul to a brighter and better life, on the condition, of course, that a man had fully pleased the gods and rendered himself worthy of such a happy lot.

Persephone, or Proserpina, as she is called in Latin, was a deity originally entirely strange to the Romans, who borrowed all their ideas of the lower world from the Greeks. Nevertheless, they identified her with Libera, an ancient rustic goddess of fertility, the feminine counterpart of Liber, under which name she signifies the same as the Greek Cora. Black, barren cows were sacrificed to Persephone as an infernal goddess, but she does not appear to have had any temples of her own.

Fig. 45.—Persephone Enthroned. Painting from Pompeii. Naples.

Persephone is of no great importance in art, and statues of her are rare. She is represented either as the fair daughter of Demeter, or as the grave, severe queen of the world of shadows. In the latter character she may generally be recognised by her sceptre and diadem Her other attributes are ears of corn, a poppy, and a torch, as a symbol of her connection with the Eleusinian mysteries, besides the pomegranate and narcissus. The engraving (Fig. 45), after a painting in the Naples Museum, represents her as the Stygian queen.

16. Hades (Pluto).—The same twofold nature which we meet with in Persephone may be observed also in her husband, Hades, or Aïdoneus (the invisible), as he is called by the epic poets, on account of the mysterious gloom in which his kingdom as well as his person was enveloped. He first appears as the unrelenting, inexorable foe of human life, on whom one cannot even think without fear and trembling. For this reason, says Homer, "he is of all the gods the most detested among mortals." This conception, however, was subsequently supplanted by one of a less dismal nature, in which the other side of his character is brought into prominence. From this point of view he is represented not only as sending nourishment to plants from the deep bosom of the earth, but also as offering unbounded riches to mankind in the shape of the precious metals which lie in his subterraneous passages and chambers. In this sense he was also called Pluto, or Pluteus—that is, the god of riches.

Hades belonged to the earliest deities of Greece, being, like Poseidon, a brother of Zeus. When the three brothers partitioned the universe among themselves, Hades received the dark regions of the earth as his exclusive kingdom, the portals of which he was said to keep closed, in order that no soul might return to the upper world without his consent. He was also termed Polydectes (the receiver of many), from the fact of his seizing on all men, without distinction, at their appointed time, and conveying them to his dismal realms. The ideas which men first entertained, as to the mode in which Hades exercised his power over mortals, exactly corresponded with their grim conception of the god. He was looked on as a powerful and dreaded robber, who, as in the case of Persephone, seizes on his prey and carries it off with his swift horses. Later, a milder conception of the god was introduced. The task of carrying the souls of the dead to the lower world was delegated to Hermes, who thus became a servant of Pluto, the Zeus of the infernal regions, just as he was otherwise a servant of the Zeus of heaven. But though the original dismal conception of this deity as the inexorable god of death was much diminished in course of time, yet Hades, nevertheless, always conveyed an idea of something grim and mysterious to the Greek mind; which is perhaps the reason why so few myths, beyond that of the rape of Proserpina, were circulated concerning him. He can, in fact, scarcely be said to have had a place in the public worship of the Greeks.

The Roman conception of this deity differed little from that of the Greeks, having been, in fact, borrowed entirely from a Greek source. By them he was called Pluto, or Pater Dis. He had no temple in Rome, but had, in common with Proserpina, a sub-terranean altar in the Campus Martius, which was uncovered and used once a-year. Only black animals were sacrificed to him.

Artists naturally hesitated to portray a being whose very name they feared to pronounce, and con-sequently antique statues of Hades are very rare. His characteristic features—a grim expression of countenance, tightly-closed lips, and long tangled hair—are em-bodied in a marble head, in the possession of Prince Chigi at Rome, of which we give an engraving (Fig. 46). His principal attributes are a sceptre, a votive bowl, and sometimes a two-pronged fork, or a key.

Fig. 46.—Head of Hades.   Palazzo Chigi. Rome.

17. The Lower World.—To our consideration of Hades we must add some remarks on the ideas which the ancient

Greeks and Romans had of the other life and of the abodes of the dead. It may be well to remark, at the outset, that the Romans do not originally appear to have believed in a kingdom of the dead in the interior of the earth, and that all their ideas on this subject were borrowed from the writings of the Greeks. Neither do their ideas on this subject, nor even those of the Greeks, appear to have been invariably the same at all times. Even in the poetry of Homer we come across two very different views as to the situation of the realms of the dead. According to that which we find in the *Iliad*, it was situated beneath the disc-shaped earth, only a thin layer separating it from the upper world. This is made evident on the occasion of the great battle of the gods in the 20th book, where we read—

> "Pluto, the infernal monarch, heard alarmed,
> And, springing from his throne, cried out in fear,
> Lest Neptune, breaking through the solid earth,
> To mortals and immortals should lay bare
> His dark and drear abode of gods abhorred."

According to another view which prevails in the *Odyssey*, the world of shadows was not situated beneath the earth, but lay far to the westward, on the other side of Oceanus, or on an island in the same ; so indefinite and vague were men's ideas as to the locality of the kingdom of death in the time of Homer, and so undeveloped were their conceptions as to the lives of departed souls. The lower world appears as a desolate, dismal region, where departed spirits lead a shadowy, dreamy existence, to reach which is no happiness. There is no difference in their lots ; for we as yet hear nothing of the judgment of the dead. The Elysian fields, to which the special favourites of the gods were transferred, form no part of the lower world in Homer, but were supposed to lie in an entirely distinct region in the far West (the isles of the blest). Later on, the outlines of the lower world become more clearly defined. It was now supposed to be a region in the centre of the earth, with several passages to and from the upper world. Through it flowed several rivers— Cocytus, Pyriphlegethon, Acheron, and Styx. The last of these encompassed the lower world several times, and could only be crossed by the aid of Charon, the ferryman, who was depicted as a sullen old man with a bristling beard. The Greeks therefore used to place an obolus (small copper coin) in the mouths of their dead, in order that the soul might not be turned back by Charon for lack of money. On the farther side of the river the portals were watched by the dreadful hell-hound Cerberus, a three-headed monster, who refused no one entrance, but allowed none to leave the house of Pluto. All souls, on reaching the lower world, had to appear before the tribunal of Minos, Rhadamanthus, and Æacus. Those whose lives had been upright were then permitted to enter Elysium, where they led a life of uninterrupted bliss; whilst those who on earth had been criminal and wicked were consigned to Tartarus, where they were tormented by the Furies and other evil spirits. Those whose lives had not been distinctly good or bad remained in the asphodel meadow, where as dim shadows they passed a dull, joyless existence.

The punishments of great criminals in the infernal regions were a fruitful theme for the imagination of the poets. The most celebrated criminals were Tityus, Tantalus, Sisyphus, Ixion, and the Danaids. We have said that the idea of the judgment of the dead is not found in the earliest legends. Hence we must expect to find, in some cases, that the crimes supposed to have drawn down the wrath of the gods were either later inventions, or had very little connection with the punishment inflicted. Thus to take the case of Tantalus, the original idea appears to have been the burning sun looking upon sweet fruits and streams of water, and drying them up instead of being able to enjoy them. It is possible that another part of the legend, the offering of his children for the gods of heaven to eat, may have a similar origin. So the story of Sisyphus seems to point to the sun daily toiling up the steep hill of heaven, yet ever obliged to recommence his weary task. So the name Ixion seems to be derived from a word meaning wheel, and to be yet another allusion to the orb of day. As men began to forget the reality underlying these words, and to think that some real person suffered these woes, it was only natural that they should try to find a reason. Generally, perhaps always, some point in the story could be twisted into a crime deserving of punishment (compare the legend of Œdipus). The punishment of Tityus, who had offered violence to Leto, consisted in being chained to the earth, whilst two vultures continually gnawed at his ever-growing liver. Tantalus, the ancestor of the Atridæ, Agamemnon and Menelaus, had been deemed worthy to hold intercourse with the gods, until he thought fit to put their omniscience to the test by setting before them the flesh of his son Pelops. This crime he was condemned to expiate by the torments of continual hunger and thirst. Above his head were suspended the most beautiful fruits; but when he attempted to snatch them, a gust of wind blew them beyond his reach. At his feet flowed a stream of the purest water; but when he tried to quench his thirst, it suddenly vanished into the ground. Sisyphus, formerly king of Corinth, had provoked the wrath of the gods by his numerous crimes, and was condemned, in consequence, to roll a block of stone up a high mountain, which, on reaching the top, always rolled down again to the plain. Ixion, a not less insolent offender, was bound hand and foot to an ever-revolving wheel. Lastly, the Danaids, or daughters of Danaus, who, at their father's command, had slain their husbands on the wedding night, were condemned to pour water continually into a cask full of holes, which could never be filled.

18. The Erinyes (Furiæ).—The Erinyes, or Furies, were denizens of the lower world, who executed the commands of Hades and Persephone. They were ultimately three in number, and their names were Tisiphone, Alecto, and Megæra; and this number, like that of the Graces, the Fates, and others, is due to the fact that the Greeks expressed any undefined number by the sacred numeral three. In their original signification they appear as the avengers of every violation, either on the part of gods or men, of the moral laws of the universe. When, at a later period, the idea of an avenging Nemesis had become more and more developed, the significance of the Erinyes diminished, and their avenging duties were confined to the family.

As the inexorable pursuers of every injury done to the sacred ties of blood—especially the murder of kindred—they received a much greater degree of attention at the hands of the Greek tragic poets, by whom they were frequently brought on the stage. The pictures thus drawn of the relentless activity of the Erinyes are both powerful and striking. Nothing can equal the keen scent with which they trace the crime, or the untiring speed with which they pursue the criminal. As a symbol of this latter quality, the poets have endowed them with brazen feet. Their appearance is wan and Gorgon-like; wild lust for blood is written in their features, and the serpents which twine round their heads in the place of hair deal out destruction and death on their unhappy victims. Flight avails them nought, for there is no region whither the avenging Furies cannot follow, no distance that they cannot compass. With torch swung on high they dog the steps of the unhappy wretch, like swift huntresses following in the track of their hard-pressed game, and never rest until they have driven him to madness and death.

What, then, was the origin of the belief in these dreadful beings? Two explanations have been given, and in each case we shall see in them the powers of nature. Whether we are to look upon them as the storm-clouds darting lightnings upon the criminal, or as the bright dawn rising over the earth and pointing out his hiding-place, we must recognise the idea of the punishment of sin, inflicted by the powers of heaven. If, as seems most probable (*cf.* the genealogy given them by Æschylus and

Sophocles), we are to take the latter explanation, we shall have some reason for the names of "kindly" and "venerable," applied to them by the Greeks, partly, no doubt, owing to the ancient custom of avoiding words of ill-omen. Yet poetical mythology treated this as a transformation of their nature, and associated it with a special event, namely, the institution of the Areopagus at Athens, and the purification of the matricide Orestes effected by this venerable court. The story relates that Orestes, after having slain his mother Clytæmnestra and her infamous paramour Ægisthus, in revenge for the murder of his father Agamemnon, wandered for a long time about the earth in a state bordering on madness, owing to the persecution of the Erinyes. At length, however, he was befriended by Apollo and Athene, the kindly deities of the luminous Æther. Apollo first purified him before his own altar at Delphi, and then defended him before the court of the Areopagus, which had been founded by Athene. Orestes was here acquitted, for Athene, when the votes for and against him were equal, declared that then and in all future time the criminal should have the benefit of the doubt. The Furies, indeed, were at first very wroth, and threatened the land with barrenness both of women and soil; but Athene succeeded in pacifying them, by promising that a shrine should be erected to them on the hill of the Areopagus. After they had taken possession of this sanctuary, they were thenceforth venerated by the Athenians, under the names of Semnæ (venerable), or Eumenides (benevolent), as propitious deities who, though they still continued to punish crimes, were ever ready to grant mercy to the repentant sinner, and to give succour to all good men.

There were different traditions concerning the origin of the Erinyes. According to Hesiod, they owed their existence to the first execrable crime committed since the beginning of the world, for they were the daughters of Earth, and sprang from the drops of blood that fell from the mangled body of Uranus. They here appear, therefore, as an embodiment of the curses which the angry father invoked on the head of his unnatural son. Sophocles, on the other hand, calls them the daughters of Gæa and Scotos (darkness of night). Æschylus simply terms them the daughters of the Night. Besides the shrine in Athens already mentioned, they had another near the city, a sacred grove in Colonus, which was celebrated as the last refuge of the unfortunate Œdipus. In Athens they had an annual festival, at which libations of milk and honey were made to them.

In art the Erinyes are represented as swift huntresses, armed with spear, bow, and quiver. Torches, scourges, or snakes were also put in their hands. They were, moreover, provided with wings on their shoulders or head as a token of their swiftness.

19. Hecate.—Among the mystic deities of the lower world we must not omit to mention Hecate. By the Romans, indeed, she was never publicly venerated, though she was not exactly unknown to them. Common tradition made her a daughter of the Titan Perseus and Asteria. She ruled principally over the secret forces of Nature, which perhaps explains the spectral and awe-inspiring form which this goddess assumed. She was supposed to preside over all nocturnal horrors, and not only to haunt the tombs and cross-roads herself in company with the spirits of the dead, but also to send nightly phantoms from the lower world, such as the man-eating spectre Empusa, and other fabulous goblins.

As her name seems to signify, Hecate (far-striking) was originally a moon-goddess, not like either Artemis or Selene, but representing the new moon in its invisible phase. The ancients not being able to account for the different phases of the moon, naturally came to the conclusion that, when invisible, it was tarrying in the lower world. The public worship of the goddess was not very extensive, but her importance in connection with the mysteries was all the greater. Men were wont to affix small pictures of her to houses and city gates, which were supposed to prevent any bad spells from affecting the town or house. On the last day of every month her image on the house doors was crowned with garlands, and viands were set before it in her honour, which were afterwards eaten by the poor, and termed the meals of Hecate. Wooden images of the goddess with three faces were generally set up where three roads met, and here dogs were sacrificed to her as sin-offerings for the dead. This usually took place on the thirtieth day after death. As in the case of other infernal deities, black lambs were sacrificed to her, besides libations of milk and honey.

Hecate was generally represented as three-formed (*triformis*), which probably has some connection with the appearance of the full, half, and new moon. In order to explain more clearly the nature of such a representation, we give an engraving (Fig. 47) after a bronze statuette in the Capitoline Museum at Rome. The figure facing us holds in her hands a key and a rope, which point her out as the portress of the lower world; over her brow is a disc, representing, probably, the dark surface of the new moon. The figure on the right holds in either hand a torch, in virtue of her character as a mystic goddess, whilst on her brow is a half-moon and a lotus-flower. Lastly, the third figure bears, as a symbol of the full moon, a Phrygian cap with a radiant diadem fastened on it, which gives forth seven rays; in her right hand is a knife, in her left the tail of a serpent, of which no satisfactory interpretation has hitherto been discovered.

Fig. 47.—Three-formed Hecate. Capitoline Museum.

20. Sleep and Death.—Sleep and Death were conceived by the ancients as twin brothers. According to Hesiod, they were children of Night alone. They dwelt in the lower world, whence they visited the earth to steal over mortals ; the former a kindly benevolent spirit, the latter grim and cruel. Apart from this conception, which was especially developed by later poets and artists, Death was sometimes depicted as quite distinct from Sleep, and in a still less amiable guise. The different forms of violent death were personified as female deities of formidable aspect, called the Ceres; or Apollo and Artemis among the inhabitants of heaven, and Pluto and Persephone among those of the lower world, were represented as the deities of death. The Romans had a personal god of death, whom they called Orcus; he was represented as an armed warrior dealing out mortal wounds among mankind. But none of these special gods of death had any great importance, either in religion or art. Artists, indeed, laboured sedulously to diminish the dreadful appearance of Thanatus (death), and to render him more and more like his brother Hypnus (sleep).

Thanatus and Hypnus often appear in company, either sleeping or standing; the former usually bears a reversed torch, the latter a poppy-stalk or a horn, out of which he is pouring some liquid. They are both generally represented in the bloom of youth. In Fig. 34, which is after a drawing of Asmus Carstens, they appear as the children of Night, and are here brought into immediate connection with the other powers, Nemesis and the Parcæ, who control the destinies of man.

Besides Sleep and Death, Hesiod also mentions Dreams as the children of Night. Other writers, however, call them the sons of Sleep, who dwell in the far West, close to the realms of Hades. This house of dreams has, in Homer's well-known description, two gates—one of ivory, through which pass flattering, deceptive dreams, and one of horn, whence the true dreams proceed. Morpheus was made the special god of dreams by the poets, and termed the son of Hypnus.

IV.—ROMAN DEITIES OF THE HOUSE AND FAMILY.

Before passing to the heroic legends, some remarks are necessary concerning the inferior deities, who played such an important part in the domestic worship of the Romans. We have already

incidentally remarked that the people of Italy generally passed
by the greater gods of the heaven and earth in anxious awe.
Their invocation and adoration was left to public worship,
whilst, in their less important domestic concerns, men had
recourse to certain inferior deities, whom they thought nearer to
them; just as in the present day, in Italy, the common people
prefer to communicate their prayers and wishes to their patron
saints rather than to the Almighty himself.

1. **The Penates.**—The Penates were the kindly domestic
deities of the Romans—the guardians of the household, who
especially provided for its daily wants. Of their name, number,
and sex nothing is known—not because the facts have been
lost to us, but because the Romans themselves were content
with this indefinite conception. Similar good spirits, exerting
an active influence in the household, were recognised by popular
German superstition, without experiencing any necessity of
having distinct names for them. The shrine of the Penates consisted of the hearth, the central point of the house, which not
only served for the preparation of meals, but was also especially
dedicated to religious purposes. It stood in the "atrium," the
only large room in the Roman house, where the family met for
meals and received visitors. On the hearth, a fire was continually kept burning in honour of Vesta and the Penates.
Around it, after the introduction of images of the gods, were
placed the statues of the Penates. These were generally small
and puppet-like, and, among the poorer classes, were only
roughly cut out of wood. There was no domestic occurrence,
either of joy or mourning, in which the Penates did not take
part. Like the Lares, of whom we shall speak presently, they
participated in the daily meal, portions being set on certain
plates for that purpose before the images. There were also
State Penates, the ancients regarding the state as nothing but an
extended family. The temple of Vesta was to the state what
the hearth was to the household. Here was the seat of their

worship, and here it was that the Roman Pontifex Maximus brought those offerings which, in private households, were the part of the head of the family. In the innermost sanctuary of the temple of Vesta there were statues of these Penates, of great sanctity, since Æneas was reported to have brought them with him from Troy. We have no trustworthy information as to their number or appearance, for, with the exception of the Pontifex and the Vestal Virgins, none ever entered the holy place. It is scarcely necessary to add that they were believed to exercise an especial influence on the welfare and prosperity of the state and people of Rome.

2. The Lares.—The Lares, like the Penates, were the tutelary deities of the house and family, and on that account often confounded with them. They were commonly supposed to be the glorified spirits of ancestors, who, as guardian deities, strove to promote the welfare of the family. The seat of their worship was also the family hearth in the atrium, where their images of wood or wax were generally preserved in a separate shrine of their own (Lararium). The Lares received an especial degree of veneration on the first day of every month; but, like the Penates, they took part in all the domestic occurrences, whether of joy or sorrow. Like the Penates, they also received their share at every meal on particular dishes, and were crowned with garlands on the occasion of every family rejoicing. When a son assumed the *toga virilis* (came of age), he dedicated his *bulla** to the Lares, amid prayers and libations and burning of incense. When the father of the house started on a journey or returned in safety, the Lares were again addressed, and their statues crowned with wreaths, flowers and garlands being their favourite offerings.

The same conception which pervades the domestic Lares may be perceived in a more extensive form in the Lares of the Gens, the

---

* A gold or silver ornament, like a medal, which was worn round the neck during childhood.

L

city, and the state itself. The Lares do not appear, in fact, to have differed in many respects from the heroes worshipped by the Greeks. At all events, Romulus and Remus, the mythical founders of the city, were regarded as its Lares, and, in the time of Augustus, the genius of the emperor was associated with them.

3. Larvæ, Lemures, and Manes.—Just as the Lares were regarded as the good and happy spirits of ancestors, the souls of others were supposed to wander about in the guise of evil demons and spectres, giving rise to weird terrors, and casting bad spells on the senses of those whom they met. Such was especially believed to be the fate of those who had not received burial, or in whose case the prescribed ceremonies had been neglected, and who being, in consequence, unable to find rest, were doomed to flit about the earth. Such spirits were called Larvæ, or Lemures. The propitiatory festival of the Lemuria, or Lemuralia, which was said to have been instituted in memory of the murdered Remus, was celebrated annually in their honour on the 9th, 11th, and 13th of May. Every pater-familias was supposed during these days to perform certain midnight ceremonies, and to repeat certain forms, which had the effect of banishing any evil spirits.

In contrast to the Lares and Larvæ, the souls of the dead were also commonly venerated as Manes, or good spirits. These were believed after burial to have been converted into beings of a higher order, who dwelt, indeed, in the interior of the earth, but exercised, notwithstanding, a considerable in-fluence on the affairs of the upper world. It was possible to summon them from the lower world by means of sacrifices. A general festival of the dead took place in February, when the Manes were propitiated with offerings and libations. These offerings were placed on the tombs of the deceased, and, of course, varied extremely, according to the means of the donors.

PART III.—THE HEROES.

I.—INTRODUCTORY.

ON passing to heroic mythology, a world still more rich in marvels than that with which we have already become acquainted presents itself to our view. The greater extent of this department of mythic lore is easily comprehensible, if we take into consideration the multitude of separate existences into which Greek life was split up, even from the earliest times. Each of the numberless countries, islands, cities, and towns endeavoured to trace back its peculiar institutions to mythical founders and ancestors; and as these were always described either as the sons or as the favourites of the gods, there accordingly sprang up, in course of time, a vast number of local heroic legends. These fabulous founders of states, however, were not the only heroes of Greek mythology. The attempt to pierce the clouds of obscurity which enveloped the early history of mankind, and the desire of a more enlightened age to bridge over the intervening gulf, and fill it with beings who should form a connecting link between the sublime forms of the great inhabitants of Olympus and the puny race of mortals, naturally gave rise to a whole series of heroic legends. These were partly the property of entire nationalities, or even of the whole Hellenic

race, and partly of a local or provincial character.   Moreover,
as the gods collectively were divided into gods proper and
dæmons—that is to say, spirits resembling the gods, but inferior
to them in wisdom and power, whose workings men saw in air
and earth and sea—even so the race of mortals was divided into
heroes and men, between whom a similar difference subsisted.
The latter are, in their nature, not different from the former—
both are alike mortal, and must at length fall a prey to inexorable death.   But the heroes are endowed with a degree of
physical strength and dexterity, courage and endurance under
difficulties, such as never fall to the lot of ordinary men.   It
was not, however, by any means all who lived in this early
mythical period who were accounted heroes ; but, just as in
Genesis vi. 2 a distinction is made between the "sons of God"
and the "daughters of men," so in the present instance the
heroes were the mighty ones—the ruling spirits of the age—
those whose marvellous exploits contributed to remove the
obstacles to civilisation and culture, who delivered countries
from cruel robbers and savage beasts, who drained marshes,
made roads through untrodden forests, and regulated the course
of rivers.   By their actions they proved themselves men of no
ordinary powers, endowed with divine strength, and, therefore,
apparently of divine origin.   It appeared, at least, that such
beings must have had an origin different from that of ordinary
men, who were made out of clay, or sprang from trees or stones.
Some of these heroes may perhaps have had a real existence,
having probably been the ancestors of the later dominant races,
to whom a dim tradition reached.   Others were undoubtedly a
product of the imagination.   To these may be added a third
class, and this is by far the most numerous, including those who
were originally personifications of various natural phenomena,
and, as such, deified and venerated in local forms of worship, but
who were later, in consequence of the birth of new political communities, expelled from their place in public worship, and only
continued to exist in the popular faith in the inferior character

of heroes. Many such heroes were afterwards again promoted to the rank of gods, though with an altered meaning (*e.g.*, Heracles).

Any real veneration of heroes by prayers and sacrifices can scarcely be said to have existed before the migration of the Heraclidæ—at least there is no mention of it in Homer. Even later, except in the case of those heroes who were raised to the rank of gods for their great deeds, and who were, therefore, worshipped in temples of their own, the worship of heroes is scarcely to be distinguished from that of the dead. Homer makes no distinction between the fate of heroes after death and that of ordinary mortals, all being doomed alike to the gloomy realms of Hades. As we have already observed, it was only certain special favourites, or sons of Zeus, who were excepted from this gloomy lot, and were transported in their bodily shape to the Isles of the Blest. Hesiod, on the other hand, says that all heroes—whom he, in the first instance, terms demi-gods—were transported to the Isles of the Blest, where Cronus ruled over them. Here, for the first time, the idea of a just retribution in the other world takes a definite shape; for Hesiod obviously conceives a residence in Elysium to be the reward of meritorious actions performed in the upper world. This idea was subsequently more fully developed, especially in the mysteries, and men were gradually elevated to a belief in the immortality of the soul. The spirits of the dead were believed, even after they were in their graves, to exert continually a mysterious influence; on which account men strove to gain their favour by means of offerings, thereby removing every real distinction between the worship of heroes and that of the dead.

Amid the multitude of legends of this kind, we shall only dwell upon those which occupy a prominent position either in poetry or in art. We shall begin with those which relate to the creation and early civilisation of mankind, after which we shall pass to the most celebrated provincial legends, and conclude with those that refer to the more important of the common undertakings of the later heroic age.

IL—THE CREATION AND PRIMITIVE CONDITION OF MANKIND.

The legends concerning the origin of the human race differ very widely. The most ancient are undoubtedly those which describe men as springing from the trees or rocks. Another tradition asserts that the human race was of later growth, having been first called into existence by Zeus and the gods of Olympus. A third account makes the Titan Prometheus, the son of Iapetus, the creator of mankind, but leaves it uncertain whether this took place before or after the flood of Deucalion. Prometheus, according to this account, made men of clay and water, after which Athene breathed a soul into them. There were likewise various accounts concerning the primeval condition of mankind. According to one, the human race raised itself, with the assistance of the gods, from a state of helpless barbarism : this progress was the subject of numerous legends. Another account represents men as living originally in a holy and happy communion with the gods (the golden age), and asserts that they first became savage after having lost this good fortune by their presumption.

Of the myths that relate to the introduction of the first elements of civilisation among mankind by divine aid, there is none, except those already mentioned concerning Dionysus and Demeter, more celebrated than the story of Prometheus. The Titan Iapetus had, by Clymene, the daughter of Oceanus, four sons—the stout-hearted Atlas, the presumptuous Menœtius, the crafty Prometheus, and the foolish Epimetheus. With the name of Prometheus is linked the idea of the first commencement of civilisation among mankind by the introduction of fire. Prometheus is said to have stolen fire from heaven, and to have taught its use to man. By being employed for all the common purposes of daily life, however, this pure celestial element became polluted ; whereupon Zeus visited the author of this sacrilege with a fearful punishment. He ordered Prometheus to be chained to a rock, where, during the day-time, an eagle devoured his liver (the seat of all evil desires), which always grew again during the night.

It is very difficult to see the origin of this series of legends, but the foundation seems to be the discovery of fire by man. At any rate, one word, closely resembling the name Prometheus, appears in India as the name of the stick used to produce fire by friction. If this be the case, we shall see in parts of the Greek legend instances of the ever-recurring principle, that when the real derivation of a word is lost, men try to give it an explanation by attaching it to the nearest word in the existing language (*cf.* the derivation of Pan mentioned p. 130). When the notion of "forethought" had once been attached to his name, it would be natural to invent a complementary legend about his brother Epimetheus (afterthought).

The legend of Prometheus appears in its grandest form in Æschylus' play, "Prometheus Bound."

The idea that, together with the introduction of civilisation, many evils which were before unknown to man came into existence, is expressed in the myth of Pandora. Zeus determined to leave mankind in possession of Prometheus' gift ; but he ordered Hephæstus to make an image of a beautiful woman, which the gods then endowed with life and adorned with all kinds of gifts, whence she was called Pandora. Aphrodite bestowed on her the seductive charms that kindle love, Athene instructed her in every art, Hermes endued her with a smooth tongue and a crafty disposition, whilst the Seasons and Graces adorned her with flowers and fine dresses. Zeus then sent her, under the guidance of Hermes, to the foolish Epimetheus, who, in spite of the warning of his brother not to accept any present from Zeus, received Pandora and made her his wife. There was in the house of Epimetheus a closed jar, which he had been forbidden to open, and which contained all kinds of diseases and ills. Pandora removed the cover and these escaped, and men who had before been free from disease and care have ever since been tormented. Pandora closed the jar in time to keep in Hope. Thus both Greek legend and Biblical tradition alike represent woman as the first cause of evil and death.

The legend of the five ages of mankind transports us to quite another region of tradition. According to this, the gods first created a golden race of men, who lived free from care and sorrow, while the earth, of its own accord, furnished them with all that was necessary to support life. Subject neither to the infirmities of age nor to the pangs of sickness and disease, men at last sank peacefully, as into a sweet sleep, to death. In what manner the golden age disappeared is not related; we are only told that this race, notwithstanding its disappearance, still continues to exist in the upper world, in the shape of good spirits, who guard and protect mortals. After this, the gods created a second (silver) race of men, who were, however, far inferior to their predecessors, both in mind and body. They passed their time in idle and effeminate pursuits, and refused to pay the gods due honours. Zeus, in his wrath, thereupon blotted them out from the face of the earth, and created the third (brazen) race of mankind out of ash wood. This race proved headstrong and violent. They were of giant stature and great strength, and took pleasure in nothing but battle and strife. Their weapons, houses, and utensils were of bronze, iron not yet being known. Zeus was not compelled to destroy this evil race, since they destroyed themselves in their bloodthirsty strife. According to another account, they were destroyed by the flood of Deucalion.

Deucalion appears to have been a son of Prometheus, while his wife Pyrrha was the daughter of Epimetheus and Pandora. Zeus having determined to destroy the corrupt race of the third or bronze age by a flood, Prometheus warned his son, who built himself an ark, into which he retired with his wife when the waters began to rise. Nine days and nights he was tossed on the waters; at length his vessel rested on Mount Parnassus in Bœotia. He disembarked, and immediately offered a sacrifice of thanksgiving to Zeus the preserver. Pleased at his gratitude, Zeus granted his prayer for the restoration of the human race ; and Deucalion and Pyrrha were commanded by Hermes to cast stones behind them, from which sprang a new race of men. Such is the legend in its most ancient form ; later writers engrafted on it still further incidents of Biblical tradition, until at last the Greek Noah was represented as having taken living animals with him into the ark, and as having let loose a dove after his landing on Parnassus.

III.—PROVINCIAL HEROIC LEGENDS.

1. The Lapithæ and the Centaurs.—We shall commence with the Thessalian legend of the Lapithæ and Centaurs, on account of its great antiquity and its importance in sculpture. We read in the Homeric poems how the hoary Nestor on one occasion boasts of having, in his younger days, taken part with his friends Pirithoüs and Cæneus, and the other princes of the Lapithæ, in their contest with the savage Centaurs. In Homer's account the Centaurs are merely depicted as an old Thessalian mountain tribe of giant strength and savage ferocity, utterly unable to control their rude; sensual nature. Nor do we find here any mention of their being half horses and half men ; they are merely said to have inhabited the mountain districts of Œta and Pelion, in Thessaly, and to have been driven thence by the Lapithæ into the higher mountain-lands of Pindus.

Their contest with the Lapithæ is sometimes conceived as a symbol of the struggle of Greek civilisation with the still existing barbarism of the early Pelasgian period. This may be the reason why Greek art, when in its bloom, devoted itself so especially to this subject. The origin of this contest is referred to the marriage feast of Pirithoüs and Hippodamia, to which the principal Centaurs had been invited. On this occasion the Centaur Eurytion, heated with wine, attempted to carry off the bride ; this gave rise to a contest which, after dreadful losses on both sides, ended in the complete defeat of the Centaurs. The Centaurs, however, since they were thus able to sit with the Lapithæ at meat, must have been endowed with purely human forms.

Theseus and Nestor, the friends of Pirithoüs, both took part in the battle. Another prominent warrior was the gigantic Cæneus (Slayer), who had been rendered invulnerable by Poseidon, but whom the Centaurs slew on this occasion by burying him beneath a mass of trees and rocks.

There is, however, also a natural explanation of the tales of these strange beings. The father of the Centaurs is Ixion, who, as we have already seen, may be interpreted to be the sun. The crime said to have been the cause of his punishment was his love for Hera (the goddess of the atmosphere). If we take these points, together with the legend that Ixion begat the Centaurs of Nephele, the cloud, we may be prepared to see in the horse-formed Centaurs a parallel to the cows of the sun, the bright clouds which pass over the sky. There is the more ground for this, as similar beings appear in Indian mythology, and their name has, with much probability, been identified with that of the Centaurs.

As we have already mentioned, the Centaurs play an important part in art. The custom of depicting them as half horse and half man came into vogue after the time of Pindar, and was quickly adopted in sculpture. In the representations of earlier art the face of a man is joined to the body and hind legs of a horse. But in its higher stage of development, after the time of Phidias, this was replaced by a more elegant conception, and the body of a man from the navel upwards was joined to the

Fig. 48.—Metope of the Parthenon.

complete body of a horse, so that the Centaurs of this period have the four feet of a horse and the hands and arms of a man. Such is their appearance on numerous extant art monuments, of which we shall mention the most important.

In the first place, there are the reliefs from the frieze of the Theseum at Athens. This temple, which is still in a good state of preservation, was converted during the middle ages into a chapel of St. George. It is supposed to have been built at the instance of Cimon, after he had brought back the bones of the Attic hero from Scyros. Besides other important pieces, which we shall mention hereafter, the temple has, on its western or hinder frieze, a representation of the contests of the Centaurs and Lapithæ at the wedding of Pirithoüs, done in Parian marble. It is executed in such a manner that it is impossible to discover which party will get the upper hand; and this has enabled the artist, whose name has not come down to us, to introduce a lively variety into the different scenes of the combat.

We have another series of most splendid representations from the battle of the Centaurs, full of life and spirit, on some dilapidated metopes* of the Parthenon at Athens. This splendid specimen of Doric architecture is 227 feet in length and 101 feet in breadth. It

Fig. 49.—From the Frieze of the Temple at Bassæ.

was ruined in 1687, during the war between the Venetians and Turks, by a shell which broke through the midst of the marble roof. A large part of the ninety-two metopes of the outer frieze contain a number of the most beautiful and life-like scenes from the battle of the Giants and that of the Centaurs. Of these metopes, thirty-nine still remain on the temple, though they are all in a terribly mutilated condition; seventeen are in the British Museum, and one in the Louvre at Paris. Those from the south side are comparatively in the best state of preservation; these are seventeen in number, the

* The squares between the triglyphs of the frieze which are intended to support the gable, every one of which is generally adorned with a separate sculpture in relief.

whole number on the south side having been thirty-two. They represent, exclusively, scenes from the battle of the Centaurs. Here a bearded Centaur is carrying off a woman, whom he holds in his powerful grasp; there, another is galloping away over the body of his fallen enemy; another is engaged in a fierce contest with a human foe; whilst a fourth lies slain on the field. The engraving we append may give a faint idea of the beauty and bold design of this splendid creation (Fig. 48). To these grand monuments of Greek art we must add the frieze of the temple of Apollo Epicurius at Bassæ, near Phigalia in Arcadia, which was discovered in 1812, and is now in the British Museum. It represents, likewise, a series of the most vivid scenes from the battle of the Lapithæ and Centaurs. In the individual groups and scenes of the battle, which is here completed before our eyes, there is the same variety and animation, so that we must ascribe it to some great artist (Fig. 49).

Besides these sculptures in relief, some splendid single statues of Centaurs have come down to us from antiquity. Among these, the first place must be assigned to the two Centaurs in the Capitoline Museum. They are executed in black marble, and were found in the villa of Hadrian at Tivoli, where so many ancient art treasures have been brought to light.

Among the Centaurs, Chiron, who was famous alike for his wisdom and his knowledge of medicine, deserves mention as the preceptor of many of the heroes of antiquity. So far superior was he to his savage kindred, both in education and manners, that he was commonly reported to have had a different origin, and was therefore described as a son of Cronus and Philyra, or Phyllira, one of the Oceanids. Homer, who knew nothing of the equine shape of the Centaurs, represents him as the most upright of the Centaurs, and makes him the friend of Peleus and the preceptor of the youthful Achilles, whom he instructed in the art of healing and gymnastic exercises. He was, moreover, related to both these heroes, his daughter Endeïs having been the mother of Peleus. Subsequently, other mythical heroes were added to the number of his pupils, such as Castor and Polydeuces, Theseus, Nestor, Meleager, and Diomedes. Music, too, was now represented as a subject of his instruction, though this is perhaps due to a misinterpretation of the name of his

Fig. 50.—Centaur teaching a Boy to play upon the Pipe.   Relief by Kundmann.

mother.   He inhabited a cave on Mount Pelion; later mythology, however, transferred his residence, after the Centaurs
had been driven from Pelion by the Lapithæ, to the promontory of Malea.   Here, by an unlucky accident, he was wounded
with a poisoned arrow by his friend Heracles, and, the wound

being incurable, he voluntarily chose to die in the place of Prometheus.

The idea of the connection of the Centaurs with the arts and sciences originated in the story of Chiron and Achilles, and has since furnished modern art with the subjects for some of its most valuable works. Fig. 50 represents a Centaur teaching a boy to play on the flute, and is after an *alto-relievo* of the Viennese sculptor Kundmann.

2. Theban Legend.—1. *Cadmus.*—Among Theban legends, none is more celebrated than the founding of Thebes by Cadmus. Cadmus was a son of the Phœnician king Agenor. After Zeus carried off his sister Europa to Crete (*vide* the *Cretan Legends*), he was despatched by his father in search of her. Accompanied by his mother Telephassa, he came to Thrace and thence to Delphi, where he was commanded by the oracle to relinquish his quest. It further ordered him to follow a young heifer with the mark of a crescent on either side, and to build a town on the place where the heifer should lie down. Cadmus obeyed, and, finding the heifer in Phocis, he followed her. She led him into Bœotia, and at length lay down on a rising ground. On this spot Cadmus founded a town, which he called Cadmea, after himself, though he had first to experience a perilous adventure. Before sacrificing the heifer, he sent some of his companions to fetch water from a neighbouring spring, where they were slain by a dragon belonging to Ares which guarded the spring. Cadmus then went himself, and slew the dragon, the teeth of which he sowed in the ground by the advice of Pallas. Hereupon armed men sprang from the ground; they immediately turned their arms against each other, and were all slain except five. Cadmus built his new town with the assistance of these men, who thus became the ancestors of the noble families of Thebes. In expiation of the dragon's death, Cadmus was obliged to do service to Ares for eight years. At the end of this period Ares pardoned Cadmus and gave him Harmonia—his daughter by Aphrodite—to wife. Harmonia became the mother of four daughters—Autonoë, Ino, Semele, and Agave. After reigning for a long time at Thebes, Cadmus was compelled in his old age to retire to the Enchelians in Illyria; but whether he was driven out by Amphion and Zethus (who appear in Homer as the founders of Thebes) or withdrew from some other cause is not manifest. He and his wife were afterwards changed into serpents, and transferred, by the command of Zeus, to the Elysian fields.

In this story we see another form of the combat of the hero with the monster, and can probably give it the same explanation. The dragon guards the waters, and the hero, by killing it, frees them. Do we not see in this the combat of the sun with the cloud; and in the armed men who turn their weapons against one another, the clouds that seem to fight with one another in the thunderstorm? Yet even admitting this interpretation, it may be that we have in the name of Cadmus an allusion to the civilisation and the arts received by the Greeks from the East. So, too, with the alphabet, the invention of which Hellenic tradition ascribed to him.

2. *Actæon.*—We have already incidentally mentioned the fortunes of three of the daughters of Cadmus—Ino, Semele, and Agave. The eldest, Autonoë, married Aristæus, the son of Apollo, and became by him the mother of Actæon. Actæon was handed over to Chiron to be reared as a stout hunter and warrior; but he had scarcely reached the prime of youth when he was overtaken by a lamentable fate. Whilst hunting one day on Mount Cithæron, he was changed by Artemis into a stag, and was torn in pieces by his own dogs. The cause of her anger was either that Actæon had boasted that he was a more skilful hunter than Artemis, or that he had surprised the virgin-goddess bathing. The latter tradition ultimately prevailed, and,

in later times, even the rock whence
he beheld Artemis was pointed out on
the road between Megara and Platæa.
He received heroic honours in Bœotia,
and his protection was invoked against
the deadly power of the sun in the
dog-days. The story of Actæon is
probably nothing but a representation
of the decay of verdant nature beneath
an oppressive summer heat.

The story of
Actæon's transfor-
mation and death
was a favourite
subject for sculp-
ture. A small
marble group, re-
presenting Actæon
beating off two
dogs which are at-
tacking him, was
found in 1774, and
is now preserved
in the British
Museum (Fig. 51).

3. *Amphion
and Zethus.*—Be-
sides the royal
family of Cadmus,

Fig. 51.—Actæon Group.   British Museum.

which was continued in Thebes after his departure by his
son Polydorus, we come across the scions of another ruling
family of Thebes which came from Hyria, or Hysia, in Bœotia,
in the persons of Amphion and Zethus. Nycteus, king of
Thebes, had a wonderfully beautiful daughter called Antiope,
whose favours Zeus enjoyed on approaching her in the form of a
Satyr. On becoming pregnant, she fled from the resentment of

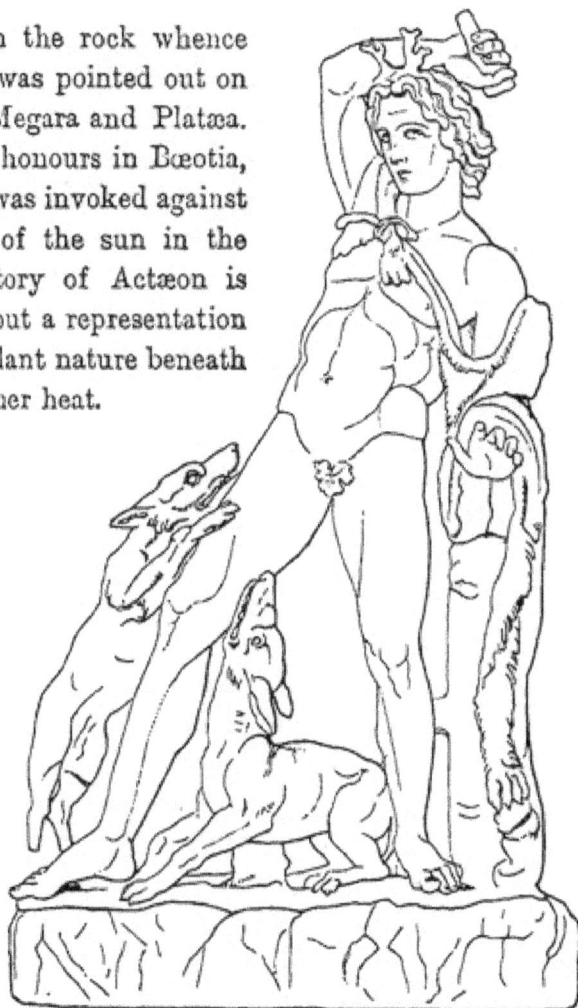

her father to Sicyon, where the king, Epopeus, received her and made her his wife. This enraged Nycteus, who made war on Epopeus in order to compel him to deliver up his daughter Antiope. He was obliged to retire without accomplishing his purpose, but, on his death, he entrusted the execution of his vengeance to his brother Lycus, who succeeded him. Lycus defeated and slew Epopeus, destroyed Sicyon, and took Antiope back with him as prisoner. On the way, at Eleutheræ on Cithæron, she gave birth to the twins Amphion and Zethus. These were immediately exposed, but were subsequently dis-covered and brought up by a compassionate shepherd. Antiope was not only kept prisoner in the house of Lycus, but had also to submit to the most harsh and humiliating treatment at the hands of his wife Dirce. At length she managed to escape, and by a wonderful chance discovered her two sons, who had grown, on lonely Cithæron, into sturdy youths. The story of her wrongs so enraged them that they resolved to wreak a cruel vengeance on Dirce. After having taken Thebes and slain Lycus, they bound Dirce to the horns of a wild bull, which dragged her about till she perished. According to another story, Dirce came to Cithæron to celebrate the festival of Bacchus. Here she found her runaway slave, whom she was about to punish by having her bound to the horns of a bull. Happily, however, Amphion and Zethus recognised their mother, and inflicted on the cruel Dirce the punishment she had destined for another. Her mangled remains they cast into the spring near Thebes which bears her name.

The punishment of Dirce forms the subject of numerous pieces of sculpture. The most important among them is the Farnese Bull (*Toro Farnese*) in the museum at Naples (Fig. 52). This world-renowned marble group is supposed, with the exception of certain parts which have been restored in modern times, to have been the work of the brothers Apollonius and Tauriscus, of Tralles in Caria, Apollonius and Tauriscus belonged to the Rhodian school, which

M

Fig. 52.—Farnese Bull. Naples.

flourished in the third century B.C. This colossal group—undoubtedly the largest which has descended to us from antiquity—was first erected in Rhodes, but came, during the reign of Augustus, into the possession of Asinius Pollio, the great art-patron. It was discovered in 1547 in the Thermæ of Caracalla at Rome, and was set up in the Palazzo Farnese. It was thence transferred to Naples in 1786, as a portion of the Farnese inheritance. The following is a brief explanation of the group, though, of course, the most complete account could give but an imperfect idea of its beauty. The scene is laid on the rocky heights of Cithæron. The position of the handsome youths on a rocky crag is as picturesque as it is dangerous, and serves not only to lend the group a pyramidal aspect pleasing to the eye, but also to set before us their marvellous strength. There are several tokens that the occurrence took place during a Bacchic festival: the wicker *cista mystica* in use at the festivals of Dionysus—the fawn skin which Dirce wears—the ivy garland that has fallen at her feet—the broken thyrsus, and, lastly, the Bacchic insignia which distinguish the shepherd boy, who is sitting on the right watching the proceedings with painful interest—all point to this fact. The lyre which rests against the tree behind Amphion is a token of his well-known love of music. The female figure in the background is Antiope.

The story goes on to relate that the two brothers, after the expulsion and death of Lycus, acquired the sovereignty of Thebes, though Amphion always figures as the real king. The two brothers were widely different in disposition and character. Zethus appears to have been rude and harsh, and passionately fond of the chase. Amphion, on the other hand, is represented as a friend of the Muses, and devoted to music and poetry. He soon had an opportunity of proving his wondrous skill when they began to enclose Thebes, which had been before unprotected, with walls and towers; for whilst Zethus removed great blocks and piled them one on another by means of his vast strength, Amphion had but to touch the strings of his lyre and break forth into some sweet melody, and the mighty stones moved of their own accord and obediently fitted themselves together. This is why Amphion is always represented in sculpture with a lyre and Zethus with a club. We can scarcely doubt that these Theban Dioscuri, like the Castor and Polydeuces of Sparta, who are well known to be only symbols of the morning and evening star, were originally personifications of some natural phenomenon; though we are no longer in a position to say what it was.

Amphion is further celebrated on account of the melancholy fate of his sons and daughters. He married Niobe, the daughter of the Phrygian king Tantalus, and sister of Pelops. Great was the happiness of this marriage ; the gods seemed to shower down their blessings on the royal pair. Many blooming and lovely children grew up in their palace, the pride and delight of their happy parents. From this paradise of purest joy and happiness they were soon to pass into a night of the deepest mourning and most cruel affliction through the presumption of Niobe—the same presumption which had led her father Tantalus to trifle with the gods and consummate his own ruin. The heart of Niobe was lifted up with pride at the number of her children,* and she ventured to prefer herself to Latona, who had only two ; nay, she even went so far as to forbid the Thebans to offer sacrifice to Latona and her children, and to claim these honours herself. The vengeance of the offended deities, however, now overtook her, and all her children were laid low in one day before the unerring arrows of Apollo and his sister. The parents did not survive this deep affliction. Amphion slew himself, and Niobe, already paralysed with grief, was turned into stone by the pity of the gods, and transferred to her old Phrygian home on Mount Sipylus, though even the stone has not ceased to weep.

Such is the substance of this beautiful legend, though its details vary considerably in the accounts of the poets and mythologists. The most circumstantial and richly-coloured account of it is contained in the *Metamorphoses* of Ovid. The poets

---

* The number of Niobe's children varies materially. Homer (*Il.* xxiv., 602) gives her six sons and as many daughters. According to Hesiod and Pindar, she had ten sons and ten daughters ; but the most common account, and that followed by the tragic poets, allows her fourteen children. Everywhere the number of sons and daughters appears to be equal. The story of Niobe was frequently treated of by the tragic poets, both Æschylus and Sophocles having written tragedies bearing her name.

have continually striven to impose a purely ethical interpretation on the story, by representing the destruction of the children of Niobe as the consequence of the great sin of their mother; but it is more probably a physical meaning which lies at the root of the legend. It is, in fact, a picture of the melting of the snow before the hot scorching rays of the sun. This incident the fertile imagination of the Greeks portrayed in the most beautiful metaphors. But just as a subject so purely tragic as the history of Niobe found its first true development in tragic poetry, so likewise it only attained its proper place in sculpture after art had laid aside its earlier and more simple epic character, and set itself to depict, in their full force, the inward passions of the soul. This tendency towards pathos and effect is characteristic of the age of Praxiteles and Scopas, and the later Attic school.

To this age (4th century B.C.) belonged the group of Niobe, which was so highly celebrated even among the ancients, and which was seen by Pliny in the temple of Apollo Sosianus at Rome, although people even then hesitated whether to ascribe it to Praxiteles or Scopas. None but one of these great masters could have been the author of this tragedy hewn in stone. Although the original figures of this magnificent group have disappeared, yet copies of most of them are still in existence. With regard to the celebrated Florentine Niobe group, the dissimilarity of its treament and the various kinds of marble employed serve to show that it is not a Greek original, but a Roman imitation. It was found at Rome in 1583, near the Lateran Church, and was purchased by Cardinal Medici to adorn his villa on the Monte Pincio. In 1775 it was brought to Florence, where it has remained since 1794 in the gallery of the Uffizi.

There has never been but one opinion as to the beauty of this group. First among the figures—not only in size, but also in artistic perfection—is that of Niobe herself. The unhappy queen displays in her whole bearing so majestic and noble a demeanour, that, even if none of the other splendid results of Greek sculpture had come down to us, this alone would bear ample testimony to the high perfection and creative power of Greek art. The following description of the arrangement of the group is taken from Lübke's *History of Plastic Art:*—

"Apollo and Artemis are to be supposed outside the group;
they have accomplished their work of vengeance and destruction
from an invisible position in the heavens. This is denoted by
each movement of the flying figures, who either gaze upwards in
affright towards the heavens, or seek to cover themselves with their
garments. One of the sons is already stretched dead on the earth;
another leans in mortal agony against a rock, fixing his eyes, already
glazed in death, on the spot whence destruction has overtaken him.
A third brother is striving in vain to protect with his robe his sister,
who has fallen wounded at his feet, and to catch her in his arms;
another has sunk on his knees, and clutches in agony at the wound
in his back; whilst his preceptor is endeavouring to shield the
youngest boy. All the others are fleeing instinctively to their
mother, thinking, doubtless, that she who had so often afforded protection could save
them also from the
avenging arrows of
the gods. Thus from
either side the waves
of this dreadful flight
rush towards the cen-
tre, to break on the
sublime figure of Niobe
as upon a rock. She
alone stands unshaken
in all her sorrow,
mother and queen to
the last. Clasping her
youngest daughter,
whose tender years
have not preserved
her, in her arms, and
bending over as though
to shield the child, she
turns her own proud
head upwards, and,
before her left hand
can cover her sorrow-
stricken face with her
robe, she casts towards
the avenging goddess
a look in which bitter
grief is blended with
sublime dignity of soul
(Fig. 54). In this look
there is neither defi-

Fig. 54.—Niobe.   Florence.

ance nor prayer for mercy, but a sorrowful and yet withal lofty expression of heroic resignation to inexorable fate that is worthy of a Niobe. This admirable figure, then, is pre-eminently the central point of the composition, since it expresses an atonement which, in a scene of horror and annihilation, stirs the heart to the deepest sympathy."

Zethus was not more fortunate than Amphion in his domestic affairs. He married Aëdon (nightingale), the daughter of Pandareos. Pandareos was the friend and companion of Tantalus, for whom he stole a living dog made of brass from the temple of Zeus in Crete, and was on that account turned into stone.

Aëdon was jealous of the good-fortune of Niobe in having so many beautiful children; she herself having only one son, Itylus. She resolved, one night, to slay the eldest son of Niobe, but she killed, in mistake, her own child instead. Zeus took compassion on her, and changed her into a nightingale. In this guise she still continues to bewail her loss in long-drawn mournful notes. Tradition says nothing as to the death of Zethus, although the common grave of the Theban Dioscuri was pointed out in Thebes. After his death, Laius, the son of Labdacus and grandson of Polydorus, restored in his person the race of Cadmus to the throne of Thebes. (See the legend of the Labdacidæ later on.)

3. **Corinthian Legend.**—1. *Sisyphus.*—Corinth, or Ephyra, as it was formerly called, was said to have been founded by Sisyphus, the son of Æolus. Its inhabitants, on account of the position of their city between two seas, were naturally inclined to deify that element, and it is not improbable that Sisyphus was merely an ancient symbol of the restless, ever-rolling waves of the sea. This interpretation, however, is by no means certain; and the idea of Sisyphus in the lower world ever rolling a huge stone to the top of a mountain might equally well refer to the sun, which, after attaining its highest point in the heavens at the time of the summer solstice, glides back again, only to begin

its career anew on the shortest day. In any case, the rolling of the stone does not appear to have been originally a punishment. It was only later—after people had become familiar with the idea of retribution in the lower world—that it assumed this character. In order to account for it, a special crime had to be found for Sisyphus. According to some, he was punished at the instance of Zeus, because he had revealed to the river-god Asopus the hiding-place of his daughter Ægina, whom Zeus had secretly carried off from Phlius. According to another tradition, he used to attack travellers, and put them to death by crushing them with great stones. The Corinthians being crafty men of business, it was natural that they should accredit their mythical founder with a refined cunning. Of the numerous legends which existed concerning him, none was more celebrated than that of the cunning mode in which he succeeded in binding Death, whom Ares had to be despatched to release.

2. *Glaucus.*—Tradition describes Glaucus as a son of Sisyphus by Merope. He also appears to have had a symbolic meaning, and was once identical with Poseidon, though he was afterwards degraded from the rank of a god to that of a hero. He is remarkable for his unfortunate end. On the occasion of some funeral games, celebrated in Iolcus in honour of Pelias, he took part in the chariot race, and was torn in pieces by his own horses, which had taken fright.

3. *Bellerophon and the Legend of the Amazons.*—The third national hero of Corinth was Bellerophon, or Bellerophontes. Here the reference to the sun is so obvious, that the signification of the myth is unmistakeable. He was termed the son of Poseidon or Glaucus, and none could appreciate this genealogy better than the Corinthians, who daily saw the sun rise from the sea. We must first, however, narrate the substance of the story. Bellerophon was born and brought up at Corinth, but was obliged from some cause or other to leave his country. That he

killed Bellerus, a noble of Corinth, is nothing but a fable arising from an unfortunate misinterpretation of his name. He was hospitably received by Prœtus, king of Tiryns, whose wife at once fell in love with the handsome, stately youth. Finding, however, that Bellerophon slighted her passion, she slandered him to her husband, and Prœtus forthwith sent him to his father-in-law, Iobates, king of Lycia, with a tablet, mysterious signs on which bade Iobates put the bearer to death. At this juncture the heroic career of Bellerophon begins. Iobates sought to fulfil the command of Prœtus by involving his guest in all kinds of desperate adventures. He first sent him to destroy the Chimæra, a dangerous monster that devastated the land. The fore part of its body was that of a lion, the centre that of a goat, and the hinder part that of a dragon. According to Hesiod, it had three heads—that of a lion, a goat, and a dragon. According to the same poet, the Chimæra was a fire-breathing monster of great swiftness and strength, the daughter of Typhon and Echidna. Bellerophon destroyed the monster by raising himself in the air on his winged horse Pegasus, and shooting it with his arrows. Pegasus was the offspring of Poseidon and Medusa, from whose trunk it sprung after Perseus had struck off her head. Bellerophon captured this wonderful animal as it descended at the Acro-Corinthus to drink of the spring of Pirene. In this he was assisted by the goddess Athene, who also taught him how to tame and use it. Here, then, he appears to have already possessed the horse at Corinth; though another tradition relates that Pegasus was first sent to him when he set out to conquer the Chimæra. The origin of the story is ascribed to a fiery mountain in Lycia; but, as all dragons and suchlike monsters of antiquity are represented as breathing forth fire and flames, we are perhaps scarcely justified in having recourse to a volcano. This characteristic is, in fact, merely a common symbol of the furious and dangerous character of these monsters.

The contest of Bellerophon is far more likely to be a picture of the drying up, by means of the sun's rays, of the furious mountain torrents which flood the corn-fields. Others, again, have thought that the Chimæra represents the storms of winter conquered by the sun.

The next adventure in which Iobates engaged Bellerophon was an expedition against the Solymi, a neighbouring but hostile mountain tribe. After he had been successful in subduing them, Iobates sent him against the warlike Amazons, hoping that among them he would be certain to meet his death. We here, for the first time, come across this remarkable nation of women, with whom other Greek heroes, such as Heracles and Theseus, are said to have fought; and it will not, therefore, be foreign to our object to dwell here on their most important features.

The Amazons appear in legend as early as Homer, though he only mentions them incidentally. They were said to be a nation of women, who suffered no men among them, except so far as it was necessary to keep up the race. The women, on the other hand, were trained from their earliest years in all warlike exercises; so that they were not only sufficiently powerful to defend their own land against foreign invaders, but also to make plundering incursions into other countries. Their dominions, the situation of which was at first indefinitely described as in the far north or far west, were afterwards reduced to more distinct limits, and placed in Cappadocia, on the river Thermodon, their capital being Themiscyra in Scythia, on the borders of Lake Mæotis, where their intercourse with the Scythians is said to have given rise to the Sarmatian tribes. Later writers also speak of the Amazons in Western Libya. Of the numerous stories rife concerning them, none is more tasteless than that of their cutting off or burning out the right breast, in order not to incommode themselves in the

use of the bow. From
the Thermodon they are
said to have made great
expeditions as far as the
Ægean sea; they are even
reported to have invaded
Attica, and made war on
Theseus. They also play
a prominent part in the
story of Heracles, by whom
they were defeated; and
in the Trojan war, when,
under their queen Penthe-
silea, they came to the
assistance of Priam against
the Greeks.

The Amazons were fre-
quently represented in Greek
art. They are here depicted
as fine, powerful women,
resembling Artemis and her
nymphs, though with stouter
legs and arms. They gene-
rally appear armed, their
weapons being a long double-
edged battle-axe (*bipennis*)
and a semicircular shield.
An anecdote related by Pliny
proves what a favourite subject the Amazons were with
Greek artists. He says that
the celebrated sculptors,
Phidias, Polycletus, Phrad-
mon, and Cresilas, made a
wager as to who should
create the most beautiful
Amazon. Polycletus re-
ceived the prize, so that
we may conclude that he

Fig. 55.—Amazon. Berlin.

brought this statue—the ideal Amazon of the Greeks—to its highest perfection. Unfortunately, we know nothing of it, except that it was of bronze, and stood with the statues of the other artists in the temple of the Ephesian Artemis. The Amazon of Phidias, we are told, was represented as leaning on a spear; Cresilas, on the other hand, endeavoured to portray a wounded Amazon. Besides these statues, we hear a great deal of the Amazon of Strongylion, celebrated for the beauty of her legs, which was in the possession of Nero. We still possess a considerable number of Amazon statues, some of which are supposed to be imitations in marble of the renowned statue at Ephesus. There are, moreover, several statues of wounded Amazons, some of which are believed to be copies of the work of Cresilas. There is also another marble statue, considerably larger than life, which takes a still higher rank. It was originally set up in the Villa Mattei, but since the time of Clement XIV. it has been in the Vatican collection. It is apparently a representation of an Amazon resting after battle; she is in the act of laying aside her bow, as she has already done her shield, battle-axe, and helmet. In doing so she raises herself slightly on her left foot, an attitude which is as charming as it is natural.

Lastly, we must not omit to mention a statue that has newly come into the possession of the Berlin Museum, which is supposed to be after a work of Polycletus (Fig. 55).

We must now return to the history of Bellerophon. After returning in triumph from his expedition against the Amazons, the life of the young hero was once more attempted by Iobates, who caused him to be surprised by an ambuscade. Bellerophon, however, again escaped, slaying all his assailants. Iobates now ceased from further persecution, and gave him his daughter in marriage, and a share in the kingdom of Lycia. Bellerophon, in full possession of power and riches, and surrounded by blooming children, seemed to have reached the summit of earthly prosperity, when he was overtaken by a grievous change of fortune. He was seized with madness, and wandered about alone, fleeing the society of men, until he at length perished miserably. Pindar says that he incurred the enmity of the gods by attempting to fly to heaven on his winged horse Pegasus; whereupon Zeus sent a gadfly to sting the horse. Pegasus cast

off Bellerophon, and flew of his own accord to the stables of
Zeus, whose thunder-chariot he has ever since drawn. The sad
fate of Bellerophon was the subject of a touching tragedy of
Euripides, some parts of which are still in existence. Heroic
honours were paid to Bellerophon in Corinth, and he also had
a shrine in the celebrated cypress-grove of Poseidon.

4 Argive Legend.—1. *Io.*—The first personage who meets
us on the very threshold of the mythic age of Argos is Inachus,
the god of the Argive river of that name. Inachus was venerated by the inhabitants as the first founder of Argive civilisation
after the flood of Deucalion. By his union with Melia, the
daughter of Oceanus, he became the father of Io, famed for her
beauty, whose history, which is of great antiquity, has been so
greatly embellished by the poets and legendary writers. The
following is the substance of the story :—

Io was the priestess of Hera. Her great beauty attracted the
notice of Zeus. On remarking this, Hera, in her jealousy,
changed Io into a white heifer, and set the hundred-eyed Argus
Panoptes (the all-seeing) to watch her. Zeus, however, sent
Hermes to take away the heifer. Hermes first lulled the
guardian to sleep with his wand and then slew him, whence he
is called Argiphontes (slayer of Argus). Hera avenged herself
by sending a gadfly to torment Io, who, in her madness, wandered through Europe and Asia, until she at length found rest
in Egypt, where, touched by the hand of Zeus, she recovered
her original form, and gave birth to a son. This son, who was
called Epaphus, afterwards became king of Egypt, and built
Memphis. The myth, as we have already remarked, has received many embellishments, for the wanderings of Io grew
more and more extensive with the growth of geographical knowledge. The true interpretation of the myth is due to F. W.
Welcker, whose meritorious researches in Greek mythology have

proved of such great value. Io (the wanderer) is the moon, whose apparently irregular course and temporary disappearance was considered a most curious phenomenon by the ancients. The moon-goddess of antiquity was very frequently represented under the figure of a heifer; and Isis herself, the Egyptian goddess of the moon, was always depicted with horns. The guardian of the heifer, the hundred-eyed Argus, is a symbol of the starry heaven. Whether we see in Hermes the dawn or the morning breeze, in either case the slaying of Argus will simply mean that the stars become invisible at sunrise. There is nothing extraordinary in representing the apparent irregularity of the moon's course, inexplicable as it was to the ancients, under the guise of mental disorder. Similar representations occur in the stories of the solar heroes, Bellerophon and Heracles. In the south-east—the direction in which Egypt lay from Greece—Io again appears as full moon, in her original shape.

2. *Danaüs and the Danaïds.*—According to the legend, Danaüs was a descendant of Io. Epaphus, the son of Io, had a daughter Libya, who bore to Poseidon two sons, Agenor and Belus. The former reigned over Phœnicia, the latter over Egypt. Belus, by his union with Anchinoë, or Achiroë, the daughter of the Nile, became the father of Ægyptus and Danaüs. Between these two brothers—the former of whom had fifty sons and the latter fifty daughters—a deadly enmity arose; this induced Danaüs to migrate from Egypt and seek the old home of his ancestress Io. He embarked with his fifty daughters in a ship—the first that was ever built—and thus came to Argos, where Gelanor, the reigning descendant of Inachus, resigned the crown in his favour. As king of Argos, Danaüs is said to have brought the land, which suffered from want of water, to a higher state of cultivation by watering it with wells and canals. He is also said to have introduced the worship of Apollo and Demeter. The story proceeds to relate that the fifty sons of Ægyptus followed their uncle to Argos, and com-

pelled him to give them his fifty daughters in marriage. Danaüs, in revenge, gave each of his daughters on the wedding day a dagger, and commanded them to slay their husbands in the night. All obeyed his command except Hypermnestra, who spared her husband Lynceus, and afterwards even succeeded, with the assistance of Aphrodite, in effecting his reconciliation with her father. Lynceus succeeded Danaüs in the kingdom, and became, by his son Abas, the ancestor of both the great Argive heroes, Perseus and Heracles. At a later period, the fable sprang up that the Danaïds were punished for their crimes in the lower world by having continually to pour water into a cask full of holes. It has been frequently remarked that this punishment has no conceivable connection with the crime. Neither must we forget that the idea of retribution in the lower world was of a comparatively late date. Originally, too, the idea prevailed that the pursuits of the upper world were continued after death in the realms of Hades. And herein lies the key to the interpretation of the myth, which is evidently connected with the irrigation of Argos ascribed to Danaüs.

3. *Proetus and his Daughters.*—Acrisius and Proetus were twin sons of Abas, the son of Lynceus and Hypermnestra. Between these two brothers an implacable hostility existed, which was said by the poets to have commenced even in their mother's womb. Proetus received, as his share of the patrimony, the kingdom of Tiryns; but he was subsequently expelled by his brother, and took refuge at the court of Iobates, king of Lycia. Iobates gave him his daughter Antea, or Sthenoboea, in marriage, and afterwards restored him to his kingdom of Tiryns. Proetus, with the aid of the Lycian workmen whom he had brought with him (Cyclopes), built a strong fortress, which enabled him not only to maintain peaceable possession of Tiryns, but also to extend his dominion as far as Corinth. The legend then passes to the history of his three

daughters, the Prœtides, whose pride was so excited by their father's greatness and their own beauty that they began to think themselves superior to the gods. Their arrogance, however, was soon punished, for they were visited with a foul disease and driven mad. They now fled the society of mankind, and wandered about among the mountains and woods of Argos and Arcadia. At length Prœtus succeeded in procuring the services of the celebrated soothsayer and purifier Melampus, who undertook the purification and cure of his daughters. It was reported of Melampus that serpents had licked his ears whilst asleep, and that he acquired, in consequence, a knowledge of the language of birds. He successfully accomplished the cure of the Prœtides, and received, as a reward, the hand of the princess Iphianassa, in addition to which both he and his brother Bias received a share in the sovereignty of Tiryns. Thus it was that the race of the Amythaonidœ, who all inherited the gift of seeing into futurity, and from whom the celebrated soothsayer Amphiaraüs himself was descended, came to Argos.

4. *Perseus.*—Acrisius, the brother of Prœtus, had a daughter called Danaë, whose fortune it was to gain the love of the great ruler of Olympus. Her father, Acrisius, was induced by an oracle, which foretold that he should be killed by his own grandson, to immure Danaë in a subterraneous chamber. Zeus, however, in his love for her, changed himself into a shower of golden rain, and thus introduced himself through the roof of her prison. Thus was the god-like hero Perseus born. There can be no doubt that this myth, too, is founded on the idea of the bridal union of heaven and earth; this is one of the pictures of nature which the mind most readily forms. Danaë represents the country of Argos; her prison is the heaven, enveloped, during the gloomy months of winter, with thick clouds. Her offspring by Zeus represents the light of the sun, which returns in the spring-time and begins, like a veritable hero, its contest

with the powers of death and darkness. The Gorgon Medusa has the same significance in the history of Perseus that the hideous Python has in that of Apollo.

The legend then proceeds to relate that Acrisius, having heard of the birth of his grandson, to avert the fate threatened by the oracle, ordered mother and child to be confined in a chest and cast into the sea. But human wisdom avails nought against the inevitable decrees of heaven. The chest was cast by the waves on the rocky island of Seriphus, where it was found by the fisherman Dictys; and Danaë and her child were hospitably received and cared for by Dictys and his brother Polydectes, the ruler of the island. The latter, however, subsequently wished to marry Danaë, and on her rejecting his advances made her a slave. Fearing the vengeance of Perseus, he despatched him, as soon as he was grown up, on a most perilous adventure. This was no other than to bring him the head of the Gorgon Medusa—a terrible winged woman, who dwelt with her two sisters, the daughters of Phorcys and Ceto, on the farthest western shore of the earth, on the border of Oceanus. Perseus set out, though he was in the greatest perplexity how to accomplish so perilous a task. Hermes, however, at this juncture came to his aid; and Athene, the special patroness of heroes, inspired him with courage. These deities first showed him how to procure the necessary means for accomplishing his undertaking, which consisted of an invisible helmet, a magic wallet, and a pair of winged sandals. All these were in the hands of the Nymphs, by whom probably the water-nymphs are meant. The way to their abode he could only learn from the Grææ. These creatures, who were likewise the daughters of Phorcys and Ceto, were reported to have come into the world as old women; their very appearance was appalling, and they had but one eye and one tooth between them, of which they made use in turn. They, too, dwelt on the outskirts of the gloomy region inhabited by

N

the Gorgons, whence they are called by Æschylus their sentinels. Under the guidance of Apollo and Athene, Perseus came to the Græœ. He then robbed them of their one eye and one tooth, and thus forced them to tell him the way to the habitations of the Nymphs. From the latter he at once obtained the objects he sought; and having donned his winged sandals, he hastened to the abode of the Gorgons, whom he fortunately discovered asleep. Athene then pointed out to him Medusa—the other two sisters, Stheno and Euryale, being immortal—and enjoined him to approach them carefully backwards, as the sight of their faces would infallibly turn any mortal into stone. With the help of her mirror-like shield and the sickle of Hermes, Perseus succeeded in cutting off the head of Medusa without looking round; and having placed the head in his wallet, he hastened away. His helmet, which rendered him invisible, enabled him to escape the pursuit of the other Gorgons, who had meanwhile awaked. From the trunk of Medusa sprang the winged horse Pegasus, and Chrysaor, the father of Geryones. On his return to Seriphus, Perseus turned the unrighteous Polydectes into stone by means of the Gorgon's head, which he then presented to Athene; and after making his benefactor, Dictys, king of the island, he turned his steps towards his native place, Argos. Such are the essential features of the myth—concerning which, in spite of its antiquity, we have no earlier sources of information—such is the original framework on which was afterwards built up the history of the further adventures of the hero. The most celebrated of these was the rescue of Andromeda, which formed the subject of a drama of Euripides, and was also highly popular among artists and poets. The following is a brief account of this exploit :—Cassiopea, the wife of Cepheus, king of Æthiopia, ventured to extol her own beauty above that of the Nereids, who thereupon besought Poseidon to avenge them. He granted their request, and not only overwhelmed the land with disastrous floods, but sent also a terrible sea-monster, which devoured both man and beast. The oracle of Ammon declared that the land could only be saved by the sacrifice of the king's daughter, Andromeda, to the monster. Cepheus, after some time, yielded to the entreaties of his people, and Andromeda was chained to a rock close to the sea. In this situation she was found by Perseus, on his return from his adventure with the Gorgons. He forthwith attacked and slew the sea-monster, and released the trembling maiden, who soon after married her preserver. Later writers, not satisfied with this adventure, added that Perseus was also obliged to vanquish a rival in Phineus, the king's brother, to whom Andromeda had been already promised. Phineus, together with his warriors, was changed into stone by means of the Gorgon's head.

The legend concludes with the return of the hero to Argos, where he was reconciled to his grandfather Acrisius, who had at first fled in terror to Larissa. On the occasion, however, of some games which the people of Larissa had instituted in his honour, Perseus was unfortunate enough to kill Acrisius with his discus, thus involuntarily fulfilling the prophecy of the oracle. In this feature of the story we recognise an unmistakeable reference to the symbolic meaning of Perseus; for the discus here represents, as in the story of the death of Hyacinthus, the face of the sun. Perseus, unwilling to enter on the inheritance of the grandfather he had slain, exchanged the kingdom of Argos for that of Tiryns, which was handed over to him by its king, Megapenthes, the son of Prœtus. He here founded the cities of Midea and Mycenæ, and became, through his children by Andromeda, the ancestor of many heroes, and, among others, of Heracles. His son Electryon became the father of Alcmene, whilst Amphitryon was descended from another of his sons. According to Pausanias, heroic honours were paid to Perseus, not only throughout Argos, but also in Athens and the island of Seriphus.

Perseus occupies a prominent position in Greek art. His common attributes are the winged sandals, the sickle which he made use of to slay Medusa, and the helmet of Hades. In bodily form, as well as in costume, he appears very like Hermes.

Among the art monuments which relate to his adventures is a marble relief from the Villa Pamfili, now in the Capitoline Museum

Fig. 56.—Perseus and Andromeda. Marble Relief in the Museum at Naples

at Rome, depicting the rescue of Andromeda. The sea-monster lies dead at the feet of Perseus, who is assisting the joyful Andromeda to descend from the rock. The attitude and expression of both figures are very striking: on the one side, maidenly modesty; on the other, proud self-reliance. It is worth remarking that Perseus, in addition to his winged shoes, has also wings on his head. The same conception is perceptible, with a few minor points of difference, in several Pompeian paintings, and on a marble relief of the Naples Museum (Fig. 56). Representations of Medusa are mostly confined to masks, which are often found on coats of mail, shields, leaves of folding doors, and instruments of all kinds. There are two types, representing an earlier and a later conception of Medusa. Earlier art set itself to depict the horrible only in the head of Medusa; and artists, therefore, strove to impart to the face as strong an expression of rage and ferocity as was possible, representing her with tongue lolling forth, and boar-like tusks. It is worthy of remark that, in the earlier examples of these masks—which are frequently met with on coins, gems, and pottery—the hair generally falls stiff and straight over the forehead, serving to render the horrible breadth of the face still more striking, while the snakes appear to be fastened round the neck like a necklace. Very different is the conception adopted by the later and more sensuous school. This laboured principally to give expression to the gradual ebbing away of life in the countenance of the dying Gorgon, an effect which was rendered still more striking by transforming the hideous Gorgon face of earlier times into an ideal of the most perfect beauty. The most splendid example of this later conception, which had been creeping in since the age of Praxiteles, is to be found in the Medusa Rondanini of the Munich collection—a marble mask of most beautiful workmanship, which was brought

Fig. 57.—Rondanini Medusa. Munich.

from the Rondanini Palace at Rome (Fig. 57). This Medusa, like many others of the later type, has wings on the head.

5. The Dioscuri.—On passing to Laconia and Messenia, the southern districts of the Peloponnesus, we come in contact with the legend of the Dioscuri. Tyndareüs and his brother Icarius were said to have founded the most ancient sovereignty in Lacedæmon. They were driven thence, however, by their half-brother Hippocoön, and were kindly received by Thestius, the ruler of the ancient city of Pleuron in Ætolia, who gave Tyndareüs his daughter Leda in marriage. Icarius received the hand of Polycaste, who bore him Penelope—afterwards the wife of Odysseus; while Leda was the mother of the Dioscuri, Castor and Polydeuces (Pollux). Tyndareüs was afterwards reinstated in his Lacedæmonian kingdom at Amyclæ by Heracles. Besides these two sons, Leda had also two daughters, Clytæmnestra and Helene (Helen), who are celebrated in connection with the Trojan war. An ancient legend also existed to the effect that Leda had been beloved by Zeus, who had approached her under the guise of a swan. The greatest incongruity prevails as to which of the children could claim a divine origin. In Homer, Helen alone is represented as the daughter of Zeus; while Clytæmnestra, together with Castor and Polydeuces, appear as the children of Tyndareüs. At a subsequent period, the name of "Dioscuri" (sons of Zeus) and a belief in their divine origin arose simultaneously. Later still, Castor was represented as a mortal, and the son of Tyndareüs; and Polydeuces as immortal, and the son of Zeus. After Castor, however, had fallen in the contest with the sons of Aphareus, his brother Polydeuces, unwilling to part from him, prevailed on Zeus to allow them to remain together, on condition of their spending one day in Olympus and the next in Hades. They thus led a life divided between mortality and immortality. The following is an account of their heroic deeds:—On attaining manhood, Castor distinguished himself by his skill in the management of horses; whilst Polydeuces became renowned as a skilful boxer, though he too had skill in riding. They first made war on Theseus, who had carried off their sister Helen, then ten years old, and set her free by the conquest of Aphidnæ. They next took part in the expedition of the Argonauts, in which Polydeuces gained still further renown by his victory with the cestus over the celebrated boxer Amycus. They were also present at the Calydonian boar hunt. Their last undertaking was the rape of the daughters of Leucippus, king of Messenia. This was the cause of their combat with their cousins Idas and Lynceus, the sons of Aphareus, to whom the damsels had been betrothed. According to others, however, it sprang from a quarrel as to the division of some booty that they had carried off together. Castor was slain by Idas, whereupon Polydeuces in his wrath slew Lynceus, while Idas himself was overwhelmed by a thunderbolt from Zeus.

The interpretation of this myth is by no means void of difficulty. It is commonly supposed that they were ancient Peloponnesian divinities of light, who, after the Dorian invasion, were degraded to the rank of heroes. They are often interpreted as personifications of the morning and evening star, or of the twilight (dawn and dusk). This view died out after the second deification that they underwent. They were venerated, not only in their native Sparta, but throughout the whole of Greece, as kindly, beneficent deities, whose aid might be invoked either in battle or in the dangers of shipwreck. In this latter character they are lauded by an Homeric hymn, in which they are represented as darting through the air on their golden wings, in order to calm the storm at the prayer of the terror-stricken mariner. It has often been remarked, and with a great appearance of truth, that these Dioscuri flitting about on their golden wings are probably nothing more than what is commonly called St. Elmo's

fire—an electric flame which is often seen playing round the
tops of the masts during a storm, and which is regarded by the
sailors as a sign of its speedy abatement; indeed the name Elmo
has been supposed a corruption of Helene. In Sparta, the
Dioscuri were regarded as the tutelary deities of the state, as
well as an example of warlike valour for the youth of the
country. Their shrines here were very numerous. Their
ancient symbol, which the Spartans always took with them on a
campaign, consisted of two parallel beams joined by cross-bars.
They had other festivals and temples besides those of Sparta;
in Mantinea, for instance, where an eternal fire was kept
burning in their honour; also in Athens, where they were
venerated under the appellation of Anaces. Their festival was
here celebrated with horse-racing. The Olympic games also
stood under their special protection, and their images were set
up in all the palæstra. They were, in fact, everywhere regarded
as extremely benevolent and sociable deities, who foster all that
is noble and beautiful among men.

The Dioscuri were believed to have assisted the Romans
against the Latins at the Lake Regillus; and the dictator, A.
Postumius, vowed a temple to them, which was erected in the
Forum, opposite the temple of Vesta. In commemoration of this
aid, the Equites made a solemn procession from the temple of
Honos, past the temple of the Dioscuri, to the Capitol every
year on the Ides of July.

In art the Dioscuri are represented as heroic youths of noble mien
and slim but powerful forms. Their characteristic marks are conical
caps, the points of which are adorned with a star. They generally
appear nude, or clothed only with a light chlamys, and nearly
always in connection with their horses, either riding, standing by
and holding them, or leading them by the bridle. The most celebrated representation of the Dioscuri that has come down to us from
antiquity consists of the marble statues called the Colossi of Monte
Cavallo, in Rome. These are eighteen feet in height, and the proportions of the figures, together with those of the horses, are exquisite.

They are set up on the Quirinal, which has received from them the name of Monte Cavallo. They are not, indeed, original works, but are probably imitations of bronzes of the most flourishing period of Greek art, executed in the time of Augustus.

6. Heracles (Hercules).—Of all the myths of the countries originally inhabited by the Æolians the myth of Heracles is the most glorious. This hero, though his fame was chiefly disseminated by means of the Dorians, was yet by birth the common property of the Æolian race—their national hero, in fact, just as he afterwards became the national hero of the whole of Greece. No other Greek myth has received so many subsequent additions —not only from native, but also from foreign sources—as this; which is, in consequence, the most extensive and complicated of all Greek myths. We shall, therefore, have to confine ourselves to the consideration of its most characteristic features, and those which are the most important in the history of art.

In Homer, who is here again our most ancient authority, the leading features of the myth are traced—the enmity of Hera towards the hero; his period of subjection to Eurystheus, and the labours by which he emancipated himself (though special mention is made only of his seizure of Cerberus); his expeditions against Pylus, Ephyra, Œchalia, and Troy. The verses in the *Odyssey* (xi. 602–4), which refer to his deification and subsequent marriage with Hebe, are probably a later insertion. In the *Iliad*, Heracles is spoken of as a great hero of olden time, "whom the Fates and the grievous wrath of Hera subdued." In Homer, too, he appears as a purely Grecian hero, his warlike undertakings having never yet led him beyond Troy, and his armour differing in no respect from that of other heroes. The description of him in Hesiod's *Theogony* and in the *Shield of Heracles* is somewhat more minute, but is otherwise essentially the same. From what source the deification of Heracles sprang—whether it was due to Phœnician influences or not—has hitherto remained an undetermined question; we only know that it appears as an accomplished fact about 700 B.C.

I. THE BIRTH AND YOUTH OF HERACLES.—This portion of the legend found its chief development in Bœotia. Amphitryon, a son of Alcæus and grandson of Perseus, was compelled to flee from Tiryns with his betrothed Alcmene—likewise a descendant of Perseus by her father Electryon—on account of a murder, and found an asylum at the court of Creon, king of Thebes. From this place he undertook an expedition against the robber tribes of the Teleboæ (Taphians), in consequence of a promise made to Alcmene, whose brother they had slain. After the successful termination of this expedition, the marriage was to have been celebrated at Thebes. But, in the meanwhile, the great ruler of Olympus himself had been smitten with the charms of Alcmene, and, taking the form of the absent Amphitryon, had left her pregnant with Heracles, to whom she afterwards gave birth at the same time with Iphicles, the son of Amphitryon. The sovereignty over all the descendants of Perseus, which Zeus had destined for Heracles, was snatched from him by the crafty jealousy of Hera, who prolonged the pains of Alcmene and hastened the delivery of the wife of Sthenelus, the uncle of Amphitryon, by two months. Not content with having subjected the hero to the will of the weak and cowardly Eurystheus, Hera, according to a subsequent account of the poets, sent two serpents to kill the child when he was about eight months old. Heracles, however, gave the first proof of his divine origin by strangling the serpents with his hands. An account of this scene has descended to us in a beautiful poem of Pindar. In Thebes, the boy grew up and was put under the care of the best preceptors. But, though he excelled in every feat of strength and valour, he made no progress in musical arts, and even slew his master Linus on account of a somewhat harsh reproof which his inaptitude entailed on him. As a punishment, Amphitryon sent him to Mount Cithæron to mind the flocks, a mode of life which Heracles continued until he had completed his eighteenth year. It was to this period that the sophist Prodicus, a contemporary of Socrates, referred his beautiful allegory of the *Choice of Heracles*. After attaining his full growth (according to Apollodorus he was four cubits in height) and strength, the young hero performed his first great feat by killing the lion of Cithæron. Whether it was this skin or that of the Nemean lion which he afterwards used as a garment is not certain. His next act was to free the Thebans from the ignominious tribute which they were compelled to pay to Erginus, king of Orchomenus, by a successful expedition, in which Amphitryon, however, lost his life. Creon, the king of Thebes, in gratitude gave the hero his daughter Megara in marriage, while Iphicles married her sister.

II. Heracles in the Service of Eurystheus—The Twelve Labours.—We now come to the second epoch in the life of the hero, in which he performed various labours at the bidding of Eurystheus, king of Mycenæ or Tiryns. The number of these was first fixed at twelve in the Alexandrian age, when Heracles was identified with the Phœnician sun-god, Baal; probably from the analogy afforded in the course of the sun through the twelve signs of the Zodiac. The subjection of Heracles to his unmanly cousin Eurystheus is generally represented as a consequence of the stratagem by which Hera obtained for the latter the sovereignty over all the descendants of Perseus. At a later period Heracles was said to have become insane, in consequence of the summons of Eurystheus to do his bidding. The following is an account of the labours of Heracles :—

1. *The Fight with the Nemean Lion.*—The district of Nemea

and Cleonæ was inhabited by a monstrous lion, the offspring of Typhon and Echidna, whose skin bade defiance to every weapon. Heracles, after using his arrows and club against the animal in vain, at last drove it into a cave, and there strangled it with his hands. He afterwards used the head of the lion as a helmet, and the impenetrable skin as a defence.

2. *The Lernæan Hydra.*—This was a great water-serpent, likewise the offspring of Typhon and Echidna. The number of its heads varies in the accounts of poets, though ancient gems usually represent it with seven. It ravaged the country of Lerna in Argolis, destroying both men and beasts. In this adventure Heracles was accompanied by Iolaüs, the son of his brother Iphicles, who, on this as on other occasions, appears as his faithful companion. After driving the monster from its lair by means of his arrows, he advanced fearlessly, and, seizing it in his hands, began to strike off its heads with his sword. To his amazement, in the place of each head he struck off two sprang up. He then ordered Iolaüs to set on fire a neighbouring wood, and with the firebrands seared the throats of the serpent, until he at length succeeded in slaying it. He then dipped his arrows in its gall, thus rendering the wounds inflicted by them incurable.

3. *The Erymanthian Boar.*—This animal inhabited the mountain district of Erymanthus in Arcadia, from which place it wasted the cornfields of Psophis. Heracles drove the boar up to the snow-covered summit of the mountain, and then caught it alive, as Eurystheus had commanded him. When he arrived at Mycenæ with the terrible beast on his back, Eurystheus was so terrified that he hid himself in a vessel. This comic scene is frequently depicted on vases. It was on this occasion that Heracles destroyed the Centaurs. On the road the hero, hungry and thirsty, was hospitably received by the friendly Centaur Pholus, who holds the same place among the Arcadian Centaurs

as Chiron does among those of Thessaly.　Pholus broached, in honour of his guest, a cask of wine lying in his cave, which was the common property of all the Centaurs.　The fragrance of the wine attracted the other Centaurs living on Mount Pholoë, and they immediately attacked the tippling hero with pieces of rock and trunks of trees.　Heracles, however, drove them back with arrows and firebrands, and completely vanquished them after a terrible fight.　On returning to the cave of Pholus, he found his friend dead.　He had drawn an arrow out of a dead body to examine it, but accidentally let it fall on his foot, from the wound of which he died.

4. *The Hind of Cerynea.*--This animal, which was sacred to the Arcadian Artemis, had golden horns and brazen hoofs, the latter being a symbol of its untiring fleetness.　Heracles was commanded to bring it alive to Mycenæ, and for a whole year he continued to pursue it over hill and dale with untiring energy.　At length it returned to Arcadia, where he succeeded in capturing it on the banks of the Ladon, and bore it in triumph to Mycenæ.

5. *The Stymphalian Birds.*--These voracious birds, which fed on human flesh, had brazen claws, wings, and beaks, and were able to shoot out their feathers like arrows.　They inhabited the district round Lake Stymphalis in Arcadia. Heracles slew some, and so terrified the rest by means of his brazen rattle that they never returned.　This latter circumstance is apparently an addition of later times, to explain their reappearance in the history of the Argonauts.

6. *Cleansing of the Stables of Augeas.*—The sixth task of Heracles was to cleanse in one day the stables of Augeas, king of Elis, whose wealth in cattle had become proverbial.　Heracles repaired to Elis, where he offered to cleanse the stables, in which were three thousand oxen, if the king would consent to give him a tenth part of the cattle.　Augeas agreed to do so ; Heracles

then turned the course of the Peneus or the Alpheus, or, according to some, of both rivers, through the stalls, and thus carried off the filth. Augeas, however, on learning that Heracles had undertaken the labour at the command of Eurystheus, refused to give him the stipulated reward, a breach of faith for which Heracles, later, took terrible vengeance on the king.

7. *The Cretan Bull.*—In the history of Minos, king of Crete, we find that Poseidon once sent up a bull out of the sea for Minos to sacrifice, but that Minos was induced by the beauty of the animal to place it among his own herds, and sacrificed another in its stead ; whereupon Poseidon drove the bull mad. The seventh labour of Heracles consisted in capturing this bull and bringing it to Mycenæ. It was afterwards set free by Eurystheus, and appears later, in the story of Theseus, as the bull of Marathon.

8. *The Mares of Diomedes.*—Diomedes was king of the Bistones, a warlike tribe of Thrace. He inhumanly caused all strangers cast upon his coasts to be given to his wild mares, who fed on human flesh. To bind these horses and bring them alive to Mycenæ was the next task of Heracles. This, too, he successfully accomplished, after inflicting on Diomedes the same fate to which he had condemned so many others.

9. *The Girdle of Hippolyte.*—Admete, the daughter of Eurystheus, was anxious to obtain the girdle which the queen of the Amazons had received from Ares; and Heracles was accordingly despatched to fetch it. After various adventures he landed in Themiscyra, and was at first kindly received by Hippolyte, who was willing to give him the girdle. But Hera, in the guise of an Amazon, spread a report that Heracles was about to carry off the queen, upon which the Amazons attacked Heracles and his followers. In the battle which ensued Hippolyte was killed, and the hero, after securing the girdle, departed. On his journey homewards occurred his celebrated adventure

with Hesione, the daughter of Laomedon, king of Troy.   This king had refused Poseidon and Apollo the rewards he had promised them for their assistance in building the walls of Troy. In consequence of his perfidy, Apollo visited the country with a pestilence, and Poseidon sent a sea-monster, which devastated the land far and wide.   By the advice of the oracle, Hesione, the king's daughter, was exposed to be devoured by the animal. Heracles offered to destroy the monster, if Laomedon would give him the horses which his father Tros had received as a compensation for the loss of Ganymedes.   Laomedon agreed, and Heracles then slew the monster.   Laomedon, however, again proved false to his word, and Heracles, with a threat of future vengeance, departed.

10. *The Oxen of Geryones.*—The next task of Heracles was to fetch the cattle of the three-headed winged giant Geryones, or Geryoneus (Geryon).   This monster was the offspring of Chrysaor (red slayer) and Callirrhoë (fair-flowing), an Oceanid, and inhabited the island of Erythia, in the far West, in the region of the setting sun, where he had a herd of the finest and fattest cattle.   It was only natural that Heracles, in the course of his long journey to Erythia and back, should meet with numerous adventures; and this expedition has, accordingly, been more richly embellished than any other by the imagination of the poets.   He is generally supposed to have passed through Libya, and to have sailed thence to Erythia in a golden boat, which he forced Helios (the sun) to lend him by shooting at him with his arrows.   Having arrived in Erythia, he first slew the herdsman who was minding the oxen, together with his dog.   He was then proceeding to drive off the cattle, when he was overtaken by Geryon.   A violent contest ensued, in which the three-headed monster was at length vanquished by the arrows of the mighty hero.   Heracles is then supposed to have recrossed the ocean in the boat of the sun, and, starting from Tartessus, to

have journeyed on foot through Iberia, Gaul, and Italy. We pass over his contests with the Celts and Ligurians, and only notice briefly his victory over the giant Cacus, mentioned by Livy, which took place in the district where Rome was afterwards built, because Roman legend connected with this the introduction of the worship of Hercules into Italy. At length, after many adventures, he arrived at Mycenæ, where Eurystheus sacrificed the oxen to the Argive goddess Hera.

Heracles has now completed ten of his labours, but Eurystheus, as Apollodorus relates, refused to admit the destruction of the Lernæan Hydra, because on that occasion Heracles had availed himself of the help of Iolaüs, or the cleansing of the stables of Augeas, because of the reward for which he had stipulated; so that the hero was compelled to undertake two more. This account does not, however, harmonise with the tradition of the response of the oracle, in deference to which Heracles surrendered himself to servitude, and which offered the prospect of twelve labours from the first.

11. *The Apples of the Hesperides.*—This adventure has been even more embellished with later and foreign additions than the last. The golden apples, which were under the guardianship of the Hesperides, or nymphs of the west, constituted the marriage present which Hera had received from Gæa on the occasion of her marriage with Zeus. They were closely guarded by the terrible dragon Ladon, who, like all monsters, was the offspring of Typhon and Echidna. This, however, was far less embarrassing to the hero than his total ignorance of the site of the garden of the Hesperides, which led him to make several fruitless efforts before he succeeded in reaching the desired spot.

His first object was to gain information as to the situation of the garden, and for this purpose he journeyed through Illyria to the Eridanus (Po), in order to inquire the way of the nymphs who dwelt on this river. By them he was referred to the treacherous sage Nereus, whom he managed to seize whilst asleep, and refused to release until he had obtained the desired information. Heracles then proceeded by way of Tartessus to Libya, where he was challenged to a wrestling match by the giant Antæus, a powerful son of Earth, who was, according to Libyan tradition, of a monstrous height (some say sixty cubits). He was attacked by Heracles, but, as he received new strength from his mother Earth as often as he touched the ground, the hero lifted him up in the air and squeezed him to death in his arms.

From Libya Heracles passed into Egypt, where the cruel king Busiris was in the habit of seizing all strangers who entered the country and sacrificing them to Zeus. Heracles would have suffered a similar fate, had he not broken the chains laid upon him, and slain the king and his son. His indulgence at the richly-furnished table of the king was a feature in the story which afforded no small amusement to the comic writers, who were especially fond of jesting on the subject of the healthy and heroic appetite of Heracles. From Egypt the hero made his way into Æthiopia, where he slew Emathion, the son of Tithonus and Eos, for his cruelty to strangers. He next crossed the sea to India, and thence came to the Caucasus, where he set Prometheus free and destroyed the vulture that preyed on his liver. After Prometheus had described to him the long road to the Hesperides, he passed through Scythia, and came at length to the land of the Hyperboreans, where Atlas bore the pillars of heaven on his shoulders. This was the end of his journey, for Atlas, at his request, fetched the apples, whilst Heracles supported the heavens. Here again the comic poets introduced an amusing scene. Atlas, having once tasted the delights of freedom, betrayed no anxiety to relieve his substitute, but offered, instead, to bear the apples himself to Eurystheus. Heracles, however, proved even more cunning than he, for,

o

apparently agreeing to the proposition, he asked Atlas just to relieve him until he had arranged more comfortably a cushion for his back. When Atlas good-humouredly consented, Heracles of course left him in his former position, and made off with the apples. Another account states that he descended himself into the garden and slew the hundred-headed dragon who kept guard over the trees.

12. *Cerberus.*—The most daring of all the feats of Heracles, and that which bears the palm from all the others, and is, in consequence, always put at the end of his labours, was the bringing of Cerberus from the lower world. In this undertaking, which is mentioned even by Homer, he was accompanied by Hermes and Athene, though he had hitherto been able to dispense with divine aid. He is commonly reported to have made his descent into the lower world at Cape Tænarum in Laconia. Close to the gates of Hades he found the adventurous heroes Theseus and Pirithoüs, who had gone down to carry off Persephone, fastened to a rock. He succeeded in setting Theseus free, but Pirithoüs he was obliged to leave behind him, because of the violent earthquake which occurred when he attempted to touch him. After several further adventures, he entered the presence of the lord of the lower world. Hades consented to his taking Cerberus, on condition that he should master him without using any weapons. Heracles seized the furious beast, and, having chained him, he brought him to Eurystheus, and afterwards carried him back to his place in the lower world. The completion of this task released Heracles from his servitude to Eurystheus.

III. Deeds of Heracles after his Service.—1. *The Murder of Iphitus and Contest with Apollo.*—The hero, after his release from servitude, returned to Thebes, where he gave his wife Megara in marriage to Iolaüs. He then proceeded to the court of Eurytus, king of Œchalia, who had promised his beautiful daughter Iole in marriage to the man who should vanquish him-

self and his sons in shooting with the bow. The situation of
Œchalia is variously given; sometimes it is placed in Thessaly,
sometimes in the Peloponnesus, on the borders of Arcadia and
Messenia, and sometimes in the island of Eubœa, close to Eretria.
Heracles gained a most complete victory; but Eurytus, nevertheless, refused to give him his daughter, reproaching him with the
murder of his children by Megara, and with his ignominious
bondage to Eurystheus. Heracles, with many threats of future
vengeance, withdrew, and when, not long afterwards, Iphitus,
the son of Eurytus, fell into his hands, he cast him from the
highest tower of his citadel in Tiryns. This somewhat treacherous
action being at variance with the general character of the
hero, the story subsequently arose that Iphitus was a friend
of Heracles, and had advocated his cause with Eurytus, and that
Heracles only treated him thus in a fit of insanity. The bloody
deed was fraught with the gravest consequences. After seeking
purification and absolution in vain among men, Heracles came
to Delphi, in order to seek the aid and consolation of the oracle.
But Apollo, with whom the royal family of Œchalia stood in
high favour, rejected him; whereupon Heracles forced his way
into the temple, and was already in the act of bearing away the
holy tripod, in order to erect an oracle of his own, when he was
confronted by the angry deity. A fearful combat would doubt
less have ensued, if the father of gods and men himself had not
interfered to prevent this unnatural strife between his favourite
sons by separating the combatants with his lightning. Heracles
was now commanded by the Pythian priestess to allow himself
to be sold by Hermes into slavery for three years, to expiate the
murder of Iphitus.

2. *Heracles in the Service of Omphale.*—This portion of the
story is of Lydian origin, but was cleverly interwoven with the
Greek legend. The Lydians, in fact, honoured a sun-hero called
Sandon, who resembled Heracles in many respects, as the an

cestor of their kings. The oriental character of the Lydian Heracles at once manifests itself in the fact that he here appears as entirely devoted to sensual pleasures, becoming effeminate in the society of women, and allowing himself to be clothed in female attire, whilst his mistress Omphale donned his lion-skin and club, and flaunted up and down before him. He did not always linger in such inactivity, however; sometimes the old desire for action urged him forth to gallant deeds. Thus he vanquished and chastised the Cercopes, a race of goblins who used to trick and waylay travellers. He also slew Syleus, who compelled all passing travellers to dig in his vineyard; which formed the subject of a satyric drama of Euripides.

3. *His Expedition against Troy.*—After performing several other feats in the service of Omphale, Heracles again became free. He now appears to have undertaken an expedition against the faithless Laomedon, king of Troy, in company with other Greek heroes, such as Peleus, Telamon, and Oïcles, whose number increased as time went on. The city was taken by storm: Oïcles, indeed, was slain, but, on the other hand, Laomedon and all his sons except Podarces fell before the arrows of Heracles. Hesione, the daughter of the king, was given by Heracles to his friend Telamon, and became by him the mother of Teucer. She received permission from Heracles to release one of the prisoners, and chose her brother Podarces, who afterwards bore the name of Priamus (the redeemed), and continued the race of Dardanus in Ilium.

4. *The Peloponnesian Expeditions of Heracles.*—The legend relates that the hero now undertook his long-deferred expedition against Augeas, which was the means of kindling a Messenian and Lacedæmonian war. After assembling an army in Arcadia, which was joined by many gallant Greek heroes, he advanced against Elis. Heracles, however, fell sick; and in his absence his army was attacked and driven back with great loss by the

brave Actoridæ or Molionidæ, the nephews of Augeas.   It was only after Heracles had slain these heroes in an ambuscade at Cleonæ, as they were on their way to the Isthmian games, that he succeeded in penetrating into Elis.   He then slew Augeas, and gave the kingdom to his son Phyleus, with whom he was on friendly terms.   It was on this occasion that he instituted the Olympic games.   He then marched against Pylus, either because its king, Neleus, had given assistance to the Molionidæ, or else because Neleus had refused to purify him from the murder of Iphitus.   This expedition against Pylus was subsequently greatly embellished by the poets, who made it into a great battle of the gods, one part of whom fought for Neleus, and the other part for Heracles.   The chief feature was the combat between Heracles and Periclymenus, the bravest of the sons of Neleus, who had received from Poseidon, the tutelary deity of the Pylians, the power of transforming himself into any kind of animal. The result of the combat was of course a complete victory for Heracles.   Neleus, with his eleven gallant sons, was slain, and only the youngest, Nestor, remained to perpetuate the celebrated race.   The Lacedæmonian expedition of Heracles, which follows close on that against Pylus, was undertaken against Hippocoön, the half-brother of Tyndareüs, whom he had expelled.   Hippocoön was defeated and slain by Heracles, who gave his kingdom to Tyndareüs.   On this occasion Heracles was assisted by Cepheus, king of Tegea, with his twenty sons, a circumstance which is only mentioned on account of a remarkable legend connected with his stay in Tegea.   Heracles is here said to have left Auge, the beautiful sister of Cepheus, and priestess of Athene, pregnant with Telephus, whose wondrous adventures have occupied artists and poets alike.   Auge concealed her child in the grove of Athene, whereupon the angry goddess visited the land with a famine.   Aleüs, the father of Auge, on discovering the fact, caused the child to be exposed, and sold the mother beyond the sea. Auge thus came into Mysia, where the king Teuthras made her his wife. Telephus was suckled by a hind. He grew up, and ultimately, after some wonderful adventures, succeeded in finding his mother. He succeeded Teuthras, and, later, became embroiled with the Greeks when they landed on their expedition against Troy, on which occasion he was wounded by Achilles. Telephus, among all the sons of Heracles, is said to have borne the greatest resemblance to his father.

5. *Acheloüs, Nessus, Cycnus.*—The next episode in the history of the hero is his wooing of Deïanira, the daughter of Œneus, king of Ætolia. Œneus is celebrated as the first cultivator of the vine in that country, and as the father of the Ætolian heroes, Meleager and Tydeus. The river-god Acheloüs was also a suitor for the hand of Deïanira, and as neither he nor Heracles would relinquish their claim, it was decided by the combat between the rivals* so often described by the poets. The power of assuming various forms was of little use to Acheloüs, for, having finally transformed himself into a bull, he was deprived of a horn by Heracles, and compelled to declare himself vanquished. Heracles restored him his horn, and received in exchange that of the goat Amalthea. After his marriage with Deïanira, Heracles lived for some time happily at the court of his father-in-law, where his son Hyllus was born. In consequence of an accidental murder, he was obliged to leave Ætolia and retire to the court of his friend Ceÿx, king of Trachis, at the foot of Mount Œta. On the road occurred his celebrated adventure with the Centaur Nessus. On coming to the river Evenus, Heracles entrusted Deïanira to Nessus to carry across, whilst he himself waded through the swollen stream. The Centaur, induced by the beauty of his burden, attempted to carry off Deïanira, but

---

* The most beautiful description exists in a chorus in the *Trachiniæ* of Sophocles, and in Ovid's *Metamorphoses.*

was pierced by an arrow of Heracles, and expiated his attempt with his life.   He avenged himself by giving Deïanira some of his blood to make a magic salve, with which he assured her she could always secure the love of her husband.

On reaching Trachis they were hospitably received by Ceÿx. Heracles first defeated the Dryopes, and assisted the Dorian king Ægimius in his contest with the Lapithæ.   He next engaged in his celebrated combat with Cycnus, the son of Ares, which took place at Iton, in the neighbourhood of the Gulf of Pagasæ. Heracles not only slew his opponent, but even wounded the god of war himself, who had come to the assistance of his son.   This contest is the subject of the celebrated poem called the *Shield of Hercules*, which goes under the name of Hesiod.

IV. DEATH AND APOTHEOSIS.—The death of Heracles, of which we learn most from the masterly description of Sophocles in the *Trachiniæ*, is generally supposed to have been connected with his expedition against Eurytus.   The hero, who could not forget the ignominious treatment he had received at the hands of Eurytus, now marched with an army from Trachis against Œchalia.   The town and citadel were taken by storm, and Eurytus and his sons slain; whilst the beautiful Iole, who was still unmarried, fell into the hands of the conqueror. Heracles now withdrew with great booty, but halted on the promontory of Cenæum, opposite the Locrian coast, to raise an altar and offer a solemn sacrifice of thanksgiving to his father Zeus.   Deïanira, who was tormented with jealous misgivings concerning Iole, thought it was now high time to make use of the charm of Nessus.   She accordingly sent her husband a white sacrificial garment, which she anointed with the ointment prepared from the blood of the Centaur.   Heracles donned the garment without suspicion, but scarcely had the flames from the altar heated the poison than it penetrated the body of the unhappy hero.   In the most fearful agony he strove to tear off the garment, but in vain, for it stuck like a plaster to his skin; and where he succeeded in rending it away by force, it tore out great pieces of his flesh at the same time. In his frenzy he seized the herald Lichas, the bearer of the unfortunate present, and violently dashed him in pieces against a rock of the sea. In this state Heracles was brought to Trachis, where he found that Deïanira, full of sorrow and despair on learning the consequences of her act, had put an end to her own life. Convinced that cure was hopeless, the dying hero proceeded from Trachis to Œta, and there erected a funeral pile on which to end his torments. None of those around him, however, would consent to set the pile on fire, until Pœas, the father of Philoctetes, happened to pass by, and rendered him the service, in return for which Heracles presented him with his bow and arrows. As the flames rose high, a cloud descended from heaven, and, amid furious peals of thunder, a chariot with four horses, driven by Athene, appeared and bore the illustrious hero to Olympus, where he was joyfully received by the gods. He here became reconciled to Hera, who gave him the hand of her beauteous daughter Hebe in marriage.

V. HERACLES AS GOD.—We have already laid before our readers the most characteristic features of the myth. To interpret it and trace it back in all its details to the original sources would be, amid the mass of provincial and foreign legends with which it is amalgamated, almost impossible. Thus much is certain, however, that, apart from the conceptions which were engrafted on the story from Tyrian and Egyptian sources, even in the case of the Greek Heracles, myths based on natural phenomena are mixed up with historical and allegorical myths. The historic element, for instance, is apparent in the wars of Heracles against the Dryopes—against Augeas, Neleus, and Hippocoön. Here the exploits of the whole Dorian race are personified in the actions of the hero. On the other hand, in most of his single combats a symbolic meaning, derived from natural phenomena, is unmistakeable. Heracles, in fact, appears to have been, originally, a symbol of the power of the sun triumphing over the dark powers in nature. Driven from Argos by the worship of the Argive Hera, he first sank to the level of a hero, but was, subsequently, again raised to the dignity of a god. This occurred at a time when the gods of Greece had altogether cast aside their physical meaning; so that he was now regarded principally from an ethical point of view. He appears as a symbol of that lofty force of character which triumphs over all difficulties and obstacles. Poets and philosophers alike vied with each other in presenting him to the youth of their country in this character, pointing to his career as a brilliant example of what a man might accomplish, in spite of a thousand obstacles, by mere determination and force of will. The well-known allegory of the sophist Prodicus,* called "The Choice of Hercules," is an instance of the mode in which the history of the hero was used to inculcate moral precepts.

In the religious system of the Greeks, Heracles was specially honoured as the patron of the gymnasia; the gymnasium of Cynosarges in Athens being solely dedicated to him. After his deification, Heracles was also regarded in the character of a saviour and benefactor of his nation; as one who had not only merited the lasting gratitude of mankind by his deeds throughout an active and laborious life—in having rid the world of giants and noxious beasts, in having extinguished destructive forces of nature, and abolished human sacrifices and other barbarous institutions of antiquity—but also as a kindly and beneficent deity, ever ready to afford help and protection to

---

* Prodicus, a native of the island of Ceos, was an elder contemporary of Socrates. Like the latter, he taught in Athens, and met with a similar fate, having been condemned to death as an enemy of the popular religion and a corruptor of the Athenian youth.

mankind in the hour of need. In this character he was known by the names of Soter (Saviour) and Alexicacus (averter of evil). He had temples and festivals in various parts of Greece. In Marathon, which boasted of being the first seat of his worship, games were celebrated in his honour every four years, at which silver cups were given as prizes. The fourth day of every month was held sacred to him, this day being regarded as his birthday. We have already mentioned the legendary introduction of his worship into Rome.* Hercules, as he was called in Italy, was identified with the Italian hero Recaranus. He had an altar in the *Forum Boarium*, established, according to tradition, by Evander. The Roman poets, of course, devoted especial attention to the stories of his journey through Italy, and his fight with Cacus.

In Heracles ancient art sought to portray the conception of gigantic bodily strength. He is, therefore, generally represented as a full-grown man—rarely as a child or youth. We may observe the manner in which the prominent idea of physical force is expressed by regarding the formation of the neck and throat in the statue of Heracles. Nothing can express better a bull-like strength than the short neck and the prominent muscles, especially if associated with a broad, deep chest. We shall be able to appreciate this distinctive character still more clearly if we compare the form of Heracles with that of the ideal god Apollo, whose neck is especially long and slender. The figure of Heracles is, moreover, characterised by a head small in comparison with the giant body; by curly hair, bushy eyebrows, and muscular arms and legs. This conception was principally developed by Myron and Lysippus. A statue of Heracles by the former artist played a part in connection with the art robberies of Verres in Sicily. Lysippus erected several celebrated statues of Heracles, the most remarkable of which was the bronze colossus in Tarentum, which the Romans, after the capture of that town, transferred to the Capitol. Thence it was brought, by order of Constantine, to his new capital of Constantinople, where it remained until the Latin crusade of 1202, when it was melted down. Lysippus portrayed in this statue a mourning Heracles, which no one had ever attempted before him. The hero appeared in a sitting posture, without his weapons, his left elbow resting on his left leg, while his

---

* There seems ground for thinking that the Italian Hercules was properly a rural deity confounded with Heracles on account of the similarity of their names; while Recaranus properly corresponded with the great Heracles in meaning.

Fig. 58.—Farnese Hercules.

head, full of thought and sorrow, rests on the open hand. The same artist, in a still greater work, depicted the twelve labours of Heracles. These formed a group which was originally executed for Alyzia, a seaport town of Acarnania, but which was, subsequently, likewise transferred to Rome.

First among existing statues is the Farnese Hercules (Fig. 58). This celebrated colossal statue, now in the Naples Museum, was discovered in 1540, on the site of the Thermæ of Caracalla. The hero is standing upright, resting his left shoulder on his club, from which hangs his lion's skin. This attitude, as well as the head drooping towards the breast, and the gloomy gravity of his countenance, clearly show that the hero feels bowed down by the burden of his laborious life. Even the thought that he is soon to be released from his ignominious servitude (he holds behind him, in his right hand, the three apples of the Hesperides, the fruit of his last labour) is unable to cheer him, and his thoughts seem to revert only to the past. On account of the conception of the piece, and the existence of another copy bearing the name of Lysippus, the Farnese Hercules is supposed to be a copy of a work of Lysippus, of which nothing further is known.

Still more important as a work of art, though it has reached us in a terribly mutilated condition—minus head, arms, and legs—is the celebrated Torso of Hercules, in the Vatican. This was found in Rome during the reign of Pope Julius II., on a spot where the theatre of Pompey, of which it was probably an ornament, once stood.

Groups.—Heracles in action was a still more favourite subject with artists, who delighted to portray the different scenes of his versatile life. Numberless representations of such scenes occur, not only in the form of statues and works in relief, but more especially on ancient vases. We mention here, in the chronological order of the events, some of the most important.

1. *Heracles and the Serpents.*—This scene was early depicted by the celebrated painter Zeuxis, who represented Heracles as strangling the serpents, whilst Alcmene and Amphitryon stood by in amazement. There are also several statues representing this feat, among which that at Florence takes the first rank. There is also a painting from Herculaneum in the Naples Museum.

2. *The Twelve Labours.*—These have naturally been treated of times out of number. We have already mentioned the groups of Lysippus, which he executed for the town of Alyzia. A still existing bronze statue in the Capitoline Museum, representing Heracles battling with the Hydra, appears to belong to this series. Among interesting remains are the metope reliefs on the Theseum at Athens. Ten on the east side of the temple represent scenes from the life of Heracles. Nine of them belong to the twelve labours, viz., the

Nemean lion, the Hydra, the Arcadian hind, the Erymanthian boar, the horses of Diomedes, Cerberus, the girdle of Hippolyte, Geryon, and the Hesperides; whilst the tenth tablet represents his contest with Cycnus. The remains of the splendid temple of Zeus at Olympia, which was completed about 435 B.C., are less important. The metopes of the front and back of the temple contained six of the labours of Heracles. Those representing the contest with the Cretan bull, the dying lion, a portion from the fight with Geryon, and some other fragments, were found in 1829, and conveyed to the museum of the Louvre at Paris. The only one which is perfect, however, is the spirited and life-like representation of the struggle with the Cretan bull.

3. *Parerga (Subordinate Deeds).*—First among these come the scenes from his contest with the Centaurs, which were frequently treated of in art. Groups of these exist in the museum at Florence; there are also various representations to be found on vases. His adventure with Nessus is represented separately on a Pompeian painting in the Naples Museum; Nessus crouches in a humble posture before Heracles, who has the little Hyllus in his arms, and he appears to be asking permission to carry Deïanira across the stream. There is also an interesting representation of the release of Prometheus on the Sarcophagus of the Capitol, from the Villa Pamfili, which is, in other respects, also worthy of mention. The seizure of the tripod at Delphi is also frequently portrayed in art.

4. *Heracles and Omphale.*—Of the monuments referring to Heracles' connection with Omphale, the most important is the beautiful Farnese group in marble in the Naples Museum. Omphale has thrown the lion's skin round her beautiful limbs, and holds in her right hand the hero's club. Thus equipped, she smiles triumphantly at Heracles, who is clothed in female attire, with a distaff in his hand.

5. *Heracles and Telephus.*—The romantic history of Telephus was also frequently treated of in art. The Naples Museum possesses a fine painting, representing the discovery of the child after it has been suckled by the hind, on which occasion, strange to say, Heracles himself is present. In the Vatican Museum there is a fine marble group, representing Heracles with the child Telephus in his arms.

7. **Attic Legend.**—1. *Cecrops.*—Cecrops, the first founder of civilisation in Attica, plays a similar part here to that which Cadmus does in Thebes. Like Cadmus, he was afterwards called an immigrant; indeed he was said to have come from Sais in Lower Egypt. In his case, however, we are able to trace the rise of the erroneous tradition with far greater distinctness.

Pure Attic tradition recognises him only as an autochthon—that is, an original inhabitant born of the earth; and further adds, that, like the giants, he was half man and half serpent. As the mythical founder of the state, he was also regarded as the builder of the citadel (Cecropia); and marriage, as well as other political and social institutions, were ascribed to him. Perhaps he is only a local personification of Hermes. The probability of this view is greatly enhanced by the fact that his three daughters, Herse, Aglaurus, and Pandrosus, received divine honours. It was under Cecrops that the celebrated contest occurred between Poseidon and Athene for the possession of Attica, and was by his means decided in favour of the goddess. We have already given an account of it, and need only here remark that the story is purely the result of the observation of natural phenomena. In Attica, in fact, there are only two seasons—a cold, wet, and rainy winter (Poseidon), and a warm, dry, genial summer (Pallas). These seem to be continually striving for the supremacy of the land. Cecrops was succeeded in the government by Cranaüs, who is represented by some as his son. The common mythological account places the flood of Deucalion in his reign. After the expulsion of Cranaüs, Amphictyon, one of the sons of Deucalion, succeeded to the sovereignty of Attica, of whom nothing more is known than that he was deprived of the government by Erechtheus.

2. *Erechtheus, or Erichthonius.*—Erechtheus, or Erichthonius, is really only a second Cecrops—the mythical founder of the state after the flood, as Cecrops was before it. Being also earthborn, he is, like Cecrops, endowed with a serpent's form. There was another very sacred legend concerning him, which stated that Gæa (Ge), immediately after his birth, gave him to the goddess Pallas to nurse. The latter first entrusted him to the daughters of Cecrops, her attendants and priestesses, enclosed in

a chest. The latter, however, prompted by curiosity, opened the chest, contrary to the commands of the goddess, and were punished in consequence with madness. Erichthonius was now reared by the goddess herself in her sanctuary on the citadel, and was subsequently made king of Athens. The same stories are then related of him as of Cecrops—that he regulated the state, introduced the worship of the gods, and settled the dispute between Poseidon and Athene.

The tomb of Erechtheus was shown in the Erechtheum, the ancient temple dedicated to Athene Polias, where the never-dying olive tree created by the goddess was also preserved.

Two among the daughters of Erechtheus are celebrated in legend. The first is Orithyia, who was carried off by Boreas, and became the mother of Calaïs and Zetes, whom we come across again in the story of the Argonauts ; the other is Procris, the wife of the handsome hunter Cephalus, who was said to be a son of Hermes by Herse, the daughter of Cecrops. Cephalus was carried off by Eos, who was unable to shake his fidelity to his wife. It served, however, to excite the jealousy of the latter, which ultimately proved fatal to her. Procris had hidden herself among the bushes, in order to watch her husband, when Cephalus, taking her for a wild animal, unwittingly killed her. After the death of Erechtheus, the tragic poets relate that Ion, the mythical ancestor of the Ionians, ruled in Athens. This means nothing more than that the primitive Pelasgian age in Attica had now come to an end, and the dominion of the Ionians commenced.

3. *Theseus.*—Theseus is the national hero of the Ionians, just as Heracles is of the Æolians. He has not unjustly been called the second Heracles ; and he has, indeed, many features in common with the Æolian hero, since the national jealousy of the Ionians led them to adopt every possible means of making their own hero rival that of their neighbours. They therefore strove

to represent him, likewise, as a hero tried in numberless contests—generous, unselfish, and devoted to the interests of mankind—and of course ascribed to him a multitude of adventurous exploits. There is no great undertaking of antiquity in which Theseus is not supposed to have taken part, and he was even sent on an expedition to hell, in imitation of Heracles.

He was the son of the Athenian king Ægeus, whom mythological tradition made a great-grandson of Erechtheus. After his father Pandion had been driven out by his relations, the sons of Metion, Ægeus betook himself to Megara, where he was hospitably received by the ruler, Pylas. From Megara, Ægeus, Pallas, Nisus, and Lycus, the sons of Pandion, undertook an expedition against Athens, which ended in the expulsion of the Metionidæ, and the restoration of the former royal family in the person of Ægeus. Such, at least, is the tradition; although it is more probable that Athens never had a king of this name, and that Ægeus (waveman) is only a surname of Poseidon, the chief deity of the seafaring Ionians. Ægeus, though twice married, had no heir, and now undertook a journey to Delphi to seek the advice of the oracle. On his way back he stopped at the court of Pittheus, king of Trœzen, and became, by his daughter Æthra, the father of Theseus. Before his departure, he placed his sword and sandals beneath a heavy stone, and commanded Æthra to send his son to Athens as soon as he was able to move the stone and take his father's sword. Theseus was carefully trained in music and gymnastics by the sagacious Pittheus, and soon developed into a stately youth. He is also supposed to have been educated by the Centaur Chiron, whose instruction had now become a necessary item in the education of a real hero.

When Theseus was sixteen, his mother took him to the stone beneath which lay his father's sword and sandals. With a slight effort he raised the stone, and thus entered on his heroic career. His earlier adventures consisted in overcoming a series of obstacles that beset him in his journey from Trœzen to Athens. They are generally supposed to have been six in number.

1. Between Trœzen and Epidaurus he slew Periphetes, the son of Hephæstus—who was lame, like his father—because he was in the habit of murdering travellers with his iron club; whence he is called Corynetes, or club-bearer.

2. He next delivered the Isthmus from another powerful robber called Sinis. He used to fasten travellers who fell into his hands to the top of a pine tree, which he bent to the earth, and then allowed to recoil; after which, on their reaching the ground, he would kill them outright; whence he is called Pityocamptes, or pine-bender. Theseus inflicted the same fate on him.

3. In the woody district of Crommyon he destroyed a dangerous wild sow that laid waste the country.

4. Not far from this, on the rock of Sciron, on the borders of Megara, dwelt another monster, called Sciron, who compelled travellers to wash his feet, and then kicked them into the sea. Theseus served him in a similar fashion.

5. In the neighbourhood of Eleusis he vanquished the giant Cercyon, who compelled all who fell into his hands to wrestle with him.

6. His last combat awaited him on the confines of Eleusis, where dwelt the inhuman Damastes. This monster used to lay his victims in a bed : if this was too short, he would hack off their projecting limbs; if too long, he would beat out and pull asunder their limbs, whence he is called Procrustes. He was also slain by Theseus.

On reaching Athens, he found his father Ægeus in the toils of the dangerous sorceress Medea, who had fled from Corinth to Athens. She was on the point of making away with the new-

P

comer by poison, when Ægeus, fortunately, recognised him by
the sword he bore, and preserved him from his impending
fate.

Medea was compelled to flee; but a new danger awaited the
hero from the fifty sons of Pallas, who had reckoned on succeeding their childless uncle Ægeus. Theseus, however, slew
some in battle and expelled the rest.

He now undertook his greatest and most adventurous feat, in
order to free his country from its shameful tribute to Minos,
king of Crete, whose son, the youthful hero Androgeos, had
been treacherously murdered by the Athenians and Megareans.
Another account says that he was sent by Ægeus against the
bull of Marathon, and thus slain. At any rate, Minos undertook
a war of revenge. He first marched against Megara, of which
Nisus, the brother of Ægeus, was king. Minos conquered him
by means of his own daughter Scylla, who became enamoured of
Minos, and cut off from her father's head the purple lock on
which his life depended. After having taken Megara and slain
Nisus, Minos marched against Athens. Here he was equally
successful, and compelled the vanquished Athenians to expiate
the blood of his son by sending, every eight or (according to
the Greek method of reckoning) every nine years, seven youths
and seven maidens to be devoured by the Minotaur. This was
a monster, half man and half bull. Twice already had the
bloody tribute been sent, and the third fell just after Theseus'
arrival in Athens; he at once bravely offered to go among the allotted victims. He was resolved to do battle with the Minotaur, and
to stake his life on the liberation of his country from the shameful tribute. Under the guidance of Aphrodite he passed over
to Crete, and soon discovered the efficacy of her protection. The
goddess kindled a passionate love for the hero in the breast of
Ariadne, the daughter of Minos. Ariadne rendered him every
possible assistance in his undertaking, and especially presented

him with a clew of thread, by means of which Theseus, after having slain the Minotaur, was enabled to find his way out of the Labyrinth. We have already narrated how Ariadne was deserted by Theseus on the isle of Naxos, only to become the bride of Dionysus, the divine son of Semele. Theseus also landed at Delos, where he instituted the festival of the Delia in honour of the divine children of Leto. On reaching Athens, he showed his gratitude to his divine protectress by the institution of the worship of Aphrodite Pandemus. In honour of Dionysus and Ariadne, he instituted the Oschophoria, in which festival Athene also had a share. Lastly, in honour of Apollo, he instituted the Pyanepsia, a festival which was celebrated on the seventh day of the month Pyanepsion (end of October).

The happy return of Theseus from his Cretan expedition, however, proved the death of his aged father. Ægeus, as he stood on the coast looking for his son's return, perceived that the ships had black sails instead of white, which were to have been hoisted in the event of his son's success; and believing that all was lost, he cast himself headlong into the sea. This story was perhaps only invented to account for the name of the Ægean Sea.

With regard to the other exploits of Theseus, there exists the greatest variety of accounts as to the order in which they took place. As king, he is said to have been the first to unite the separate districts of Attica into one political community, with one state Prytaneum, and to have instituted the festival of the Panathenæa in commemoration of this event. The following, among his later exploits, are worthy of mention :—

1. He captured the bull of Marathon (said to have been the same which Heracles brought alive from Crete), and sacrificed it in Athens to Apollo Delphinius.

2. He assisted his friend Pirithoüs, the prince of the Lapithæ, in his contest with the Centaurs.

3. He undertook with Pirithoüs an expedition to Lacedæmon, in which they carried off Helen, the sister of the Dioscuri.

4. At the request of Pirithoüs, he accompanied him to the lower world to carry off Persephone; but Hades, enraged at their audacity, caused them both to be bound in chains and fastened to a rock. Theseus was rescued from this plight by Heracles, but during his absence the Dioscuri had released their sister from Aphidnæ, where she was confined.

5. He next joined Heracles in his expedition against the Amazons, and received, as the reward of victory, their queen Antiope, or Hippolyte. Another tradition asserts that Antiope followed him of her own free will to Athens, where she was married to him, and became the mother of Hippolytus, famed for his unhappy fate. His great beauty caused his step-mother Phædra, a later wife of Theseus, and a sister of Ariadne, to fall in love with him. As he withdrew himself from her dishonourable proposals by flight, she accused him to his father of attempts on her virtue. Theseus, in his wrath, besought Poseidon to punish his faithless son; and the god, who had sworn to grant any request of Theseus, sent a wild bull (*i.e.*, a breaker) out of the sea as Hippolytus was driving in his chariot along the sea-shore. This so terrified his horses that Hippolytus was thrown from his chariot, and dragged along the ground till he was dead. This story—the scene of which was afterwards transferred to Trœzen, whither Theseus was supposed to have fled on account of a murder—was dealt with in a touching manner by the tragic poets. The *Hippolytus* of Euripides is still extant.

6. As a result of the carrying off of Antiope, a second contest with the Amazons was subsequently invented, in which Theseus was engaged alone, and which took place in the immediate neighbourhood of Athens. The Amazons are supposed to have invaded Attica, in order to release their queen. Antiope, however, was so enamoured of Theseus that she refused to return,

and fought at her husband's side, against her kindred, until she was slain.

Lastly, Theseus is said to have taken part in the Calydonian boar hunt, and also in the expedition of the Argonauts, of which we shall have more to say hereafter.

The death of Theseus is commonly agreed to have taken place in the following manner:—He had been deprived of the sovereignty of Athens by Menestheus, who was aided by the Dioscuri; and then withdrew to the island of Scyros. Here he was at first hospitably received, but subsequently murdered in a treacherous manner by Lycomedes, the ruler of the island. Demophoön, the son of Theseus, is said to have afterwards recovered his father's kingdom. At a still later period the bones of the hero were brought to Athens by Cimon, at the command of the Delphic oracle. Cimon is also supposed to have caused the erection of the temple of Theseus, which still exists in Athens, and serves as an art museum. The eighth day of every month was held sacred to Theseus, besides which he

Fig. 59.—Elgin Theseus. British Museum.

had a special festival, called the Thesea, on the eighth of Pyanepsion.

Art has followed the example of the poets and mythologists in depicting Theseus as a second Heracles. Here, however, the characteristic differences that existed between the Doric and Ionic races become apparent. Just as the latter race surpassed the former in elasticity, both of mind and body, so their national hero gives token not only of a higher intellectual being, but also of a body more lithe, and capable of greater swiftness and dexterity, than that of the Doric hero. The slighter and more elegant form of Theseus lacks, perhaps, the sheer brute strength of Heracles, but is compensated by the possession of a far greater degree of activity and adroitness. The expression of face is more amiable and the hair less bristling than that of Heracles, while there is generally no beard. Such is Theseus as depicted by Greek art at the epoch of its full development; later art strove

Fig. 60.—Theseus Lifting the Rock. Relief in the Villa Albani.

to render the form of the body still more litl.e and graceful. The costume of Theseus consists, like that of his prototype Heracles, of a lion's skin and club; sometimes also of the chlamys and petasus of the Attic youth. Existing art monuments arc far less numerous in his case than in that of Heracles. If the explanation is correct, the British Museum possesses a Theseus of priceless value. Among the statues of the Parthenon which have been preserved, there is one of a figure negligently reclining on a lion's skin, which, with the exception of the nose, hands, and feet, is in a tolerably good state of preservation (Fig. 59). It belonged to the great group of the east gable, which represented the first appearance of the new-born Athene to the astonished gods. It is the figure of a youth in his prime, somewhat larger than life, and altogether a perfect ideal of manly beauty.

A representation of the conflict of Theseus with the invading army of the Amazons still exists on a large piece of frieze-work, which, together with the representations of the battle of the Lapithæ and Centaurs (which have been already mentioned), formerly decorated the walls of the shrine of Apollo's temple in Phigalia, and is now the property of the British Museum. Among the Greek warriors Theseus may be easily recognised by his lion's skin and the club, which he is in the act of swinging against a mounted Amazon, probably the leader of the hostile army. We give an engraving of the scene where Theseus obtained the sword and sandals of his father from beneath the rock, after a relief in the Villa Albani (Fig. 60).

8. Cretan Legend.—1. *Minos and the Minotaur.*—Cretan

myths are both obscure and difficult of interpretation, because Phœnician and Phrygian influences made themselves felt at a very early period, and native sources fail us. Minos is commonly supposed to have been the first king of the country. He was the son of Zeus and Europa, who is called in Homer a daughter of Phœnix. This Phœnix was subsequently made into Agenor, a Phœnician, king of Sidon; and the story then arose that Zeus, in the form of a white bull, had carried off Europa, and arrived with his lovely prey in Crete. Europa is there said to have given birth to Minos, Rhadamanthys (Rhadamanthus), and some say Sarpedon. She afterwards married Asterion, who brought up the sons of Zeus as his own children, and, at his death, left the kingdom to Minos. He, after expelling his brothers Sarpedon and Rhadamanthus, became sole king of Crete. Of his brothers, Sarpedon went to Lycia, whilst the pious Rhadamanthus found a refuge in Bœotia. Minos next married Pasiphaë, a daughter of Helios and Perseïs, by whom he became the father of Catreus, who succeeded him, Deucalion, Glaucus, and Androgeos, besides several daughters, of whom the most celebrated are Ariadne and Phædra. Minos gave wise laws to his people, and became supreme at sea among the isles of the Ægean Sea, and even as far as Attica. In his name we find the same root (meaning " to think ") which we have seen in Minerva, and which appears in the name of the Indian lawgiver Manu.

In order to vindicate his right to the crown, Minos besought Poseidon to send him a bull out of the sea, which he was then to sacrifice to the god. Poseidon granted his prayer, but Minos was induced by the beauty of the animal to place it among his own herds. As a punishment of his perfidy, Poseidon kindled in the breast of Pasiphaë an unnatural love for the bull, and the fruit of their connection was the Minotaur. This was a monster, half man and half bull, which Minos shut up in the labyrinth that had been made by the skill of Dædalus. The food of the monster consisted of human beings, who were partly criminals and partly youths and maidens, sent as tribute from the subjugated countries. This lasted until Theseus came to Crete, and, with the aid of Ariadne and Dædalus, destroyed the Minotaur. Such is the substance of this perplexing mythical tradition, of which the simplest interpretation is that the Minotaur was originally an ancient idol of the Phœnician sun-god Baal, which had the form of a bull, and to which human sacrifices were offered. The destruction of the Minotaur by Theseus is a symbol of the triumph of the higher Greek civilisation over

Phœnician barbarism, and the consequent abolition of human sacrifices.

Closely connected with the royal family of Crete we find Dædalus, the most celebrated artist of the legendary period. He is said to have been a son of Metion, and a descendant of Erechtheus, and to have fled from Athens to Crete after murdering his nephew Talus in a fit of professional jealousy. During his residence in Crete he constructed the Labyrinth, an underground building with an endless maze of passages, as a dwelling-place for the Minotaur; besides many other wonderful works of art. For having aided Theseus in his combat with the Minotaur, Dædalus and his son Icarus were both imprisoned in the Labyrinth of Minos. The story of his flight, which he accomplished by means of the artificial wings that he made for himself and his son, is well known from the *Metamorphoses* of Ovid. Icarus fell into the sea that is named after him, and was drowned, but Dædalus reached Cumæ in safety. From this place he passed over to Sicily, where he was hospitably received by Cocalus. When Minos, however, pursued the fugutive and demanded his surrender, not only was his request refused, but he was even put to death by the contrivance of the king's daughters.

Of the other sons of Minos, Deucalion is celebrated as having taken part in the Calydonian boar hunt, and also as the father of the hero Idomeneus, who fought against Troy. Glaucus was killed, while yet a boy, by falling into a cask of honey as he was pursuing a mouse. He is reported, however, to have been restored to life by the Corinthian augur Polyidus, or, according to others, by Asclepius himself.

2. *Talos.*—The legend of Talos, the brazen man, betrays likewise a Phœnician origin, and refers to the cruel practice of offering human sacrifices. This Talos was made of brass, and was invulnerable. Hephæstus, or, as others say, Zeus gave him

to Minos as guardian of the island of Crete, round which he travelled thrice a-day. If he perceived any strangers approach he would spring into the fire, and, after becoming red-hot, he would clasp them to his breast, until they expired beneath the sardonic chuckle of the demon. He attempted to drive off the Argonauts with stones, but was destroyed by the skill of Medea. Talos had a single vein, which ran from his head to his feet, and was closed at the top with a nail. This nail Medea cleverly succeeded in extracting, in consequence of which Talos, bled to death.

IV.—COMBINED UNDERTAKINGS OF THE LATER HEROIC AGE.

1. The Calydonian Hunt.—The story of Meleager and the Calydonian boar hunt was undoubtedly, in its origin, nothing more than a provincial myth based on natural phenomena, like other myths that we have already explained. In this case the physical significance involved in the myth soon disappeared, owing to the treatment it received at the hands of the epic and dramatic poets. The poets, in fact, succeeded in introducing some striking ethical conceptions, which absorbed all higher interest.

Œneus, king of Calydon in Ætolia, on the occasion of a great festival which was celebrated after a successful vintage, had accidentally or purposely omitted to sacrifice to Artemis. To punish this neglect she sent a huge wild boar, which devastated the fields of Calydon, and seemed invincible by any ordinary means on account of its vast size. Meleager, the brave and heroic son of Œneus, therefore assembled men and hounds in great number to slay it. The boar was slain; but Artemis stirred up strife over the head and hide between the Ætolians and the Curetes of Pleuron. At first the former were victorious; but when Meleager withdrew in wrath from the battle because his mother had cursed him for the death of her brother, they were no longer able to keep the field, and soon saw their city closely invested by their enemies. In vain did the elders and priests of Calydon beseech Meleager; in vain did his father, sisters, and even mother beseech him to aid his hard-pressed countrymen. Like Achilles in the Trojan war, when he was wroth with Agamemnon on account of the loss of Briseis, Meleager long refused to stir. At last his wife—the beautiful Cleopatra— succeeded in moving him. He donned his armour, and put himself at the head of his countrymen for a sally against the besiegers. Brilliant, indeed, was the victory of the men of Calydon; but the hero Meleager did not return from the battle, for the cruel Erinyes, who had heard his mother's curse, destroyed him with the arrows of Apollo.

Such is the earliest form of the legend, as it exists in the *Iliad*. In time, however, Meleager was said to have called together against the boar all the renowned heroes of Greece. Among others there came the Dioscuri, Castor and Pollux; Theseus and his friend Pirithoüs; Idas and Lynceus, the sons of Aphareus; Admetus of Pheræ; Jason, from Iolcus; Iphicles and Iolaüs, from Thebes; Peleus, the father of Achilles; Telamon, from Salamis; Ancæus and the beautiful huntress Atalante (Atalanta), from Arcadia; besides the soothsayer Amphiaraüs, from Argos. After Œneus had entertained his guests royally for nine days, the hunt began, and the huge beast, which was as large as an ox, was surrounded and driven from its lair. Atalante, the swift huntress, was the first to inflict a wound. Ancæus then advanced with his battle-axe, but the enraged beast, with one stroke of his dreadful tusks, tore open his body and killed him on the spot. At length the monster received a mortal wound from a spear hurled by the powerful arm of

Meleager, and was soon despatched by the rest. Meleager received as his due the head and hide of the slaughtered animal, but resigned the prize to Atalante, of whom he was enamoured, on the ground that she was the first to wound the boar. This act excited the bitter jealousy of Plexippus and Toxeus, the sons of Thestius, king of Pleuron, and brothers of Althæa, the mother of Meleager. They accordingly lay in wait for Atalante, and robbed her of the present. Enraged at this, Meleager slew them both. But Meleager's death, though caused by the wrath of his mother, was worked out differently in the time of the tragic poets. The Fates had appeared to Althæa, soon after the birth of Meleager, and informed her that her son would only live until a certain brand, which was then burning on the fire, was consumed. Althæa immediately snatched the brand from the flames and carefully treasured it up. After Meleager had slain her brothers, in the first outburst of grief and indignation against her son, she placed the brand again in the fire, and thus cut off the noble hero in the prime of his youth and beauty. Althæa, on learning the unhappy fate of her son, full of sorrow for her hasty deed, put an end to her own life.

2. The Argonauts.—The story of the Argonauts experienced a similar fate to that of the Calydonian hunt. It was originally nothing but a myth based on natural phenomena; but in the hands of the poets it swelled to a mass of legends common to all the tribes of Greece, the nucleus of which was the history of the golden fleece. Athamas, the son of Æolus, was king of the Minyæ. He put away his first wife, Nephele (cloud), in order to marry Ino, the daughter of Cadmus; though he still kept Phrixus (rain-shower) and Helle (ray of light), his children by Nephele, with him. By Ino he had two other children, Learchus and Melicertes, whom their mother naturally preferred to her stepchildren, and for whose sake she endeavoured to drive the latter from their father's house. Soon afterwards, either at the command of Nephele, whom some represent as a goddess, or in consequence of her prayers for the punishment of Athamas, the land was visited with a long drought, and Ino persuaded her husband to sacrifice Phrixus as a sin-offering to Zeus, in order to put an end to the calamity. Whether Helle was to have shared her brother's fate we cannot tell, for, before Ino could accomplish her purpose, Nephele came to the assistance of her children, and gave them a winged ram with a golden fleece, which Hermes had presented to her for that purpose. Seated on this ram they fled over the sea to Colchis. On the way Helle fell into that part of the sea which bears her name, and was drowned, but Phrixus arrived safely in Colchis (Æa), where he sacrificed the ram to Zeus, who had preserved him in his flight. The fleece he hung up in the grove of Ares as a sacred treasure, setting over it a terrible, ever-watchful dragon as its guardian. To fetch this treasure from a foreign land, and thereby to release the country and people of the Minyæ from the calamity with which they were oppressed, was the task of the heroes of the race of Æolus. Athamas was so grieved at the evil he had brought on his country that he became insane, and sought to slay Ino and her children. He did, indeed, kill Learchus by dashing him against a rock, but Ino succeeded in saving herself and her younger child Melicertes by leaping into the sea (*cf.* Ino Leucothea). Athamas then fled to Epirus, and the kingdom devolved on his brother Cretheus. Cretheus married Tyro, the daughter of his younger brother Salmoneus, king of Elis. Tyro bore him three sons, the eldest of whom, Æson, succeeded his father in the kingdom, but was soon after expelled by his step-brother Pelias, who is described as a son of Tyro and Poseidon. Æson with difficulty managed to rescue his little son Jason from the hands of Pelias, and brought him to the Centaur Chiron to be educated. In Chiron's cave the young hero grew up, a

favourite with gods and men. After completing his twentieth
year, he betook himself to Iolcus to demand of his uncle his
rightful inheritance. Pelias, not daring to use violence to the
sturdy youth, endeavoured to get rid of his unwelcome guest by
involving him in a most dangerous adventure. He declared that
he would gladly resign the crown if Jason would recover the
golden fleece from Colchis. Jason, like a true hero, at once
accepted the perilous adventure. In the harbour of Iolcus he
caused a large ship with fifty oars to be constructed, which he
called the "Argo," after its builder, Argus. He then called
together the heroes, who had consented at his invitation to take
part in the expedition. In the original version of the story, the
expedition was stated to have been undertaken only by the
heroes of the race of the Minyæ—such as Acastus, Admetus,
and Periclymenus. At a later period, however—when the date
of the expedition had been fixed at one generation before the
Trojan war—no hero of any note was allowed to be absent from
the undertaking. In this manner were added the Dioscuri, the
sons of Boreas, Calaïs and Zetes, Telamon, Peleus, Meleager,
Tydeus, Iphitus, Theseus, Orpheus, Amphiaraüs, and even
Heracles. In the last case, the incongruity of allowing the
hero to play only a subordinate part was soon felt, and his
name was withdrawn. He was said to have been left behind in
Mysia, where he had landed in order to search for his favourite
Hylas, who had been carried off by the Naiads. The number
of the Argonauts was finally computed at fifty, tallying with the
number of oars.

The expedition proceeded from Iolcus to Lemnos, and thence
through the Hellespont to Cyzicus, where they were kindly
received by the Doliones. From Cyzicus they proceeded to
Bithynia, where they were opposed by the Bebryces, whose
king, Amycus, was slain by Pollux in a boxing match. Their
greatest difficulty lay in the passage of the Bosporus, there

being at the entrance of the Pontus (Black Sea) two terrible rocks, which were in constant motion—now retreating to the shore on either side, now hastily dashing together again ; whence they were called the Symplegades. This occurred so rapidly that even the swiftest vessel had not time enough to get through. The Argonauts were in great perplexity. At length the blind seer Phineus, who dwelt in Thracian Salmydessus, and whose gratitude they won by delivering him from the Harpies who had tormented him, assisted them with his advice. By means of a stratagem he recommended they were enabled to bring the Argo through without any considerable damage, after which the Symplegades remained stationary. After this they stood along the south coast towards their destination, which, in the original legend, appears to have been the utterly fabulous Æa, subsequently converted into Colchis. This was the residence of the mighty king Æetes, a son of the sun-god. To rob him, either by craft or by violence, of the golden fleece was the task of Jason, the leader of the Argonauts.

The second prominent character in the story, Medea, the daughter of Æetes, now makes her appearance. It was, in fact, only through her love that Jason was enabled to surmount the vast obstacles which stood between him and the possession of the golden fleece. When the hero demanded the fleece of Æetes, the latter declared that he would deliver it up to him after he had accomplished two tasks. The first was to harness two brazen-footed, fire-breathing bulls, which Æetes had received from Hephæstus, to a plough, and with them to till an uncultivated field. The second was to sow in the furrows the dragon's teeth that Æetes would give him, and to destroy the armed men which would then spring up. Jason's heart failed him on hearing these conditions, but Medea, who was an enchantress and priestess of Hecate, was equal to the occasion. She gave the hero a magic salve to protect him against the fiery breath of the bulls and to endow him with invincible strength, which enabled him to accomplish his first task successfully. In the case of the armed men who sprang from the dragon's teeth, by the advice of Medea he followed the example of Cadmus, and cast among them a heavy stone, whereupon in blind fury they turned their arms against each other, and were all destroyed.

The conditions imposed upon him by Æetes were thus accomplished; but the king, who perceived that Jason had only succeeded through the aid of his daughter, made this a pretext for refusing to surrender the fleece. Jason then removed it by night from the grove of Ares, after Medea had, by means of her enchantments, lulled the watchful dragon to sleep. That same night the Argonauts embarked on board their ship and put to sea, Medea accompanying them as the future wife of Jason. The wrathful Æetes attempted to overtake the fugitives, but Medea succeeded in staying the pursuit by slaying her younger brother Apsyrtus, whom she had brought with her, and scattering his limbs in the sea.

The most diverse accounts exist as to the road taken by the Argonauts on their homeward journey. Some say that they sailed up the Phasis to the Eastern Sea, and then, passing through the Red Sea and Libyan desert, over which they had to carry the Argo twelve days' journey, came to Lake Tritonis, and thence to the Mediterranean. According to another account, they sought to pass through the Ister (Danube) and Eridanus (Po) to the Western Ocean; but the object of this account was manifestly to subject them to the same vicissitudes and adventures as Odysseus and his companions.

At length Jason landed happily in Iolcus, and delivered the golden fleece into the hands of his uncle. Pelias, however, still refused to surrender the kingdom to Jason, and Medea therefore determined to make away with him by craft. Having persuaded the daughters of Pelias that she possessed a means of making the old man young again, she directed them to slay their father, cut him in pieces, and boil the limbs in a cauldron filled with all manner of herbs; this they did in the vain expectation of seeing him restored to youth. Jason now took possession of his father's kingdom, but was soon afterwards expelled by Acastus, the son of Pelias, and took refuge in Corinth. His subsequent misfortunes are well known. Thinking to better his condition, he was about to marry Creüsa, the daughter of the king of Corinth, when he was arrested by the fearful vengeance of his first wife. Medea sent the bride a poisoned garment, which caused her to die an agonising death, and then slew her own children by Jason; after which she fled in her chariot drawn by winged dragons to Athens, where she long found protection at the court of Ægeus. Jason either put an end to his own life, or was killed by the fall of a rotten beam of the Argo.

In the history of the golden fleece we have one of the most widely spread myths of all, namely, that of the loss and recovery of a treasure. In Teutonic tradition we have the treasure of the Nibelungs, in which the very name is almost identical; and if we include the stories of women carried off and rescued, the list becomes endless. And the treasure of all those stories has been interpreted to be the golden clouds. The Dragon which guards the treasure again appears in the story of the apples of the Hesperides, and is closely allied to the Sphinx.

3. **The Theban Cycle.**—The highly tragic history of the Theban house of the Labdacidæ, teeming as it does with important characters and events, has at all times furnished subjects for Greek art and poetry, and has given birth to a whole series of epic and dramatic works. The former, which would have conduced far more to an exact acquaintance with the legend, have, unfortunately, perished, with the exception of a few unimportant fragments; although many important works of the great tragic poets, Æschylus, Sophocles, and Euripides, relating to the subject, still remain. The common account runs thus:—Laius, a great-grandson of Cadmus, was warned by the oracle to

Q

beget no children, as he was doomed to perish by the hands of his son, who would then marry his mother. When his wife Iocaste gave birth to a son, Laius accordingly exposed the child, with its feet pierced, on Mount Cithæron. The child, called Œdipus from the swelling of its feet, did not die, but was found by some Corinthian shepherds, who brought it to Polybus, king of Corinth. Polybus, having no children of his own, adopted Œdipus, whc grew up in the belief that Polybus and Merope were his real parents, until one day a taunt of his companions as to his mysterious origin raised doubts in his mind. In order to solve his misgivings, he went to consult the oracle of Delphi, but he here received only the obscure direction not to return to his country, since, if he did, he would kill his father and marry his mother. Fearing on this account to return to Corinth, he took the road to Thebes, and thus, by his presumptuous prudence, brought about the very consequences he was so anxious to avoid. On the road he was met by Laius, who was on his way to the oracle to ask its advice concerning the Sphinx. A quarrel arose, in a narow defile, between Laius and Œdipus; and Œdipus slew his father without knowing who he was. On arriving at Thebes he succeeded in delivering the country from the Sphinx. This monster, which had the combined form of a woman and a lion, had been sent by Hera, whom Laius had in some way offended, from Ethiopia to devastate the land of Thebes. Seated on a rock close to the town, she put to every one that passed by a riddle, and whoever was unable to solve it, she cast from the rock into a deep abyss. This calamity induced Creon, on the death of his brother-in-law Laius, to proclaim that whoever solved the riddle should obtain the crown and the hand of Iocaste. Œdipus succeeded in solving it, and thus delivered the country from the monster, who cast herself into the abyss.

The Sphinx belongs to the same family as many of the monsters we have spoken of already; she is called by Hesoid the child of Orthros and Chimæra, whom we have seen to be the daughter of Typhon and Echidna. It would seem, therefore, probable that the contest between her and her opponent may be interpreted in the same way as that of Bellerophon and the Chimæra, or of Zeus and Typhon. In support of this, the following considerations may be adduced. Since we know that thunder was supposed to be a warning or encouragement to men, it is easy to see in it the mysterious voice of the cloud, only intelligible to the wisest of men. Hence the conqueror of the cloud was called the man who understood her language. (It would not a little help this idea, that Œdipus might seem derived from a word meaning "to know.") Then the death of the Sphinx will be the cloud falling upon the earth in the shape of rain. Œdipus, on the other hand, will be the same antagonist as we have before seen victorious over the cloud dragons ; the sun, born helpless, rising to take the kingdom after the slaughter of his enemies, yet at last sinking blinded into an unknown grave. This, however, does not cover the crimes laid to his charge. But they have been explained in this way : that when people lost consciousness of the real meaning of the misfortunes of Œdipus, they cast about for some adequate cause, and found one in the two great crimes of incest and parricide. We have seen something similar to this in the case of Ixion. Further, the names of the wives assigned by various writers to Œdipus are connected with the light, and the name Laius has been interpreted as "enemy" of the light. Sphinx itself signifies "throttler."

In art, the Sphinx had the form of a lion, generally in a recumbent position, with the breast and upper part of a beautiful woman. When the Greeks saw similar figures in Egypt, they naturally gave them the name of Sphinx. But name, family, and meaning of the Sphinx are alike Greek, although the Egyptian statues have taken too firm possession of the name ever to lose it. Ancient Egyptian art revelled in the creation of colossal Sphinxes, which were carved out of granite. A notable example of this kind exists in the giant Sphinx near the Pyramids of Gizeh, which is eighty-nine feet long. From such monstrous figures as these, Greek art held aloof.

Œdipus was rewarded with the sovereignty of Thebes and the hand of Iocaste ; and for several years he enjoyed uninterrupted happiness, surrounded by four blooming children, the fruit of his incestuous marriage. By the secret agency of the goddess, the dreadful truth was at length discovered. Iocaste hanged herself, and Œdipus, in despair, put out his own eyes. Not content with this voluntary penance, the hard-hearted Thebans compelled him besides to leave their city and country, while his sons Eteocles and Polynices, who were now grown up, refused to stir a foot in their father's behalf. Œdipus, after invoking bitter curses on their heads, withdrew, and, guided by his faithful daughter Antigone, at last found an asylum in the grove of the Eumenides at Colonus, near Athens. His grave there was regarded, in consequence of an ancient response of the oracle, as a national treasure.

The curse of their father took effect on his unnatural sons. The elder, Eteocles, drove out his brother Polynices, who then sought the assistance of Adrastus, king of Argos. Adrastus was a grandson of Bias, of the race of the Amythaonidæ, and by his marriage with the daughter of the wealthy Polybus acquired the sovereignty of Sicyon. He not only hospitably received the fugitive Polynices, but gave him his daughter in marriage, and promised to assist him in recovering the crown of Thebes. In this expedition Adrastus sought to gain the aid of the other Argive heroes. They all declared their readiness to accompany him, with the exception of Amphiaraüs, his brother-in-law, who was equally renowned for his wisdom and courage. Amphiaraüs was a great-grandson of the celebrated seer Melampus, and inherited from him the gift of prophecy. He was thus enabled to perceive the disastrous termination of the war, and strove to hinder it. But Polynices and the fiery Tydeus—likewise a son-in-law of Adrastus—were so unceasing in their entreaties, that he at length sought to escape their importunity by flight. Polynices, however, bribed his wife Eriphyle, by the present of a magnificent necklace, which had formerly been given to Harmonia on the occasion of her marriage with Cadmus, to betray his place of concealment. Hereupon Amphiaraüs was obliged unwillingly to join the expedition, which ended as he had prophesied. The attack on Thebes was not only repulsed, but all the Argive leaders, with the exception of Adrastus, who was saved by the fleetness of his horse, were slain. Polynices and Eteocles fell in single combat with each other. The flight of Adrastus to Attica, where he procured the assistance of Theseus in compelling the Thebans to grant the fallen heroes a solemn burial, is a feature unknown to the original legend, and may be ascribed to the patriotic impulses of the Athenian dramatists. The celebrated tragedy of Sophocles, called *Antigone*, is based on the assumption that Creon, the new king of Thebes, allowed the burial of the other heroes, but left Polynices to lie unburied on the field like a dog, and condemned Antigone to death because she ventured to bury her brother in despite of his command. Creon was destined to meet with a dreadful retribution, for his own son, who was betrothed to Antigone, killed himself in grief at her fate.

Ten years later, the sons of the fallen heroes are said to have combined with Ægialeus, the son of Adrastus, to avenge their fathers' defeat. This expedition has therefore been called the war of the Epigoni (descendants), and not being undertaken, like that of their fathers, in manifest opposition to the will of the gods, proved successful. Laodamas, the savage son of Eteocles, who was now king of Thebes, was defeated in a decisive battle near Thebes, and, after Ægialeus had fallen by his hands, was himself slain by Alcmæon, the son of Amphiaraüs. The Thebans were unable any longer to hold their city, and, following the advice of the blind seer Tiresias, they withdrew under the cover of darkness and mist. The aged Tiresias expired on the road, at the fountain of Tilphusa ; of the rest, some took refuge in Thessalia, and some sought other lands. The victorious Argives, after plundering and partly destroying the city, dedicated a great portion of the booty—among which was Manto, the daughter of Tiresias—to the oracle of Delphi. They then made Thersander, the son of Polynices, king of Thebes; upon which many of the fugitive inhabitants returned. Thersander subsequently took part in the Trojan war, and there perished.

4. The Trojan Cycle.—We now come to the Trojan war, the fourth and most celebrated of the common undertakings of the later heroic age. Here the sources of our information are far more plentiful than in any former period of mythic history, because both the grand national epics, the *Iliad* and the *Odyssey*, which are commonly ascribed to Homer, relate to the Trojan war. As the contents of these immortal poems are probably well known to our readers, we shall only dwell on the most essential features of the story.

I. THE HEROIC RACES OF THE TROJAN WAR.—1. *The Dardanidæ, or race of Dardanus.*—The royal family of Troy were descended from Dardanus, a son of Zeus by Electra, a daughter of Atlas. Dardanus is said to have emigrated from Samothrace, or, according to others, from Italy to Arcadia, to the north-west portion of Asia Minor, between the range of Ida and the Hellespont, where he received from king Teucer some land to form a settlement. By a daughter of the river-god Simoïs, or, as others say, of Scamander, Dardanus had a son called Tros, from whom the Trojans derived their name. Tros had three sons—Assaracus, Ilus, and Ganymedes. The last, who, like all the scions of the race of Dardanus, was possessed of wonderful beauty, was raised by Zeus to the dignity of cup-bearer to the gods, and thus became immortal. Ilus and Assaracus became the founders of two different branches of the Dardanian race. The latter remained in his native settlement of Dardania, where he became the father of Capys and the grandfather of Anchises, the father of Æneas. Ilus, on the other hand, emigrated to the plains of the Scamander, where he founded the city of Ilium, or Troy. After completing the town, he begged Zeus to bestow on him a sign of his favour. The next morning he found in front of his tent the celebrated Palladium—an image of Pallas Athene, carved in wood. On the possession of this depended the fortune and welfare of the city. After the death of Ilus, his son Laomedon became king of Troy. At his request, Poseidon and Apollo built the citadel of Pergamum. We have already related how this king, by his faithless conduct provoked the wrath of Heracles, and the first capture of the city. Of his sons only Priam remained ; in him the race of Dardanus flourished afresh, for by his wife Hecuba and by his concubines he had a great number of sons and daughters.

2. *The Pelopidæ, or race of Pelops.*—The Pelopidæ, who were chiefly instrumental in the destruction of Troy, were descended from the Phrygian king Tantalus, who was renowned alike for his unexampled good fortune and his subsequent unhappy fate. He was the son of Zeus and Pluto (rich plenty), and inhabited a citadel on Moûnt Sipylus, whence his rich pasture-lands and fruitful corn-fields extended twelve days' journey, as far as Ida and the Propontis. The very gods honoured him with their friendship, and lived on such intimate terms that they invited him to eat at their table. This unheard-of good fortune, however, begot in the puny mortal such presumption, that he began to indulge in the grossest outrages on gods and men. At length he went so far as to cut his son Pelops in pieces to boil them, and set them before the gods in order to test their omniscience. The cup of his iniquity now seemed full, and the gods brought down a heavy retribution on the head of the criminal by his well-known punishment in the lower world, where, though surrounded by the most delicious fruits, and standing up to his neck in water, he was nevertheless condemned to suffer the pangs of continual hunger and thirst. Another tradition relates that he was kept in constant anxiety by a huge rock which was suspended over his head. (See pp. 149, 150.)

The children of Tantalus were Pelops and Niobe. The unhappy fate of the latter has already been described in the mythic history of Thebes. Pelops was restored to life by the art of Hermes ; and a portion of his shoulder, which had been consumed by Demeter, was replaced by the gods with a piece of ivory. Pelops is said to have grown up in Olympus, amongst the blessed gods. On being restored to earth, he proceeded to Elis, where he became a suitor for the hand of Hippodamia, the beautiful daughter of the king Œnomaüs. The latter had promised his daughter to the man who should vanquish him in a chariot race: whoever failed was obliged to expiate his temerity with his life, as Œnomaüs transfixed him with his unerring lance as he passed. Thirteen noble youths had already suffered this fate, when Pelops appeared to undergo the dangerous ordeal. By means of the untiring winged horses which had been given him by Poseidon, and also by bribing Myrtilus, the King's charioteer—who, before starting, withdrew the linch-pins from his master's chariot or replaced them with wax—he came off victorious. Œnomaüs either was killed by the breaking down of his chariot, or put an end to his own life on seeing himself vanquished. Pelops now obtained both Hippodamia and the kingdom of Elis; but he ill rewarded Myrtilus, who had rendered him such valuable service, by casting him into the sea, in order to release himself from his obligations. Hermes, whose son he is reputed to have been, set him amongst the stars as charioteer.

The sons of Pelops by Hippodamia were Atreus and Thyestes, whose history, which is full of the most revolting crimes, formed a favourite subject with the tragic poets. First, Atreus and Thyestes murdered their step-brother Chrysippus, and were compelled to leave their country in company with their mother. They were hospitably received at Mycenæ by their brother-in-law Sthenelus, the son of Perseus, or by his son Eurystheus. On Eurystheus' death, they inherited the sovereignty of the Persidæ in Argos, and Atreus now took up his residence in the proud capital of Mycenæ, whence, strange to say, the most ancient specimen of Greek sculpture has come down to us in the so-called Gate of Lions. Soon an implacable enmity arose between the two brothers, and Thyestes, in consequence, was banished from Argos. He took with him, in revenge, Pleisthenes, the young son of Atreus, brought him up as his own son, and despatched him, later, to Mycenæ to kill Atreus. His design was discovered, and he expiated his intended crime with his life. When Atreus learned that it was his own son whom he had condemned to death, he determined on a dreadful revenge. Pretending to be reconciled, he recalled Thyestes and his children to Mycenæ; and

Thyestes, trusting to his brother's word, returned. Atreus then privately seized the two young sons of Thyestes, slew them, and set this horrible food before their father. Horror-struck at this inhuman cruelty, the sun turned his chariot and went back in his course. Thyestes, uttering fearful curses against his brother and the whole race of the Pelopidæ, again escaped, and took refuge with Thesprotus, king of Epirus. Later, he succeeded, with the help of his only remaining son Ægisthus, in avenging himself on his brother. Atreus was slain by Ægisthus whilst offering up a sacrifice on the sea-shore, and Thyestes now acquired the sovereignty of Mycenæ. The sons of Atreus, Agamemnon and Menelaüs, fled from their barbarous uncle to Sparta, where Tyndareüs, the king, received them kindly, and gave them his daughters, Clytæmnestra and Helen, in marriage. With his aid Agamemnon recovered his father's kingdom, slew Thyestes, and drove out Ægisthus. Menelaüs remained in Sparta—where he succeeded Tyndareüs—until the carrying off of his wife Helen by Paris gave rise to the Trojan war.

3. *The Æacidæ, or race of Æacus.*—After the sons of Atreus, the Æacidæ play the most important part in the Trojan war; in fact, we are almost justified in saying that the war was an exploit of these two races of heroes and their peoples, the Achæans of Argos and the Hellenes of Phthia. The ancestor of the Æacidæ was Æacus, who was renowned alike for his wisdom and justice, and on this account subsequently made a judge in the lower world. Æacus was a son of Zeus by Ægina, a daughter of the river-god Asopus. He ruled over the island of Ægina, and married Endeïs, the daughter of the wise Centaur Chiron. She bore him two sons, Peleus and Telamon. On reaching manhood they were compelled to leave their country, because, like the sons of Pelops, they had murdered, in a fit of jealousy, a step-brother who was a favourite with their father. Peleus betook himself to Phthia, where he was kindly received

by Eurytion, who bestowed on him the hand of his daughter and a third part of his kingdom. Peleus afterwards took part in the boar hunt of Calydon, on which occasion he had the misfortune to kill his father-in-law. In consequence of this, he left Phthia and proceeded to Iolcus, where he took part in the funeral games which Acastus was celebrating in honour of his father Pelias, who had perished by the treachery of Medea. Here he experienced a similar fate to that of Bellerophon at the court of Prœtus. Astydameia, the wife of Acastus, finding herself unable to seduce him, slandered him to her husband, who thereupon sought to take his life. After hunting on Pelion one day, Peleus fell asleep, and was left thus unprotected by Acastus, who hoped by this means to get rid of him. He would, indeed, have been murdered by the Centaurs, if the gods had not taken pity on him, and sent him by Hermes a sword of wonderful power, with which he was enabled to repel the assaults of the wild inhabitants of the forest. Peleus, with the help of the Dioscuri, subsequently took Iolcus, and put the treacherous Acastus and his wife to death. As a reward for his chastity, the gods gave him the goddess Thetis—a beautiful daughter of Nereus—to wife. She bore him one son, Achilleus (Achilles), the greatest and bravest hero of the Trojan war. A later tradition asserts that Thetis left her husband soon after the birth of Achilles, because he had disturbed her when she was about to render her child immortal in the fire, just as Demeter intended to do to the child of Celeüs; but this story is unknown to Homer. According to a still later legend, she plunged her son into the Styx, and thereby rendered him invulnerable in every part except the heel by which she held him. Like all noble heroes, Achilles was instructed by Chiron, under whom he acquired such wonderful skill in all feats of strength and agility that he soon surpassed all his contemporaries. In addition to Chiron, Homer names Phœnix, the son of Amyntor, as the instructor of the youthful hero. Achilles proceeded to the Trojan war with cheerful determination, although he knew beforehand that he was not fated to return alive. The story that his mother Thetis, in order to avert his fate, sent him, disguised in women's clothes, to the court of Lycomedes, king of Scyros, where he was discovered by the craft of Odysseus, is a post-Homeric invention.

From Telamon, the second son of Æacus, was descended Aias or Ajax, a hero of but little less importance. Telamon, after his flight from Ægina, found a new home in Salamis, where he married the daughter of the king Cychreus. On the decease of Cychreus, he succeeded to the crown. After the death of his first wife, he married Periboea, a daughter of Alcathoüs, king of Megara, who bore him Ajax. Tradition tells us much of the intimate friendship of Heracles and Telamon, who took part in the Trojan expedition of his mighty friend. Heracles, in return, gave him Hesione, the daughter of Laomedon, by whom he became the father of a second son, Teucer. Like every celebrated hero of antiquity, he is said to have taken part in the Calydonian hunt and the expedition of the Argonauts. Nothing inferior to this brave and doughty father was his son Ajax, on whom the mighty hero Heracles had invoked the blessing of his father Zeus, when as a child he held him in his arms. He was of greater size and strength than any of the other heroes ; though he appears somewhat uncouth and clumsy when contrasted with the swift and agile form of Achilles. His mighty shield was as characteristic of him as the ponderous deadly spear was of Achilles. Beside him, his brother Teucer ranks as the best archer among the Greeks.

4. *Nestor, the Locrian Ajax, Diomedes, and Odysseus.*—
Associated with the heroes of the race of Pelops and Æacus were some other renowned chieftains. First among them was the aged Nestor, of Pylus, whose wise counsels were as indispensable to the Greeks before Troy as the dauntless courage of

an Achilles or an Ajax. Nestor was the youngest of the twelve sons of Neleus, who was himself a son of Poseidon and Tyro, and twin-brother of Pelias. Neleus, having been driven out by Pelias, took refuge in Messenia, where he became the founder of a new kingdom. Later, however, both his sovereignty and the glory of his house were well-nigh extinguished by the hostility of Heracles, who slew all the sons of Neleus except Nestor. When quite young, Nestor defeated the neighbouring tribes of the Epei and Arcadians, and restored the dominions of his father to their former extent. He likewise took part in the contest between the Lapithæ and the Centaurs, in the Calydonian boar hunt, and in the expedition of the Argonauts. Though so far advanced in years—having ruled over three generations of men—he could not withstand the desire to take part in the Trojan war.

The Locrian Ajax—also called the Lesser Ajax, to distinguish him from his mighty namesake—was a son of the Locrian king Oïleus, of whom nothing more is known than that he took part in the expedition of the Argonauts. Ajax was renowned among the Greeks for his skill in hurling the spear and for his great fleetness, in which he was surpassed only by Achilles. He always appears in a linen corslet, and his followers, the Opuntian Locrians, are also light-armed troops.

Diomedes was a member of the oft-mentioned race of the Æolian Amythaonidæ. His father was the hot-headed Tydeus, who was killed in the war of the Seven against Thebes. Diomedes, who inherited no small portion of his father's wild, untameable disposition, of course took part in the war of the Epigoni, and subsequently succeeded his grandfather Adrastus in his Argive sovereignty at Sicyon. He also restored his paternal grandfather, the aged Ætolian king Œneus, who had been dethroned by the sons of his brother Agrius, to his kingdom. In the *Iliad* he appears as a special favourite of Pallas

Athene, and Homer makes him play an important part in the contests of the Greeks before the walls of Troy. In post-Homeric story he is represented as having carried off the Trojan Palladium.

Finally, Odysseus (Ulysses), the most popular of the Greek heroes of the Trojan war, was a son of Laërtes, king of Ithaca, by Anticlea, the daughter of Autolycus. Autolycus inhabited a district on Mount Parnassus, and was renowned for his cunning. His grandson seems to have inherited no small part of his grandfather's disposition. Through his noble and virtuous wife Penelope, Odysseus was closely related to the Atridæ; Penelope being the daughter of Icarius, who was a brother of the Spartan king Tyndareüs. He was therefore obliged—though much against his will—to comply with the request of Menelaüs, and join the expedition against Troy. On account of his wisdom and eloquence, his dexterity in all feats of strength, and his dauntless valour in the midst of danger, he also was a special favourite of Pallas.

II. THE WAR.—The *Iliad* of Homer, the most important source of our information with regard to the Trojan war, does not deal with the events of the first nine years; and of those of the tenth and last year it only gives such episodes as relate to the quarrel of Achilles and Agamemnon. Of the origin of the war, and the events of the first nine years, it speaks only incidentally, for the sake of explanation. The gap has to be filled up from the works of those writers who had access to other epic poems of the Trojan cycle, which are now no longer extant.

Eris, the goddess of discord, not having been invited to the marriage festivities of Peleus and Thetis, avenged herself by casting into the assembly a golden apple, with the inscription—"To the fairest." The three rival goddesses—Hera, Athene, and Aphrodite—each claimed the apple for herself, but were referred by Zeus to the decision of Paris. Paris was a son of Priam, the

Trojan king. Immediately after birth he was exposed on Mount
Ida, in consequence of an ill-omened dream which his mother
Hecuba had during her pregnancy. He was found, however,
and brought up by some shepherds. He decided in favour of
Aphrodite, who had promised him the most beautiful woman
on earth as his wife. Soon afterwards, at some games given by
the king, the youth, who was equally distinguished for his
handsome person and his bodily dexterity, after having wrested
the prize from all his brethren, was recognised by the prophetess
Cassandra, and received into his father's favour. He next
undertook a journey across the sea to Greece, and, among other
places, visited the court of Menelaüs, king of Sparta, by whom
he was hospitably received and entertained. Aphrodite kindled
in the breast of the young wife of Menelaüs a fatal love for their
handsome guest, who dazzled her as much by the beauty of his
person as by the oriental splendour of his appearance. While
Menelaüs was absent in Crete, and her brothers, the Dioscuri,
were engaged in their strife with the sons of Aphareus, Helen
fled with her seducer to Troy. On the refusal of the king of
Troy to surrender Helen, Menelaüs succeeded in rousing the
whole of Greece to a war of revenge. This task was the more
easy, as most of the Grecian chieftains had been suitors of Helen,
and had bound themselves by an oath to Tyndareüs to unite in
support of the husband whom Helen should choose, in the event
of his ever being injured or attacked. The well-manned ships
of the Greeks assembled in the Bœotian port of Aulis. Their
number amounted to eleven hundred and eighty-six, according
to Homer; of which Agamemnon, who had been chosen leader
of the expedition, alone furnished over one hundred. Agamemnon, however, having offended Artemis by killing a hind
sacred to the goddess, the departure of the expedition was
delayed by continuous calms, until at length, at the command of
the priest Calchas, Agamemnon determined to appease the wrath

of the goddess by sacrificing his daughter Iphigenia on her altar. At the fatal moment Artemis rescued the victim, and, after substituting a hind in her stead, conveyed Iphigenia to Tauris, where she became a priestess in the temple of the goddess. The fleet now sailed with a fair wind. The expedition first stopped at Tenedos, opposite the coast of Troy. Here, on the occasion of a banquet, Philoctetes, who possessed the bow and arrows of Heracles on which the conquest of Troy depended, was bitten in the foot by a serpent, and on account of his cries and the offensive smell of the wound was carried to Lemnos, and there left to his fate. The Greeks next effected a landing on the coast of Troy, in spite of the opposition of Hector and Æneas; for Protesilaüs devoted himself to death for the Greeks, and sprang first on the Trojan shore. Even Cycnus, the mighty son of Poseidon, who was king of Colonæ in Troas, and came to the assistance of the Trojans, was unable to stem the advance of the Greeks; and his body being invulnerable, he was strangled by Achilles by means of a thong twisted round his neck.

After the Greeks had made a station for their ships, the war began in earnest. Several of their attacks on the town having been successfully repelled by the Trojans, the Greeks now confined themselves to making inroads and plundering excursions into the surrounding country, in which Achilles was always the most prominent actor. The first nine years of the war were by no means fruitful in important events, and the wearisome monotony of the siege was broken only by the single combat between Achilles and Troïlus, the youngest son of Priam, in which Troïlus was slain, and by the fall of Palamedes of Eubœa, the head of the Greek peace-party, which was brought about by the treachery of Odysseus. At length, in the tenth year of the war, a quarrel broke out between Achilles and Agamemnon respecting a female slave who had been taken captive, and gave for the time quite another aspect to affairs. It is at this point that the *Iliad* commences. Achilles, in his wrath, retired to his tent, and refused to take any further part in the war; whilst the Trojans, who feared him more than all the other Greeks, became bolder, and no longer kept to the protection of their walls. Zeus, at the request of Thetis, gave them the victory in their first engagement with the Greeks. Hector drove the latter back to their ships, and was already about to set them on fire, when Achilles consented to allow his friend Patroclus to don his armour and lead his Myrmidons to the assistance of the Greeks. The Trojans were now driven back, but Patroclus, in the ardour of pursuit, was slain by Hector, and deprived of his armour, and Menelaüs, with the help of the greater Ajax and other heroes, only succeeded in rescuing his corpse after a bloody and obstinate struggle. The wrath of Achilles was now entirely diverted by the desire of avenging on Hector the death of his much-loved friend Patroclus. He was scarcely willing even to wait for the new armour which his goddess-mother procured him from the workshop of Hephæstus. No sooner was he in possession of it than he again appeared on the field, and Hector—the bulwark of Troy—soon succumbed to his furious onslaught. Achilles, however, was generous enough to surrender his corpse to the entreaties of Priam. The *Iliad* concludes with the solemn funeral of Hector.

The succeeding events, up to the death of Achilles and the contest for his arms, were narrated in the *Æthiopis* of Arctinus of Miletus, with the contents of which we have some slight acquaintance, although the work itself is lost. All kinds of brilliant exploits are reported to have been performed by Achilles before the walls of Troy, which were manifestly unknown to the earlier story. In the first place, immediately after Hector's death, Penthesilea, the queen of the Amazons, came to the assistance of the Trojans, and fought so bravely at the head of her army that the Greeks were hard pressed. Achilles at length overcame the heroic daughter of Ares. After her fall, a new ally of the Trojans appeared in Memnon, king of Æthiopia, who is called a son of Eos, because the Æthiopians were supposed to dwell in the far East. Among those who fell by the hand of this handsome and courageous hero was Antilochus, the valiant son of Nestor. When Memnon, however, ventured to meet the invincible Achilles, he also was vanquished, after a brave struggle. The fresh morning dew, which springs from the tears of Eos, proves that she has never ceased to lament her heroic son. But death was soon to overtake him before whom so many heroes had bitten the dust. In an assault on the Scæan gate, Achilles was killed, at the head of his Myrmidons, by an arrow of Paris, which was directed by Apollo. According to later writers, whose accounts were followed by the tragic poets, he was treacherously murdered here on the occasion of his betrothal to Polyxena, the beautiful daughter of Priam. A furious contest, lasting the whole day, took place for the possession of his corpse and armour: at length Odysseus and Ajax succeeded in conveying it to a place of safety. Mourning and confusion reigned among the Greeks at his death. During seventeen days and nights Thetis, with the whole band of Nereids, bewailed his untimely fate in mourning melodies, so sad and touching that neither gods nor men could refrain from tears.

> " See, tears are shed by every god and goddess, to survey
> How soon the Beautiful is past, the Perfect dies away !"

The death of the bravest of the Greeks was followed by an unhappy quarrel between Ajax and Odysseus respecting his arms. Ajax, on account of his near relationship to the deceased hero, and the great services he had rendered to the cause of the Greeks, seemed to have the best claim ; but Agamemnon, by the advice of Athene, adjudged them to Odysseus. Ajax was so

mortified at this decision that he became insane, and put an end
to his own life. An entire tragedy of Sophocles, treating of
the mournful fate of the son of Telamon, has come down to
us.

After Ajax had quitted the scene, Odysseus became decidedly
the chief personage among the Greeks. It was he who captured
the Trojan seer Helenus, and extorted from him the secret that
Ilium could not be taken without the arrows of Heracles. Hereupon Philoctetes, who was still lying sick at Lemnos, was
fetched, and his wound healed by Machaon. Paris soon afterwards fell by his hand. It was Odysseus, moreover, who, in
company with Diomedes, undertook the perilous task of entering
Troy in disguise and stealing the Palladium, on which the safety
of the city depended. It was he who fetched Neoptolemus, the
young son of Achilles, from Scyros to the Trojan camp, it having
been decreed that his presence was necessary to the success of
the Greeks. Lastly—and this was his greatest service—it was
Odysseus who devised the celebrated wooden horse, and the
stratagem which led to the final capture of the city. In the
belly of the horse, which was built by Epeüs, one hundred
chosen warriors of the Greeks concealed themselves. The rest
of the Greeks set fire to their camp, and sailed away to Tenedos;
whereupon the Trojans, deceived by the assurances of Sinon,
dragged the fatal horse, amid cries of joy, into the city. In
vain did the Trojan priest of Apollo, Laocoön, seek to divert
them from their folly. None would give heed to his warnings;
and when, soon afterwards, both he and his sons, whilst sacrificing
to Poseidon on the sea-shore, were strangled by two serpents that
came up out of the sea, the Trojans regarded this as a punishment sent by the gods for his evil counsel, and were the more
confirmed in their purpose.

The death of Laocoön and his sons forms the subject of one of the
most splendid of the creations of Greek art that have come down to

ιs from antiquity.   The group was found, in the year 1506, by a
Roman citizen in his vineyard, close to the former Thermæ of Titus,
and was made over by him, for a considerable annuity, to Pope Julius
II., who then placed it in the Vatican collection.   The right arm of
Laocoön, which was wanting, has, unfortunately, been incorrectly

Fig. 61.—Laocoön. Group.

restored.   This is attested by a copy of the group which was subsequently discovered in Naples.   We give an engraving of the group
in its original form (Fig. 61).

It treats really of three distinct incidents, which have been skil-
fully incorporated, by the artists to whom we owe the work (the

Rhodians Agesander, Athenodorus, and Polydorus), into one harmonious group. The eldest son is as yet unhurt, and appears to be so loosely held by the coils of the serpent that he might easily escape his impending fate, if he were not more effectually restrained by his loving sympathy with his noble father, on whom he gazes with piteous looks. Laocoön himself, who naturally forms the centre of the group, is depicted at the moment in which, mortally wounded by the serpent, he sinks on the altar, to rise from which he vainly exerts his last remaining strength. With his left arm he still mechanically seeks to repel the serpents. His hitherto energetic resistance has begun to fail, and his noble head is raised in mournful resignation to heaven, as though to ask the gods why they had condemned him to so terrible a fate. The dignified and resolute aspect of his countenance forms a beautiful contrast to that of his body, which is manifestly quivering in the keenest agony. The younger son on his right is already in the last agonies of death, and though his left hand grasps instinctively the head of the snake, he is evidently incapable of further resistance. He is drooping like a plucked flower, and in one more moment will have breathed his last.

On the night succeeding Laocoön's horrible end, and the rejoicings of the Trojans at the apparent departure of the Greeks, the Greek fleet returned in silence at a signal given by Sinon. The heroes who were hidden in the wooden horse then descended and opened the gates to the Greek host, who rushed into the doomed city. A terrible scene of plunder and carnage ensued, the Trojans, in their dismay and confusion, offering no resistance. The fate of the sacred city was fulfilled; Priam perished before the altar of Zeus by the hand of Neoptolemus, and with him the glory of Troy was laid in the dust. The men were put to death, the women and children, together with the rich booty, were carried off, the former being destined to the hard lot of slavery. Among them was the aged queen Hecuba, with all her daughters and daughters-in-law. Helen—the cause of all this misfortune—was found in the house of Deïphobus, whom she had married after the death of his brother Paris.

The city was burnt to the ground, and, long after, other cities rose on its site. Still the tradition of the siege remained among the inhabitants, though, even in Roman times, learned men had begun to declare that Old Troy must have had another site. And now when the last Ilium had been no more for many centuries, and the very existence of Homer's Troy had been declared a fable, the palace and the traces of the conflagration have been found. Dr. Schliemann has excavated the legendary site, and we know now that Athene was worshipped in the city, and that it perished by fire. We can hardly tell at present the full importance of these discoveries, nor of those at Mycenæ, where the traditional tombs of the Grecian leaders have been examined, and their long-buried wealth brought to light.

Yet this, too, the greatest of all the Grecian legend series, dissolves into the phenomena of nature. That there was a Trojan war, and that we have some historical facts about it, we can hardly doubt; but so many myths have crystallised round it, that to us it must be merely legend. The very names of Achilles, and Paris, and Helen, upon whom the whole story turns, have been recognised in Indian legend. Point after point in their history is found in the legend history of every nation of the Aryan family. The only conclusion that we can draw is, that such stories must have come into being before the separation of the Aryan family, and cannot therefore contain the later history of any one branch.

III. THE RETURN.—The Greeks, after sacrificing Polyxena on the grave of Achilles at Sigeum, prepared to return to their country. Few, however, were destined to reach their homes without some misfortune, or, even when arrived there, to experience a kindly welcome. Of the two sons of Atreus, Agamemnon, after escaping a storm on the cost of Eubœa, landed safely on his native shores, but was soon after murdered by his wife and Ægisthus, who had, during his absence, returned to Argos and married Clytæmnestra. Cassandra, the Trojan prophetess, who, in the division of the spoils, had fallen to Agamemnon, shared his fate. She had continually predicted the unfortunate end of the war and the ultimate fate of the city, but had always been laughed to scorn by her incredulous countrymen. The fate of the commander of the Greeks, with its eventful consequences, was a favourite subject with the tragic poets. His murder did not go unavenged. Orestes, the only son of Agamemnon and Clytæmnestra, had been hastily removed from the scene by his sister Electra, and sent to his uncle, Strophius, king of Phocis. Strophius had him carefully educated with his own son Pylades, who was about the same age. A most intimate friendship soon sprang up between the two youths, which, from its faithfulness and constancy, has become proverbial. On reaching manhood, the sole thought of Orestes was to avenge his noble father's treacherous death at the hands of the crafty Ægisthus and his mother Clytæmnestra. Accompanied by his friend Pylades, he returned, in the eighth year of his exile, to Mycenæ, and there slew both Ægisthus and Clytæmnestra. Although in so doing he had only fulfilled a duty, he yet incurred the deepest guilt by the murder of her who gave him birth, and at once found himself pursued by the avenging Furies. They dogged his steps, and ceased not to pursue him through all the countries of the earth, until he was at length directed by the oracle at Delphi to convey the statue of Artemis from Tauris to Attica. After he had, with the help of his newly-found sister, successfully achieved this task, he was purified by Apollo (see page 152). Of the numerous dramas that were written on the subject of the fortunes of the Pelopidæ, which we have here briefly touched on, the *Agamemnon*, *Choëphoræ*, and *Eumenides* of Æschylus, the *Electra* of Sophocles, and the *Electra* and *Iphigenia in Tauris* of Euripides, are still extant.

We must now turn to the fortunes of the other Greek leaders. Agamemnon's brother Menelaus was overtaken, off Cape Malea, by a fearful storm, which carried him to Crete and Egypt, whence, after seven years of wandering, he returned to Sparta with Helen and his share of the spoils of Troy.

The Locrian Ajax experienced a still more unhappy fate. On the night of the destruction of Troy he had penetrated into the temple of Pallas, and had not only torn away the priestess Cassandra, who was clinging for safety to the altar and statue of the goddess, but had also overturned the statue of Pallas herself. As a punishment for this offence, his ship was wrecked on Cape Caphareus. He would still have been able to escape with his life—having succeeded in getting hold of a rock—if he had not given such offence to Poseidon by his impious boast that he needed not the help of the gods, that the god split the rock with his trident, whereupon Ajax fell into the sea and was drowned.

Diomedes, Philoctetes, and Idomeneus reached their homes in safety, but were all soon afterwards driven out, after which they all three emigrated to Italy. Here Diomedes founded many towns, and was long worshipped with heroic honours.

Teucer also succeeded in reaching Salamis in safety, but his father Telamon was so wroth because he had not better protected his brother Ajax, or at least avenged his death, that he refused to receive him. He was, therefore, likewise obliged to leave his country, and subsequently settled on the island of Cyprus.

But of all the Greek heroes Odysseus experienced the most reverses, while at home his faithful wife Penelope and his son Telemachus were hard pressed by the suitors. It was only in the tenth year after the fall of Troy, and after numerous wanderings and vicissitudes, that he was permitted to return to his native Ithaca and punish the shameless suitors who had wasted his substance and goods. The story of his adventures is so well known that we need not dwell on it here, further than to mention that, according to post-Homeric accounts, Odysseus was killed by the hand of Telegonus, his own son by Circe.

The events of the Trojan cycle have supplied not only the poet, but also the artist and the sculptor, with a large number of their most acceptable subjects. Single scenes, such as the judgment of Paris, have been continually selected, ever since the time of Raphael, as favourite subjects of representation. Of modern masters, Carstens, Thorwaldsen the great Danish sculptor, Cornelius, Genelli, and Preller (Landscapes of the *Odyssey*) have illustrated the story of Troy in a series of splendid compositions. We give an engraving of a relief by Thorwaldsen, representing Priam before Achilles (Fig. 62).

Fig. 62.—Priam before Achilles.   Relief by Thorwaldsen.

Of the more important extant works of antiquity, we may mention the wedding of Peleus and Thetis, depicted on the Français vase in the Naples Museum; the abduction of Helen, depicted on a marble relief in the former Campana collection, now in the Louvre (Fig. 63); the marble group in Rome, known by the name of "Pasquino," which represents Menelaüs raising the corpse of Patroclus; and, lastly, the celebrated Ægina marbles in Munich. These last are the remains of a marble group from the gable of a temple of Pallas at Ægina, representing a battle between the Greeks and Trojans. They were discovered at Ægina in the year 1811; King Ludwig I. of Bavaria, who was a great patron of art, bought the Ægina marbles, and, after having them restored by Thorwaldsen, placed them in the Munich collection. The Laocoön, the most important of all the works relating to the Trojan cycle, has already been discussed.

V.—MYTHIC SEERS AND BARDS.

We have already incidentally mentioned most of the seers of antiquity—Melampus, the son of Amythaon, who figures in Argive legend; likewise Amphiaraüs, Tiresias, and Calchas. Concerning Tiresias, we may remark that the ancients ascribed to him a fabulous age, extending over seven or even nine generations; so that he was thus a witness of all that happened to Thebes, from the foundation of the city to its destruction by the Epigoni. Like all celebrated soothsayers, he was acquainted with the language of birds, and could penetrate the most hidden secrets of nature ; on which account he enjoyed up to his death an ever-increasing reputation among the Thebans. We have already related how, in extreme old age, when his native city could no longer withstand the assaults of the Epigoni, he experienced the bitter lot of having to take refuge in flight, and at length succumbed beneath the hardships of the journey. In the second century A.D. his grave was still shown in the neighbourhood of Haliartus.

Among the fugitive Thebans who fell into the hands of the Argives is said to have been Manto, the daughter of Tiresias, who was likewise renowned as a prophetess. She was dedicated, together with a large portion of the spoils, to the oracle at Delphi. By the command of the god she was sent into Asia Minor, where she founded the oracle of Claros, near Colophon. She here married the Cretan Rhacius, and became by him the mother of Mopsus, who afterwards founded the oracle of Mallos in Cilicia.

Among the names of the mythic bards that have been handed down to us are undoubtedly to be found some recollections of those who first cultivated the art of poetry ; partly, however, they are nothing more than personifications of certain tendencies

and modes of poetry. Such is probably the case with the
mythic bard Linus, who was celebrated in Argos, Thebes, and
Eubœa. Nothing is more common than for an unsophisticated
people to burst forth in lamentation over the decay and final
extinction of the blooming life of nature. This, as we see in
the myth of Hyacinthus, was often portrayed under the meta-

Fig. 64.—Orpheus and Eurydice.   Marble Relief in the Villa Albani.

phor of a beautiful boy slain by a quoit or by savage dogs—both
symbols of the scorching heat of the sun. The dirges which
from time immemorial were sung over the beautiful boy Linus,
at the season of vintage, probably gave rise to the myth which
makes Linus himself the singer.

Similar doleful memories are linked with the name of Orpheus, who is often termed a brother of Linus, though he was really not an Æolian, but a Thracian of Pieria. That which is best known of him is the story of his love for the beautiful nymph Eurydice. She was bitten in the foot by a snake, and thus snatched away from him by death. Orpheus then filled mountain and valley with songs of lamentation so piteous, that the wild beasts of the forest were enchanted at the sound, and followed him like lambs ; and the very rocks and trees moved from their places. His yearning towards his beloved Eurydice induced him to descend to the lower world, to beg her release from the grim king of shadows. Here his piteous lay caused even the Erinyes to shed tears of compassion, and moved the hard heart of the Stygian king. He released Eurydice on condition that Orpheus should not look back on her till he reached the upper world. Orpheus, however, violated this condition, and Eurydice was once more lost to him. He himself, not long afterwards, whilst wandering in his despair over the Thracian mountains, was torn in pieces by some women in the mad excitement of their nightly Bacchanalian orgies.

A splendid representation of the second parting of the lovers by Hermes, the guide of souls, has come down to us on a marble relief, which is preserved in the Villa Albani (Fig. 64).

INDEX.

s

www.ingramcontent.com/pod-product-compliance
Lightning Source LLC
Chambersburg PA
CBHW030347270326
41926CB00009B/993